Answering my HEART'S CRY

Valerie Lee
Baker Clayton

WINEPRESS WP PUBLISHING

Printed in the United States of America
Illustrations by Marcus Lee Baker Clayton

Packaged by WinePress Publishing, PO Box 1406, Mukilteo, WA 98275. The views expressed or implied in this work do not necessarily reflect those of WinePress Publishing. Ultimate design, content, and editorial accuracy of this work is the responsibility of the author(s).

ISBN 1-57921-137-2
Library of Congress Catalog Card Number: 98-61051

DEDICATED TO
JANET SYLAR

A woman who made the decision
not to procrastinate, but to act
when the Lord prompted her.

To God I give the glory.
To Janet I give my unending gratitude.

Janet Sylar
1954 - 1997

Contents

Part I

Chapter 1:
    Heart of Stone—Heart of Flesh 7

Part II

Chapter 2:
    Sold with Faith—Bought with Obedience 25
Chapter 3:
    The Deadline 33
Chapter 4:
    Little, Ordinary, Everyday Things 43
Chapter 5:
    Tiny Shadow of a Doubt 53
Chapter 6:
    Grind, Whine, Rattle & Clunk 65
Chapter 7:
    The Jigsaw 79

Chapter 8:
     The Prison, the Picture, the Promise 87
Chapter 9:
     Only One Word 99
Chapter 10:
     The Attacker Brought Popccorn? 107
Chapter 11:
     A Tropical Answer 119
Chapter 12:
     God Loves Me! 129
Chapter 13:
     The Security Blanket 137
Chapter 14:
     A Little Self-Grandeur 145
Chapter 15:
     Exceeding Expectations 155
Chapter 16:
     God Deserves an "A" 165
Chapter 17:
     Yes? No! Wait 177

Epilogue 187
Bibliography 191

1

Heart of Stone—Heart of Flesh

Healing Touch of Jesus

This is the end of the line for me, God . . . do you hear me? I can't take it anymore! It's not even worth trying. I'd rather be buried in a sewage tank than keep living like this. God! Are You *listening* to me? Do You even care? Answer me, will you!? You make changes in people . . . then why not me? Why! What have I done to deserve this? Oh, God, please do something . . . p-l-e-a-s-e!"

A line from the novel *Madame Bovary* by Gustave Flaubert describes the substance of what my life had become:

"The future was a totally dark corridor with a solidly locked door at its end."

Try as I might, there was no escaping that dark tunnel I called my life. I lived a depressingly pitiful existence; a hell that had no relief. Many times, more often than not, I wished

I was dead. Yet life went on . . . and on . . . and on. Every day brought pain. Pressures swarmed around our lives like bees at a picnic—never relenting, never going away, always there.

I wrote this while trying to search for who I was:

A Thousand Vases

I am like a thousand vases of flowers.
Each vase is different;
Each vase has its purpose.
The flowers are used by others;
Different flowers for different reasons.
Flowers are desirable to own.
Although some may have thorns and cause pain,
They are still loved.
My vases are many colored,
Odd shaped;
Some are even strange.
My vases were full of flowers;
So full they ran over with their brilliance.
But my flowers are no longer real.
My flowers are artificial;
Their brilliance is faded from the pain of living.
Water is the life support of all living things.
But the artificial flowers in my vases are thirsty,
For I have no water in my vases.
And my vases full of artifical flowers
Are dying.

Dying. Sometimes I feel like I'm in the middle of a relentless swirling death that seems to have no end. When will this grievous life end? Why can't I just have peace—life without so much pain?

I read there is suppose to be a peace that passes all understanding. I didn't understand why I didn't have any. When I was a child, my mother faithfully took my four brothers and me to church. As an adult, except for occasional periods of rebellion or laziness, I too have been actively involved in our church. But somewhere, somehow, God seemed to miss me and my family when it came to passing out the peace that comes from knowing Him. Somewhere deep inside, I figured if I did enough, if I tried exceptionally hard and made an impression with my good deeds at church, then maybe, just maybe, God would take notice of me and my family. Then, somehow our lives would be just a little bit easier.

I taught toddlers in Sunday School (now that is a noble calling!). I sang in the church choir and worked in nearly every children's program offered: Vacation Bible School, Girls in Action, AWANA, choir, summer camp, and the list continues. Despite all the work I did on Sundays and Wednesdays, I was still miserable. I despised myself and scorned my life. I spent nearly all my time crying out to God to rescue me from my agony, but God seemed too far away to hear . . . too intangible to be of any real help.

I married when I was only nineteen. Eighteen months into the marriage, I gave birth to a son. Ten months later I was abandoned by my husband, the same day my daughter was born. In my misery, I again married, this time to John who had three children of his own. Now I was the mother of five children; the oldest being 9 years of age, the youngest 4 and the three in the middle were all 8 years old. From the wedding on, my life turned from being just plain miserable to disastrous. I loved my new family, but I was unable to cope. I turned to God for help, but He seemed too elusive. I still could not find Him anywhere.

Like a black kettle on an open flame, I begin to boil inside. There was no satisfaction, no comfort, and I felt little, if any, love. I clung to my life at church like one clinging to a lifeline in the ocean. The church *had* to be my lifeline! Somewhere within those walls was an answer. I was sure if I stuck it out long enough, I would find it. Unfortunately, I did not find it soon enough. I began to yell, hit, kick, cuss, throw things—with my children as the recipients. I had become an abuser. The more my life around me crumbled, the more hateful I became. I lived in a prison that I had created; only in my creation, I did not put in a door of escape. I was trapped.

Several years passed, and I did not feel any different about my life. In fact, it was worse. In an effort to find some happiness, John and I bought into a time-share vacation plan; to be accurate, we bought two. Then we purchased retirement property on Lake Livingston, which we never went back to see again. Next we bought a pop-up travel trailer, a vacation travel club membership, a new van to pull the pop-up, and a brand-new red car for me. Along with these came unsolicited credit cards with incredibly high limits, which I had no problem taking to the limit. Still, I did not find any satisfaction to life. I continued faithfully to volunteer for every committee at church and the children's school, but inside I became less and less able to effectively handle my life.

A bright spot during this time was the birth of our two daughters, Cariane in 1984 and Marleigh in 1985. As much as I adored these precious daughters of ours, there was still something missing . . . a void. I wasn't even sure *what* was missing. How does one find something, if one cannot put a name to it?

A family can only live for so long in a spending frenzy before it catches up to them. Filing for bankruptcy went against everything John and I believed in, but I had left us with little choice. Without the pressure of so many bills, I felt certain that life would be a little more gentle with me, but I was mistaken. I felt like a duck in the water. To my friends and extended family, I was gliding along through life as smoothly as you please. But my own family could see that I was actually the feet of the duck, paddling for all my might, going in circles without end just to keep from drowning. Panic attacks were a daily occurence, causing me to lose all control and logic.

Not wanting to be away from the babies during the day, I took a newspaper route to earn extra money. I worked from about 3:30 A.M. until 6:30 A.M. seven days a week for eleven years. During those wee hours of the morning as I relentlessly tossed papers out the windows, I spent a lot of time praying. My family had become highly dysfunctional, with a screaming wife and mother and a house full of rebellious children. Unable to cope with the internal stress and pressures, I would cry out, "God where are You? I feel I am going to explode! Can You not help me? Where are You anyway?

It was a *very* long time in coming, but I came to realize that God had been there all along. He had been helping me, but only as much as I would allow Him. I was expecting God to turn around one day, notice that I was drowning in my own pain, and zap me into a new creation. He could do that if He so desired, but God had another plan. One in which I was responsible for my actions and well-being. God, in His gentle, loving care, used several different ways or avenues to aid in the much-needed changes in my life and to call me to become the person He originally planned. For true to His Word, He was the light that guided me on my path to becoming whole.

Moreover, I will give you a new heart and put a new spirit within you; I will remove the heart of stone from your flesh and give you a heart of flesh. (Ezek. 36:26)

There are valleys
and there are mountains so high.
It used to seem that no matter where I was,
my love for Jesus was always there.
But it seems that of late
that when I look up
I cannot see even the lowly valley.
Could it be that I am below the level of the sea?
I try to climb out of the depths that I'm in.
Even if its to just reach the valley.
For if I can reach the valley which I search for,
the mountain top surely can't be far behind.

-Written by the author

Avenue #1

During the paper route each morning at 4 A.M., I listened to a radio program called *Unshackled*. It emulated the old radio dramas from the 1940s, with pipe-organ music and people acting from a script. At first I thought it was corny, but strangely, I was drawn to it. Each episode was the real-life story of an individual caught in a circle of sin. Through the drama, the actors would tell of the struggles they encountered and the miserable mistakes they made. Many times they would end up a drug addict or alcoholic, landing in prison or trying to commit suicide. At rope's end, the individual would turn and find the answer in the waiting, ready-to-rescue-and-forgive open arms of Jesus. The lives portrayed were wretched with sin, but the victory from Christ was incredible! Best of all, they were true.

One episode of *Unshackled* portrayed an especially shady character. Afterward, while praying, I made the comment to myself, "I'm glad I'm not like that person. My life may be pretty sorry, but it's not that bad!" The exact moment those words were out of my mouth, I felt a presence like I have never felt before. So strong was the feeling, I had to pull off to the side of the road and shut off the motor. I did not *hear* anything, but these words came to mind:

> Your life is no different from every life story you have listened to for the past few years. What made these others sin is the same that is within you. You are no better, for your sin is just as great. Your attitude and self-centeredness is what drives you away from Me. I have not turned from you for a second. But you, wallowing in your sinful ways, have turned from Me.

I knew this was God speaking to me! Great wells of sobbing wracked my entire being, and for the first time in my life, I really and truly began to come face-to-face with my sin. At first, I tried to rationalize some of my behavior: I never took drugs, I didn't drink. There are others worse than me, such as rapists, murderers, and child molesters. When I finally ceased trying to make excuses, shame and remorse started weighing heavily on me. As wave after wave of memories of my behavior flooded my mind, I couldn't stop weeping. *God said there was no difference between the heart action of the worst sinner and my own heart of sin.* I knew it was true!

From that point on with nearly every *Unshackled*, I would find a similarity between the life being portrayed and my life. That morning, as my memory dug up all the abusive behaviors I tried so hard to hide, I sought forgiveness and repented right there in the car. During the weeks and months which followed, there were many times when I again had to pull off to the side of the road as the pain of my actions became overwhelming. A box of tissue stayed by my side as God's conviction brought cleansing tears. Slowly, the constricting bands on my heart started to break lose, ever so little.

I began to understand it is not the *action* I do that is so offensive in God's sight, as much as the *motive* within my heart that put the action into motion. I saw my heart and the dirt that was in it. My heart was ugly. And it was black. I always knew I was a sinner, as is everyone. But this "look inside" was frightening! This was the first time I can remember having a revelation from God, and I did not take it lightly. Maybe it *wasn't* too late for me to make some changes in my life. I already knew I didn't have the strength by myself, but maybe, just maybe with God's help I had a chance.

Avenue #2

After listening to *Unshackled* for some time, I began to wonder if other Christians went through similar struggles with sin, or if I was the only one who was so despicable. Rationally, I knew this was not true, but feelings are seldom based on reason. Even though I had been asking forgiveness all along, I did not feel forgiven and I certainly could not forget. God again used a radio program, *Focus on the Family* with Dr. James Dobson, to greatly influence my life. Although many times the subject matter did not pertain to me specifically, I could often identify with Dr. Dobson's guests on the show. Intellectually it sounds strange, but I found solace in the fact that I was not the only person who was desperately seeking God and could not seem to find Him. *Focus on the Family* plainly and honestly showed the way to God in the midst of a stormy life. Could this be part of the lifeline for which I had been searching?

Subtle changes began to take place. Using the radio programs, God continued in His own special way to reveal unhealthy attitudes, thoughts, and feelings that I harbored in my heart. Crying stayed a daily part of my life. Waves of conviction rolled over me while I prayed for not only forgiveness, but also the understanding of *"why?"*

The more I cried out to God, the more He revealed. The more He revealed, the more I asked forgiveness. The more forgiveness I asked for, the more changes started taking place both outwardly (actions you could readily see) and inwardly (the motives behind the actions). Some of the changes that needed to take place in my heart were obvious; others were hidden—some times even from myself. The shame and remorse over my horrendous behavior was almost more than I could bare. I didn't think I could go on any longer. I wanted to stop living in all this torment. I began to wonder if death was the only way out.

"God do something! I don't think I can take this anymore! I've *had* it! Is there a way to make sense of all of this? If there is, You have to show me because I just can't continue like this much longer! I mean it this time . . . either show me a way out of this mess or I will just end this misery. God I need You NOW!"

No lightening bolts came from heaven . . . no *zap*. So I made the decision that Monday would be the last day of my life.

Avenue #3

That night I received a phone call from a rather wealthy acquaintance of ours. Janet told me of a seminar being held at a Lutheran church about a forty-minute drive from our house. The guest speakers were Fred and Florence Littauer, well-known authors and speakers around the US, Canada, and Australia. While praying for the seminar, Janet felt God wanted her to invite us, so she took the liberty of registering both John and me. I was in no mood to attend a seminar and I told Janet.

Janet was insistent, but then so was I. She even offered to pick us up if we needed a ride. Finally, she said the one thing that made me determined to go: "If you don't have the money, I would be willing to pay for you both. After all, it is only fifty dollars each." That did it! To Janet, fifty dollars might have been an "only," but to us, it was a lot of money. I already was intimidated by Harry and Janet's wealth, good looks, and life, which they seemed to have all together. Just being around them and the confidence they displayed made me feel insignificant. I know it wasn't anything *they* did that made me feel this way, it was my own insecurities and jealousies being manifested. For whatever reason, I paid the money (with a hot check) and dragged John to the seminar, "Freeing Your Mind from Memories That Bind."

My life was transformed . . . forever changed through Fred and Florence. I walked into the seminar with confusion and shame; I walked away with the dawning of understanding and an ability to begin to forgive myself. A private meeting with Fred helped me to uncover reasons why I was unable to handle or cope with my own life—why I felt it necessary to always hurt those I loved the most; why I had a real need to control my family and situations. I came to grasp the concept that it was my emotions binding me, keeping my mind captive. Until I was free of the emotional bondage, I would be unable to live a full, healthy life. I learned every aspect of life has an emotion that goes with it. Even though I may forget an incident from the past, my emotions have not forgotten. People, actions, or words can trigger an emotion causing a reaction that is not welcomed. *My past was the reason for the emotional and physical abuse of my children; it could no longer be the excuse.*

Looking back I remember wondering if even *God* could heal our broken family. John's daughter ran away at 17 and now, eight years later we still do not have contact with her. We know Charlean has a toddler, I can only pray she is a better mother to Miranda than I was to her. My own daughter tried to commit suicide when she was sixteen. My son sits in prison. I threw our middle boy out of the house at 15 years of age. He came back to see us only once; he stole our charge card and ran up a large bill and we have not heard from him since. Then on his 13th birthday, John's youngest

17

son was snatched away from us by child welfare and never returned. With the combination of the way I treated him and the unstable life he had with the state, Robert to this day, struggles to function in a world he has not been prepared to handle.

Although a lot of the healing took place that weekend with the Littaurers, the restoration process is taking many years. The hurt I caused others could never be restored in a moment. It is my constant prayer that God will work in all of our hearts to bring about healing, a sense of wholeness and purpose as well as sparks of forgiveness and understanding. I cling to the hope that one day, we all will be blessed with the ability to have a healthy family-relationship with each other.

Over the next year, I read, studied, and reread Fred's books, *Freeing Your Mind from Memories That Bind* and *The Promise of Restoration*. Whereas before my life resembled murky swamp water it was now more like dirty bathwater. There were still issues to deal with, and I was not without sin in my life. Some times old habits would revisit. But I saw the real me—the one God created—begin to emerge like a butterfly from a cocoon. Although I could not excuse away my past actions, I now had understanding. I was learning to accept God's forgiveness and receive the grace to forgive myself.

Avenue #4

Radio and the Littauers were not the only vessels God used to touch my hardened heart. Our church started a twelve-week study called "Experiencing God = Knowing and Doing the Will of God." The study was a five-day-a-week individual workbook to help one get a better understanding of God in our own life. Each day there was scripture, an explanation, and questions to answer. At first, I thought the study was too elementary, much too simplified to make it worth my time and effort. I felt almost silly answering the questions, and many times just skimmed parts I felt I already knew. I even smugly told our study group that I thought it was a little *too* fundamental—it should be geared more toward new Christians, not for me. Using godly wisdom, our group leader Frank Gillespie only said, "Trust God. Keep working through the questions. God wants to reveal more of Himself through this study if you will let Him. By the time you finish all twelve weeks, God will completely and forever change your life. I know He will. Trust me. No . . . trust Him."

True to his statement, as I began to work through the pages God began to reveal Himself to me. I read about His deep, abiding love for me regardless of what I have done. I discovered God desires a love relationship with me that goes beyond church, reading the Bible, and praying. I learned that I was not created just for an earthly life, but for an eternal life as well. For the first time that I could remember, I tasted what it felt like to be cherished. That elusive peace was not just a dream any more, but it hinted at being just around the corner.

I already knew God reveals Himself (through scripture, prayer, and the Holy Spirit). What I didn't understand was that the Lord reveals not only Himself, but His plans and purposes for me. That creates a crisis of belief. Do I believe, adjust my life and obey, or do I just ignore His plan and go my own way? This was a phenomenal revelation to me. It was almost as if I had been blinded, but now a gray mist was emerging and becoming clearer with each day.

God doesn't just sit in heaven and allow things to happen; He reveals parts of Himself and allows me to make decisions on what to do with the revelation. I always thought I just had to pray and God more or less pushed a "yes" or "no" button, then I would have my answer. I didn't realize I had a daily part in God's ultimate plan for me and my family; a part that went beyond just a quick prayer and then waiting for God to push one of His buttons.

Toward the end of "Experiencing God," we studied the cost of obedience. Just like a steak is beaten until it becomes tender, my heart had been beaten by conviction until it was becoming tender enough to be pliable. I no longer saw obedience as a burden I *had* to do, but rather as a privilege. I *almost* wished God would ask me to obey Him at a great cost so I could prove my new found love for Him. I believed I would burst with all the new insights I was receiving. I realized I no longer hated myself, but was discovering the wonderful, lovable, talented person God created me to be all along.

Avenue #5

Again, God used something unusual to get my attention: Preteen camp for third through sixth graders. As a counselor, I was responsible to teach Bible truths to the children, yet it seemed every word I heard was a new arrow that pierced my heart yet again. I didn't think the Holy Spirit could go any deeper, but there He was in full force, digging His way down to the very depths of my soul.

Each night, long after the evening service was over and the children had scampered away, I would sit on the grassy field alone and pray. As my heart was pierced from the Holy Spirit's revelation of my still-ugly heart, I couldn't stop the flow of tears, which was becoming an all too familiar part of my prayers. I was afraid if anyone saw me, they would see the pain still on my face, so I stayed outside until time for lights to be out in the cabins.

The last night at camp, after all the children had gone to sleep, I again sat on the grass, unable to sleep. My boiling point had hit a full roll; I felt I was going to explode any second.

"God! What do You want from me? You keep showing me all this crud in my life, and I am dealing with it the only way I know. I see my sins and the pain it has brought. I've asked Your forgiveness. You have brought about lots of changes, and I am grateful for that. But is there no end? What more do You want from me? Tell me, and I will gladly do it. I am so exhausted, Lord. Tell me what else I can do to please You. What *more* can I give You?"

"I want all of you."

I knew what I had heard in my mind was the silent voice of God. "You have me Lord. You know I love you."

But again I heard, *"I want all of you."*

Now I knew God was asking for more, much more than I had given to date. It had been hard work uncovering the layers of rubbish in my life. Like a garbage dump, the junk stays until it is comfortably packed down and is no longer an intruder but part of the dump itself. That is how the trash in my life had become. For several years, God relentlessly hounded me. Just as relentlessly, I dealt with the junk. I didn't know what else to do.

Again I replied, "Lord, you have all of me. All that I am, I give to you."

"I want all of you," I heard for a third time.

The story of Simon Peter and Jesus from the Book of John flashed to mind. Three times Jesus asked Simon Peter if he loved Him. Three times Peter answered yes. Now three times God said, *"I want all of you"*. He wanted more; but what more could I give?

I sat there for some time thinking about my life. I reviewed all the damage and pain I had caused. I did all I thought God was asking of me; so what more did He want? As I voiced these thoughts more to myself than to the Lord, I suddenly knew. He was asking for a complete, absolute, total surrender of myself to Him . . . not just what I was willing to give to Him, but absolutely everything! This was my crisis of belief. Do I continue to argue using my life of failures as an excuse? I was sure I would just fail again, but . . . could God really change all that? Can I trust that He knows what He is doing and asking of me? As I sat pondering these thoughts I knew my answer . . . I had to trust Him . . . completely.

"Father, I have no earthly idea why you want me, but all that I am, all that I ever will be, I give wholly and completely to you. You can have all of me."

Almost immediately, I sensed that inner voice again speaking to me. *"I want you to serve Me full-time in missions."*

Stunned, I sat there for a long time. I felt confusion. Why would the Lord say that? Even I knew I was not missions material. That's reserved for decent, fine, upstanding Christians, not someone with a shame-filled past. Inside, I knew the decision was already made. For me, at this moment in my life, there was no alternative but to obey. God knew what He was doing. Besides, my past was now my past; I was no longer the same person.

"OK, Lord. You show me what You want and I will do it."

The next afternoon, I drove home with great excitement; I could barely wait to see John and share with him the incredible experience I had had with the Lord at camp.

But my quiet, soft-spoken husband was bubbling with his own news.

"Valerie, you will not believe what happened while you were gone. I had the most amazing time with God. It was as if He was asking me to give Him all of me—no holds barred. He wants to be part of our lives, just like we have been learning in 'Experiencing God.' You won't believe it, but I think that we are to join Youth with a Mission—you know, the Mercy Ships. For whatever reason, God wants us to go into full-time missions. I don't think we should wait; the time for us to do this is now."

Try as I might, I was unable to express what was going on inside. Gratitude that God took such an interest in our lives? Yes. Relief that what I heard at camp really was the voice of God calling our family into missions? Yes. But there was something else as well: fear. Fear that I would fail. Fear that I did not have enough faith. Fear that I would stop believing. I knew I could never take away the fear, and I knew that I could not guarantee that I had enough faith. So I laid the burden on the One who *was* enough.

"I am at a loss. I know that You are calling my family into missions. We are willing to follow wherever You lead. But I am afraid. I know You in my mind; Your Holy Spirit lives in my heart. But I need more. I need to know You so well that there will never, and I mean *never*, be a time that I doubt You. I want—no, I *need* to know You as well as Job knew You. Nothing could turn his face from You. With every ounce of my being I need to know you so well that if the trials of Job fall on me, I will not turn to the right or to the left, but stay on the path you've set my feet on. That is what I need.

"I don't care if I lose faith in myself and fail, but I want to know You intimately enough that I will never lose faith in You. Show me in such a way that I will never doubt You. I desperately desire to know more of who You are. So I challenge You, Lord, to show me who You are in such a way that fear or doubt will no longer be a part of who I am."

In a way, that was a dangerous prayer—God could very well take me up on the challenge I gave Him. And He did just that. The circumstances (I call them miracles) that happened over the next two years were so incredible they could only have been orchestrated by God. He revealed His faithfulness, His power and His incredible love for me and my family. Through His intimate involvement in our lives, we have all been drawn into a deep, abiding faith that otherwise, for me at least, might never have occurred.

Hearing God's voice is something that I am still in the process of learning. I know for certain that He asked me to write these miracles—these great deeds of His, into a book, so that you, His precious child, could experience as I did the amazing awesome love He has for you.

God is the same God today as He was of old; His miracles still take place. Need a miracle right about now? Are you in need of experiencing God's intimate involvement in your life? This may be my life I wrote about, but these are your miracles. The principles are the same . . . God loves you and He will never leave or forsake you. He will express the same love for you that He did for us. Come . . . stand in awe with me as I share with you the many different ways the Lord went about . . .

Answering My Heart's Cry

> I pray also that the eyes of your heart may be enlightened in order that you may know the hope to which He has called you. (Eph. 1:18)

2

Sold with Faith—
Bought with Obedience
Obedience

The holiday spirit is nearly impossible to keep when the results of tragedy are spread throughout the house. My parents, Cary and Marie Baker, were trying their best to be brave—to put up a good front—but I knew they were experiencing a heart-wrenching pain that went beyond words. Heaped throughout the house were stacks of paperwork on every available spot, mattresses on the dining-room floor, boxes piled almost to the ceiling, and clothes draped over everything. My parents (who had lost their home and the majority of their personal belongings in a flood) salvaged items above the three-foot water line and were in the long, painful process of sorting through what remained.

Mom and Dad never complained about my feeble efforts to make them comfortable. John and I both desired for my folks to feel like this was their home; to stay with us for as long as it took them to rebuild their shattered lives. But reality kept setting in: None of us could stay—not my parents, not John or myself, not our daughters. We would all have to leave. Our family knew the Lord wanted us to serve Him full time; we felt it was to be with the Mercy Ships, an arm of Youth With A Mission (YWAM). In a few short months we needed to have our house sold, our belongings packed, and leave our hometown to begin our training for a life of mission work. Whatever preparations needed to be done for our move, however, would have to wait; right now my parents needed our help and support. And with the paperwork to fill out, the county officials to see, and the decisions to be made, there was little time for anything else. The aftermath of the flood was consuming all of our lives.

As I stuffed our Thanksgiving turkey for the next day, my mind wandered back to that disastrous night just a few short weeks ago. Several times during the past thirty-plus years, warnings of possible floods were issued, but the floods never came my parents' way. This time however, my mom was nervous. When the unusually heavy rains lasted several days, Mom started to put furniture up on blocks or stacked on the beds. Neither my four brothers nor I were particularly concerned about our folks flooding, but still Mom worked into the night. Two of my brothers, Rodney and Bobby, who had come to help Mom, decided to sleep over. The guys were not afraid it would flood, but they wanted to pacify Mom's growing uneasiness.

Sure enough 4 A.M. brought the floodwaters . . . forty-five miles an hour . . . right through the house. Without the strong arms and quick thinking of Rodney and Bobby, our precious parents would have been swept away in the dark of night as they tried to escape the rising floodwaters. With no insurance to replace or repair, losing the house was traumatizing not only for Mom and Dad, but also for the rest of the family as well. Yet in the midst of the turmoil, our hearts were grateful for the lives of our loved ones, who had been spared. These hodgepodge of memories certainly would make for a bittersweet Thanksgiving.

From the flood, my wandering thoughts came full circle to all that needed to be accomplished prior to the listing and selling of our house. Having contacted a real-estate agent, we were dismayed by the number of things that needed to be completed before we could even *list* the house. Until the house was made ready, no real-estate company would even hang a "for sale" sign. The realtor suggested making the house appear more spacious. This could be accomplished by painting the inside of the house white, and boxing and storing the majority of our belongings. Because a good first impression can happen only once, there needed to be a considerable amount of time and money spent on the bushes, flowerbeds, and grass, which covered nearly one-and-a-half acres. The back quarter-acre housed John's mechanic shop; to say the word *disaster*, when referring to it, was being kind.

Making a list of all we had to do was enough to give me a headache. Yet here we were with little, if any, progress being made. I knew we could not get the house ready to put on the market while my parents lived with us; and I knew they were not leaving soon. Selling a house takes time, and time was one thing we did not have. As panic hovered near the surface, I spent a lot of time in prayer. Should we put off our missions training until next year? What was the best way to help my parents? How could we get *all* this work finished on our house, sell it, and be ready to leave in a few short months?

The ringing phone interrupted my worried thoughts. On the other end, a lady introduced herself as Dawn Ross.

Her family also lost everything to the flood. Because their home had flooded numerous times, the county banned the rebuilding of her house, along with several of their neighbors' homes. Dawn and her husband were searching different neighborhoods, looking for a suitable lot on which to build a new house and piece their lives back together again. Dennis and Dawn, also Christians, prayed, asking the Lord to direct their search. Their search led them down our country road and to the front of our house. Sitting in their car staring at our home, they felt the Lord nudge them to talk to us. Getting our name from the mailbox, they looked up our number in the phone book and called.

"We are thinking of building in your neighborhood and we like the way your house looks. May we come over and see the layout of your place?" asked Dawn.

I thought this was a rather strange request; and I really didn't care to have people traipse through my messy house, even if they were strangers. I explained to Dawn that although we did not personally go through the flood, my house right now certainly looked as if it had. Dawn said she understood and insisted that she and her husband be allowed to come walk through our home. Giving in, a time was set for Friday, the day after Thanksgiving.

Friday at 8:00 A.M., Dennis and Dawn arrived at our house. Carefully stepping around the (now neatly stacked), clutter of boxes, I ushered them from room to room. With barely a word, the Rosses expressed their thanks and left. I was surprised when two hours later we receive another phone call from Dawn asking if they could again see the house. This time Dennis and Dawn brought both sets of their parents along with them. As before, they walked through the rooms, only this time all the closets, cupboards, as well as the attic were inspected. Again with barely a word, they thanked us and left.

That evening Dawn called a third time.

"My husband and I like your house; in fact we have fallen in love with it. We have drawn up our own floor plan for the new house we want to build, full of all the extras we'd like. Going through your house, we realize that your place already has everything in it! My husband works nights and sleeps days. The way the bedrooms are set up, your bedroom will aford the quietness he needs without hearing the children; it if perfect for us. There is a blue bedroom for our son. Our youngest will want the front bedroom as she is crazy about Barbie Dolls and will love the wallpaper and the purple walls. The gray and pink flowers in the back room will be ideal for our oldest daughter. And there is even a room without carpet for our parrot! We like your house so much, we want to buy it instead of building one. I know it's probably a long shot, but are you in the market to sell your house anytime soon?"

A feather could have knocked me over! How was I to respond? My first instinct was to say no. Then I thought I'd say, not now, but you can call me another time. Yet, hadn't I been praying for an answer? Was *this* the answer we were searching for? Knowing John and I needed to really seek the Lord's guidance, I told Dawn we would meet with them on Monday morning. We could discuss the prospect of selling the house then.

Not knowing anything about selling a house, John had invited our friend Ron Rausin, a real estate broker, to join us on Monday to answer any technical questions that might arise. Before the Rosses arrival, Ron discussed with us the amount of money we would be satisfied with if we decided to sell. Because the figure was $89,000, Ron suggested making the asking price $95,000, thus leaving room for negotiations. With Ron sitting in the family room, the four of us, Dennis, Dawn, John, and I, sat at the breakfast table. As no one knew exactly where to start, we sat for a few moments in awkward silence.

Dennis started out first by saying, "Dawn and I felt God confirm to us over the weekend, we are not to build a house. We feel it is right to buy this one and make it our own."

Dennis looked to Dawn for a moment, and then she added, "We would like very much to buy your house. With our insurance money we will even be able to pay cash."

At the word *cash* my heart sank. In Texas, you take possession at the time you pay for the house. Paying cash would mean that we would have to move out immediately. I could feel panic making its way up my throat, blocking off the air passage, threatening to choke me. My near panic was premature though.

Dawn continued, "We have been talking, and feel it would be best if you all keep living in the house through Christmas and New Years. It will be easier on all of us if we are the ones to find temporary housing until the first of the year. This will give you and your parents one last Christmas holiday together. We know what they have gone through; staying here will be easier on them than trying to move out in a hurry. It would be too emotionally draining on all of us if we try any other way. After the first of the year, maybe the middle of January, we would like to move in. Do you think that will give you enough time to find another place?"

Our minds were whirling with thoughts, but neither John or I could find words to say. Instead we just sat there like a couple of dummies staring at Dennis and Dawn.

At this point, I began to share with the Rosses our call into missions. I explained the dilemma of my parents staying with us and how their coming into our lives at this time seemed to be part of the perfect answer to many anxious prayers.

"Well, in that case," piped in Dennis, "since your only source of income is your mechanic shop out back, you can continue to keep your business open until you leave for your missions training in March. We will not charge you rent; all we ask is to make sure you have garage liability insurance. Well, what do you think?" Tears were threatening to fall and the lump in my throat blocked all attempts at speaking. We both realized we were hearing God's answer, yet we were unable to utter even one word of response.

Dawn broached the subject that was at the top of all our minds. How much were we asking for the house? Posing my answer as a question and not at all with confidence, I squeaked more than said, "$95,000?" The silence that followed was almost deafening. No one moved, each of us looking down at the table or nervously fiddling with our hands.

Quietly, Dennis said, "I'm sorry. I can't pay $95,000."

There it was—the moment of truth. Now what?

Looking to John, I motioned for him to say something, anything . . . just break the silence! After what seemed like ten minutes (but in reality was probably only ten seconds), John asked that ominous question, "How much *can* you pay?"

Dennis was quiet for a few moments as he glanced at his wife. Dawn smiled at her husband. Dennis inhaled deeply and replied, "Dawn and I have prayed all weekend. We feel the Lord specifically told us to offer you $98,000."

Thinking he had misunderstood, I quickly injected, "We are not asking $98,000, we are asking $95,000."

For a brief moment, Dennis seemed to be struggling. He tipped his head toward heaven as if he was praying. Then, with a determined look in his eyes, Dennis looked straight at me and answered, "I know. But this was the amount the Lord gave to Dawn and me as we prayed. Our desire is to be obedient to Him without compromise. Are you willing to sell us your home and accept the offer to live here through the holidays?"

Dennis and Dawn were looking at us; I think our faces must have had blank stares. Dennis continued, "The offer on the price, however, is firm, we cannot pay a penny less than $98,000."

A loud *clunk* from the living room brought a halt to our conversation. Ron, sitting in John's recliner straining to hear what the four of us said, leaned too far over, causing the recliner to tip sideways, nearly spilling him to the floor. After making sure Ron was not hurt, we invited him to join us in the breakfast room.

Again, we were all silent, not sure what to say and who should speak first. Slowly, the details were worked out, handshakes given, and papers signed. I realized that no matter what happened next, this miracle would add a softness to the memory of the tragedy we had been living with.

God was here in the midst of us. Thanksgiving suddenly seemed a whole lot sweeter!

For thou are great, and doest wondrous things; thou are God alone. (Ps. 86:10)

3

The Deadline
Prayer of the Fleece

There it was . . . in the midst of all the dust, hidden behind the bedside stand, forgotten . . . that awful reminder: We were being sued! My husband, who owned a mechanic shop, was being unjustly sued by a disgruntled customer. Since Quality Automotive was not incorporated, as the owners, we were personally responsible for the lawsuit. I didn't want to deal with this notice six months ago when we received it and I certainly did not want to deal with it now.

Christmas was over and the new year had begun. Mom and Dad had temporarily moved back into their previously flooded house. Although it was too badly damaged to repair, we labored to make several of the rooms livable while construction was underway to convert their garage into a new home for them. With my parents somewhat settled, I was busy cleaning, sorting, throwing out, and packing everything in the house. Our house had been sold; in a few days the closing would take place and everything had to be moved out. At this moment I didn't have time to worry about this lawsuit. Setting the notice aside, I continued cleaning.

We were excited about working full-time with Mercy Ships, International. In a few months we would attend a Crossroad's Discipleship Training School in Tyler, Texas, a three-hour drive from our hometown. Afterward, our family would go to Costa Rica to continue our training in a practical hands-on manner. It seemed there were a hundred and one details involved in selling our house, closing the business, and disposing of the majority of our belongings. There were times when things seemed so overwhelming I wish I had a year to deal with everything instead of only months. However, knowing how I am, a few months or a few years, I wouldn't be anymore ready to leave. That's the problem with procrastinators (those who put things off until later); the length of time one has doesn't make a difference in the amount of work completed. It's sad to say, but I am a chief among procrastinators.

Several days later, while finishing the last of our bedroom packing, I again came across the notice from the courthouse. I knew this lawsuit would have to be dealt with before we moved. *Maybe I should call someone for advice*, I thought. Not having a personal lawyer, I telephoned Yogi, my brother's wife, who works for a tax law firm and explained the situation.

Yogi, whose real name's Marilyn, promised to do some research using her legal contacts. Later that afternoon Yogi called back with what she had discovered. "It seems that Fred Fischer (not his real name) and his wife are in the middle of a divorce. At this time, they are not actively pursuing the lawsuit as they have too much to deal with. But the judge has set a court hearing for July. It's imperative that John be at the hearing or he'll be held in contempt."

For just a second I was elated; Fred was getting a divorce! Maybe now he would be too distraught to worry about the lawsuit and just let it drop. I could hope anyway. As if I had been struck with a lightening bolt, the Holy Spirit jolted my whole being. My flippant attitude brought a force of conviction that was overwhelming. Into my mind came these thoughts,

> What is money other than a dream that is gone tomorrow. I would rather give You all the earthly treasures You desire than to see those I love hurting from the pain of divorce. Do you not know that marriage is a sacred vow that I do not take lightly. Neither do I take your attitude about Fred's marriage lightly!

Shame, grief, and sorrow racked my body as tears of repentance poured out. For several hours I alternated between praying and crying. Finally, I started to feel the Lord's forgiveness for my ungodly attitude and was able to think clearly again. Since I knew the law firm Yogi worked for could not help us, I flipped through the phone book, chose a name at random, made a phone call, set an appointment with the lawyer and turned back to the work of packing.

"What do you mean we lost! We haven't even been to court yet! Explain to me how I can owe $100,000 when the car is only worth $2,500 . . . and that's stretching it!" John hollered.

"Calm down," the lawyer said. "Like I already explained, in the state of Texas, when the plaintiff's attorney, that's Fred's attorney, sent you a petition, it is mandatory that the defendant, that's you, Quality Automotive, retain a lawyer and file an Answer. Since you failed to do that, the judge proceeded without you; only Fred's side of the story was given. It's too late to explain or try to prove that Fred trumped up charges out of vindictiveness. The judge can only make his decision on the information provided to the court. The final hearing will be in July, but it is only a formality. The judge has already decided John, you're guilty of the charges you are accused of. Whether you like it or not, you have to appear in court in July and you have to somehow pay the judgement amount the court has set—$100,000."

In shocked disbelief, we left the lawyer's office. My procrastination really got us in trouble this time. Here we were preparing to travel the world tending to the business of spreading the gospel, and we couldn't even handle our own personal affairs. I knew this was my fault. In our family, I am the one to pay the bills, make vacation plans, and handle any family matters. I should have made an appointment for John, or at least encouraged him to call a lawyer, months ago. Now what were we to do? The profit from the sale of our house would only be around $30,000. If the judge took that we would not have the money to go into missions. Nor would we have a place to live. Because John's mechanic shop was in our backyard and our house was already sold, neither would we have a source of income. We would be a penniless, jobless, homeless family. We would have nothing left but each other.

Desperately, I spent time in prayer asking the Lord for guidance, for wisdom, for a solution. "Lord, show us what to do. Our desire is to serve You. Wherever You ask us to go, we'll go; whatever You ask us to do, we want to do. But we're in trouble. It seems our unwillingness to face our problems may stop us from going anywhere. We may even lose everything we have worked for all these years. We need You. Please tell us what to do."

"I want you to go to Hawaii for your Crossroads."

Hawaii!? Where did that come from? I'm a daydreamer, and many times I find myself off on some wild tangent sometimes even in the middle of my prayers. Disgusted with myself for allowing my mind to wander during my prayers again, I dismissed it as nothing more than a foolish thought and went back to packing. Over the next days and weeks, I continued to seek the Lord concerning the lawsuit. Yet, with each prayer, the same thought came to my mind, *"Go to Hawaii."* This had nothing to do with the lawsuit, so why did I keep hearing this? Where was this thought coming from?

I know God speaks to us in our thoughts, and I was learning how to hear Him, but what I was hearing did not make any sense; I wasn't even sure this *was* from God. Hawaii offered the same Crossroad Discipleship Training as Tyler, with their outreach going to Ukraine instead of Costa Rica. Feasibly, John could fly back from Costa Rica for the hearing, but he certainly couldn't fly back and forth from Ukraine; the cost would be astronomical. Yet, the words kept coming into my mind, *"Go to Hawaii."*

In frustration, not sure of what to do, I cried out, "God, I'm so confused! I keep thinking You are telling us to go to Hawaii for our Crossroads, but that's ridiculous. What about the lawsuit? If the court takes our money, we won't even be able to go to Tyler, let alone Hawaii. Besides, I checked into going to Hawaii. Did you know it will add about $6,000 more to the cost of our training? I don't see how we can go, so why do I keep hearing *"go to Hawaii?"* I am trying to hear Your voice, but I am not sure that if what I am hearing is from You. It doesn't make sense. Let me hear You, Lord. Speak loud and clear."

Quietly, I heard, *"Go to Hawaii."*

Deciding to make sure once and for all whether or not this was from the Lord, I again prayed, only this time differently. "God, I have to know one way or another if this is You speaking to me. So I am going to lay down the fleece like it was done in the Old Testament. You are the same God today as You were yesterday, so I am asking You to speak to me as You did with Gideon—through the fleece. This is Monday. By Friday at five o'clock, I want Fred to call us to say he has changed his mind, he is canceling the lawsuit, and he doesn't want the $100,000. If Fred calls, then we will go to Hawaii. Otherwise, if I don't hear from Fred, we are headed to Tyler, and I do not want to hear the words telling us to go to Hawaii anymore."

To this day, I am not sure why I prayed this way, except I was at a loss to know what else to do, and time was getting short for our final decision concerning our Crossroads. I was so sure this was the end of my hearing "go to Hawaii," I never mentioned my fleece prayer to John. I just continued to pack our boxes and prepare for the move. I was confident that in some way God would help us with the lawsuit. I did not, however, seriously consider that He would take me up on my prayer and make it disappear. It was ridiculous I even asked, but to expect it to happen? Never.

Thursday, 7:30 P.M.

About to walk out the door, I heard the phone ring. As I answered it, a man at the other end said, "Hello, Mrs. Clayton. I don't know if you remember who I am, but my name is Fred Fischer. I have a lawsuit pending against Quality Automotive. I need to talk to your husband. Can I meet with you and John tomorrow afternoon at the cafeteria in Shenandoah? It's really important. Say about three o'clock?"

To say I was in shock is a vast understatement. Thoughts were racing around in my mind as I tried to figure out what this all meant. Tomorrow we were meeting Fred at three; I gave God until five tomorrow to help us out of this jam if He wanted us to go to Hawaii. Was this from God?

Walking to the car, I told John of our pending meeting with Fred. Not wanting his hopes to soar over tomorrow's meeting, I still did not tell him of my prayer. If this was God working, then I did not want to interfere. I must admit, though, that the phone call from Fred had me wondering what God was *really* up to.

Friday afternoon, 3:00 P.M.

I think John was worried Fred would try to cause more trouble. I am not sure what I was feeling . . . or even thinking. To say the least, we both were a little nervous as we walked into the cafeteria that day. As Fred—the target of a lot of my worry these past weeks—walked in, I could not help but feel sorry for the man. With head down, a dejected look over his entire countenance, Fred slowly walked over and slid into the booth across from us.

After polite formalities, Fred started right in, "I need to tell you something. I have not been to church for a number of years; I seldom even pray anymore. But on Monday I felt something so strange, yet so real. It was the presence of God right there in my office. It was almost like a physical presence. The feeling was so strong. I felt as if I was punched in the stomach and could not move. All I could do was stop what I was doing and stand still.

"I don't know if you believe in God talking to people or not, but I promise He was talking to me this past Monday. He said He wants me to come back to Him, to quit running away. He said I need to look to Him for answers to my messed up life and to quit blaming everyone and everything else for my troubles. I knew this was God speaking to me. I told my secretary to hold all my calls, then spent some time praying and seeking Christ's forgiveness for my sins— for my self-righteous attitude and ignoring Him for so long.

"Then God spoke to me about something that concerns you and me. I felt—no, I plainly *heard*—that I am to drop the lawsuit against you. He said I am to tell you I have changed my mind about the money.

"I can tell you, I didn't sleep at all Monday night, Tuesday, or Wednesday. By Thursday I was a wreck and could barely work. My boss did not know what was going on with me, but he told me I was useless to him this way and I should take off work until I got my head on straight. I won't lie to you, John. I was depending on that money from the lawsuit to help with some financial trouble I am in. But God is right: My life is a wreck. I have lived independently from Him, trusting in myself, and that has got me nowhere except a ruined marriage and a messed up, miserable life.

"I've done a lot of serious thinking and praying. I know my answers lie with God leading my life instead of me. I felt the Lord's assurance that He would be with me, helping me walk though this confusing time in my life. That's when I finally called you. I can't fight God anymore, John. What I am trying to say is . . . I am dropping the lawsuit. You will not have to pay the $100,000. Monday I'll have the papers drawn up and filed. You should have a copy mailed to you within a few days.

"One other thing, John. I'm sorry for all the trouble I caused you and your family over this lawsuit; it should never have been. I just let my wife push me into it and then didn't know how to gracefully get out. What happened to the car was our fault; it had nothing to do with the work you did. We needed money, but that is not an excuse."

After a quick prayer together and a handshake, Fred walked out the door. Only this time there was an obvious difference. By his very demeanor, Fred exhibited a man with a lighter heart and a clearer conscience. A man who in obedience was walking into a new beginning with the Lord he had for so long shunned. In dazed silence we both sat there, each in our own thoughts.

Finally, John shaking his head asked, "I wonder what got into him?"

I could only sit there trying to sort it all out. Glancing at my watch, I saw it was exactly 4:00, one hour before the deadline I had given God. It was then everything fell into place and I realized God had miraculously answered my prayer. With all my doubts gone, I turned to my husband and said, "John, I have something I need to share with you. We're not going to Tyler or Costa Rica. We're going to do our outreach in Ukraine. But first, we're going to Hawaii!"

> And we know that all things work together for good to them that love God, to them who are called according to His purpose. (Rom. 8:28)

4

Little, Ordinary, Everyday Things
Silly Prayers

The emotions of moving out of our house were not as traumatic as I figured they would be. Several years ago when John turned forty, he got the itch to move on and find the *meaning of life*. While he yearned, planned, and dreamily spoke of that perfect far-off place, I spent my time alternating between being depressed, rolling in self-pity, and getting angry. How could John even consider moving!

When we purchased our property in 1983, we built our house with the vision of living there until the day we died; we had no intentions of moving . . . ever! When John started talking about leaving, I chalked it up to his turning forty. Moving away seemed to be a "fortyish thing" with men. In his forties, John's Dad moved his family from Chicago to Houston. At the same age, my dad moved our family from Gary, Indiana, to Houston. There was just something about turning forty that makes a man want to do crazy things. I was just grateful that whatever crazy thing John wanted to do, he wanted to do with me and the girls beside him!

Yet every time John talked about moving, I burst into tears. My heart told me I would never find another church where I felt I belonged as much as I did at Oak Ridge Baptist. In our home I'd walk from room to room and try to picture someone else sleeping in our bedrooms and I'd sob for hours. Just the thought of leaving my older children and my granddaughter, Nikki, brought hysteria. Now, what I had considered unthinkable was happening; I was moving. Strange as it seems, I was as cool as a cucumber. Only when *God* asked me to follow Him did a calmness take over my presence; I knew this was right. I never once cried over what I thought I was giving up; nor did I linger over all that I was leaving behind. I was preparing to face the future and all that God was setting before us.

Between the time the house was sold Thanksgiving weekend and January 10th when we moved out, John had constructed makeshift housing from my brother's flooded mobile home. Rodney had also been a victim of the flood, losing nearly everything he owned. Although Rodney's mobile lay in ruins, John felt sure that he could make it safe enough for us to stay in for the two-and-one-half months until we left for Hawaii. Rodney and John replaced the floor, the doors, and made numerous other repairs. Yet with all the scrubbing, bleaching, and sterilizing I did, I never quite felt clean while we lived there. The day we moved in, we had no water, as the well was still contaminated from the sewage. That meant no showers or toilet facilities. Ever try to cook without water? But then the propane tank had floated down the road with the river so we were unable to cook anyway. In our part of Texas in January, you need the air conditioner during the day and the heater at night. We had neither. It really wasn't a very pleasant place to live; I felt dirty all the time and itched as if tiny bugs were crawling over my skin, yet we tried to make the best of it.

We laughingly joked that this was preparing us for life as missionaries. Who knew what living conditions we may encounter over the next years. Even traveling to Hawaii, we would soon be facing the unknown. Ukraine—I had no idea what to expect. Needless to say, I spent a lot of time in prayer. As a family, we needed clear direction and discernment if we were to traipse around the world with our nine- and eleven-year-old daughters!

Our YWAM training, which is called Crossroads Discipleship Training School (CDTS), was held in Hawaii. I still was not sure why God had called John and me into missions. I was certain that there were many more families in our church alone, who were better qualified to be in full-time ministry than either of us. But call us He did. Of that, we had *no* doubt. We prayed diligently for all the changes we needed in our life to be successful in what God had planned for us.

Our daughters, Cariane and Marleigh, would have their training at the Foundation School on the Hawaiian YWAM base. Although it taught several regular school subjects, its main objective was to help prepare the children for life away from home and for the upcoming trip to a foreign country. We prayed a lot about Cariane and Marleigh's school. As parents, we were concerned about not only the scholastic side of our children, but also the spiritual and the emotional side. We prayed for the school, the teachers, and for the other students who would attend. Like our girls, these children would leave grandparents, home, and their pets to come to an unknown place. That can be scary. Specifically, we prayed for a child for each of our girls to befriend—special girls who could bond easily and become good friends in a short amount of time. In this way, we hoped to alleviate some of the homesickness and the tears we knew would inevitably come.

I also prayed for the place where we would live. Since I love water, I asked God for a room in Hawaii with a view of the ocean. While I was at it, I prayed that, if possible, could the room face the sunset? I would relish watching the sun dip its shining face in the horizon of the Pacific.

I told John and the girls of my prayers for their school, their soon-to-be friends, and our room. Was it silly to ask God about something so trivial as the view from our window? John didn't think so as he prayed and asked, if we couldn't have an ocean view, how about a view of the mountain, as that would be his preference. I did not know how close we were to the ocean or where we would be in comparison to the mountain top, so in a way it was a silly prayer. But it was said earnestly, and I knew God would honor that.

However, thinking this kind of prayer just might work, Cariane and Marleigh jumped in, adding their own postscript to our prayers. Could they please have a room overlooking the swimming pool? Of course we had no idea if there even *was* a pool. Praying this way though aided in focusing our thoughts on the fun things ahead and helped to alleviate the fears and stave off questions for which I had no answers.

Sunday, April 2nd, was our going-away party. Food, friends, tears, hugs, and well-wishes filled the day. We basked in the love we felt as many of our close friends and family came to say their goodbyes. Even my brother Robin, who makes his living selling his handmade, hand-painted vases, pottery, and frames at weekend craft shows, gave up his prepaid booth and its profits to come spend the day with us. All too soon, everyone left, the dishes were washed, and the day was over. Monday, we finished our packing and attended to last-minute details. The alarm went off at 4:15 A.M. Tuesday, announcing the time had finally come to leave.

Saying good-bye was tough. My mother and oldest brother Randy drove us to the airport. I felt as if I were floating in slow motion through a crazy dream. One in which I was watching a family about to fly off into the unknown and leave behind everything and everyone they held dear to their hearts. Our best friends, Gary and Laura Montgomery and their two children, Megan and Melissa made the early-morning trip to bid us farewell and God-speed. Just their presence, the fact that they cared enough to get up at 4 o'clock in the morning to ride with us, strengthened the knowledge that we were doing the right thing. Laura's tears as we hugged good-bye and her sweet words was all the encouragement I needed. I may be facing the unknown, but I had my family by my side, was accompanied by many prayers and was being directed by the Lord Himself. What more could I ask?

Believe it or not, it took us twenty-two hours to get to Hawaii! Talk about total exhaustion! Although it was only 9:00 P.M. Hawaiian time when we arrived, our bodies' time clocks said 2 A.M. and *way* past bedtime. While John and I waited for the luggage to come down the baggage carousel, Cariane and Marleigh fell asleep on the concrete sidewalk, too exhausted to keep their eyes open any longer. Storing our luggage in the back of the waiting van, we half carried, half dragged our sleeping children to the van and headed for the YWAM base, which was to be our home for the next twelve weeks. The ride from the airport was not much more than a blur as we tried to keep our red eyes open and our heads from nodding off into the land of slumber.

At the base we were greeted by cheerful people offering us coffee, punch, or pizza; but all we wanted was to lay our heads down. We were ushered to a table where we met our school leader, Dr. Doug Kinne. I am sure that Doug thought we were a couple of strange Texans as he asked us questions, because nothing more than slurs came out as our answers. I tried to focus on what Doug was saying, but between the girls draping their tired bodies over me and my own head trying to nod off, I wasn't doing a particularly good job of coherently answering Doug's questions.

Doug was talking about our assigned room. He said that as he prayed about the students and their rooms, he felt he was to move us from the original room assigned to us. We were to go to building one, room nineteen. In checking over the room however, he noticed that room nineteen had a cracked bathroom sink in need of repair. Doug put in a work order for a new sink; the old one was taken out, but the new one was not in place yet and might not be for several days or even a week. Doug said he did not want to put us in a room that was not ready. Would we like to go see the two different rooms and decide which one we liked the best? At this point I didn't care if we *ever* had a sink. I told

Doug if he just gave us a room with beds, we would brush our teeth in the shower; just get us beds!

Everyone hopped into a pickup along with our luggage and were driven to room nineteen. Even in the growing darkness, John and I could see that the rooms faced the mountain. God had given us a mountain view! Maybe our prayers weren't so silly after all. Dragging our luggage and our feet up the stairs, I didn't know if we could stay awake long enough to get undressed. Forget showers and brushing our teeth tonight; just show us where we can lie down. As we stepped into room nineteen, all dreams about sleeping were forgotten. There it was. Although it was almost dark, it was still visible in all its glory: the ocean. And not just a window-size view of the ocean either. The entire fourth wall was not a wall at all; it was a giant ceiling-to-floor, wall-to-wall screen facing the ocean. We not only had a view of the mountains from the door, but we also had a perfect view of the ocean from every corner of the room, no matter where we were standing! I also learned from our driver that from this particular room we could see the sun set right on the ocean's horizon; just as I had prayed.

Running to the screen to get a better view of the campus and the ocean, the girls began to squeal with delight. Looking out they saw that we were literally right over the pool area. In fact, we had the *only* family room that directly overlooked the pool. Now we knew why Doug Kinne had been prompted to move us to this particular room. God had answered each of our prayers concerning our accommodations, and all with this one little room!

Morning came much too early, but up we arose too excited to sleep in. We walked downstairs to meet the girls' new teachers and classmates, of which there were ten. It didn't take long before it was obvious God had done it again. First, the six boys were introduced. Next came the girls: Cariane, Marleigh, and two other girls. Blair was ten and Rachel was twelve, as close to the same ages of Cariane and Marleigh as one could get. True to my request, the four quickly became friends and could be found together day and night.

In retrospect, the mountain was already there. God did not put it there just for us. Whether or not we prayed for a mountain view, we would have gotten it. The same with the ocean; it has been there since the creation, as were the fabulous sunsets with all their splendor. These things were already in place before our prayers. But the question is, what prompted Doug to move us to room ninteen instead of leaving us where we were originally assigned which was *not* over the pool? Did God really care about the fun, silly little prayers of children that He arranged this room over the pool just for them? And what about Rachel and Blair? Was it a fluke that there were only two other girls in Cariane and Marleigh's class? Not one, not three or four, but two? Two girls the right ages, and two who got along famously with our daughters? Were these all coincidences, or was the hand of the Lord working on behalf of our family?

God had recently answered some big prayers in our life. He literally brought home buyers to our front door. He had the lawsuit dismissed, thus answering the question if we were to go to Hawaii. Now God was showing us that He is the God of everything in our life, even the little, ordinary, everyday things.

I think if you had asked me if I knew that God was concerned for the little details in our lives, I would of answered yes. But honestly, I don't think I *really* believed it—not on a gut level of really knowing. But now I do. I know for sure, that God cares and is intimately involved in every aspect of our lives, whether those aspects are important or seemingly insignificant. Our family, although being Christians for many years, had just begun to discover the awesome truth in this very important concept.

> If you remain in Me, and My words remain in you, ask whatever you wish and it shall be given you. (John 15:7)

5

Tiny Shadow of a Doubt
Divine Healing

It's mine! I got it!" John leaped high as the white ball came sailing over the net. It had been fifteen years since he'd played volleyball, and he was enjoying every moment. This was Memorial Day weekend and John and a few other men were taking this last opportunity to play at Magic Sands Beach before leaving for the country of Ukraine.

This tiny, snowy-white beach seemed to have a magical quality all its own, with lava rock blanketing the beachfront. The coal-black rocks laying over the white sand made its own special beauty, while rhythmic waves crashed over the lava, emitting a lovely musical sound. Nestled on this tiny strip of white beach, stretched between two palm trees, was a volleyball net where the men were playing. *This is really living,* thought John. *Nothing could spoil this.*

John leaped into the air, driving the ball with the full force of his 255-pound frame back over the net. Twisting slightly on the way back down, John sensed more than felt a *r-r-rip!* For the fraction of a second it took to come down from the jump, John wondered what that strange feeling was in his knee. Attempting to land on his feet, his leg buckled under from his weight. Falling to the sandy, hot ground, searing pain shot from his knee to his foot and back up to his thigh. Rolling from side to side on the sand, John felt as if his entire leg was on fire; this was the most excruciating pain he had ever felt. Immediately, the men came running from all directions surrounding John. Kneeling in a circle around him, the men started to pray for the throbbing agony to subside.

Amazingly, as the men prayed, the pain ebbed away. Looking at his knee, John was startled by the huge bulge, the size of a man's fist, just above his kneecap. Being careful not to harm him further, the men helped their injured buddy hobble to the van and back to the YWAM base.

Hopping on his good leg, John was helped up the stairs and into bed, his injured leg propped up with a stack of pillows. I was shocked at the ugly huge knot directly above my husband's knee. My first reaction was to find transportation and immediately drive him to the hospital emergency room, but John refused to go. I sent Marleigh downstairs to ask Rochelle, one of the nurses at our school, to take a look at the knee. Although the injury was definitely serious, Rochelle felt the hospital would only tell us to go home, prop the leg up, and make an appointment with an orthopedic doctor on Tuesday. So this is what we did.

"It doesn't look very good," Dr. Simon (not his real name), the orthopedic sports doctor, told us the next week. "Look here. Right at the base of your knee is where your patella tendons are attached. Tendons are the wonderful little things that allow your elbows and knees to bend back and forth while holding them in place. Usually when an injury occurs to the knee, it is a tear to the tendon. You, however, have ripped all three cords of your tendons completely out of their socket. You can see them here at the top of your knee. It's similar to a rubber band when you stretch it, then let it go. Your tendons have snapped out of place; like the rubber band, they have landed in a wad right at the top of your kneecap. What I don't understand is why you do not have any pain. This is a quite painful injury to have. Are you sure you aren't hurting?"

"No, I'm not. I'm fine. My friends prayed, asking God to take away the pain. And He did," assured John.

With a shrug, Dr. Simon continued with his exam, "This is serious but not impossible to fix. We do not have the facilities to do the surgery on this island; so it will have to be performed on Oahu. Afterward, we'll place you in a cast for several months. When the cast comes off, you will require three to six months of physical therapy. I'll arrange to have the surgeon fly in from Honolulu at the end of next week to make all the arrangements. Until then, stay off that leg. I hope you have good insurance; this is an expensive injury to have. Are there any questions?"

Only about a dozen! We knew no amount of questions or answers would help us right now. With only $500 to our name and no insurance, our situation had no easy solution. In three weeks we were scheduled to leave for Ukraine; it looked like this injury could very well prevent us from going. Back in our room, laying prone with his leg elevated, John was pleased as numerous classmates stopped by our room to pray for him. Strange as it sounds, although everyone prayed specifically for divine healing, they all left our room expressing their sorrow that we would now have to miss going to Ukraine with the rest of the team. By now we were both saddened and somewhat discouraged over this unexpected turn of events.

Amanda Harlow, a doctor from New Zealand, and her husband Paul were among those who visited us. While in our room, Amanda examined the knee, agreeing with the same bleak diagnosis of the specialist. Like others who had visited, Amanda and Paul asked if they could pray for John. For a few minutes they prayed just like the others had, but then they asked our permission to pray in "tongues." Raised as Southern Baptists, we had neither been taught about this practice of praying, nor did we know anyone first-hand who did. Although personally we knew very little about praying in tongues, we had learned that it is called a prayer language from the Holy Spirit; it is one of the gifts of the Spirit that not everyone possesses. We couldn't imagine it hurting, so we gave our consent. About ten minutes into the prayer, Amanda surprised us by saying, "I feel God just confirm to me that John will be healed—without surgery." To say the least, we were stunned into silence.

Thoughts of doubt intermixed with hope, tumbled together in our minds as Amanda continued. "Valerie, every day I want you to kneel right alongside John's bed. Place your hand on his knee and pray in faith that God will heal this injury right here while John's laying in this bed. You need to pray everyday until the healing takes place." Having left her instructions, Amanda and Paul turned and walked out of our room, leaving us with not only questions, but also with a great sense of hope tangled with uncertainty: hope that God would really miraculously heal; uncertainty that He would actually do it.

I knew God has the power to divinely heal, but we'd always relied on the Lord healing through the special skills of doctors. I had no doubt John would be made well again, but I assumed it would be a combination of surgery, physical therapy, and lots of time. But to just . . . heal? I didn't know if I really believed that would happen. However, I decided to do as Amanda recommended.

That evening I followed Amanda's directions. I knelt next to the bed, placed my hand on John's knee, and started to pray.

"Lord, I know You can heal without surgery and even without doctors. I have never seen this happen, but I have heard of You still doing that from time to time. It's not that I don't believe You can, it's . . . I don't know . . . I don't think You will. Forgive my unbelief. If You want to heal John through a miracle, don't let me and my doubts stand in Your way. If You don't divinely heal, that too will be OK. But then You will need to provide the money for the surgery and the physical therapy, as we do not have any left; it all went for our plane fare to Ukraine. Whichever way You choose, we will thank you for Your help and for Your care. You are such a good God. Thank You, too, for taking away John's pain."

Finishing the prayer, I got up from the floor and went down to get John his dinner tray.

About thirty minutes later, I heard John holler, "Valerie! Come here. Quick!" Jumping to my feet, I hurried to the bed and looked where John was pointing: his injured knee. There, like a butterfly in a cocoon, the wadded up tendons were wiggling! Not going anywhere, just wiggling. After a few minutes, maybe three or four, the wiggling stopped. I took a quick glance to catch John's reaction; all I saw was his puzzled brow. What were we to think? Was this a good sign? Was this even supposed to happen? All evening we stared at the knee, but no more movement occurred.

The next night, again kneeling next to the bed, I laid my hand on John's knee and prayed. "Father, the tendons moved yesterday. What does this mean? I prayed a little longer finishing with, "Lord, help my unbelief." To our complete surprise, thirty minutes after I finished praying the tendons again started to move. Only this time instead of only wiggling around, they started to make a direct move downward toward the kneecap moving in the same fashion as an inchworm. At first, we stared with disbelief, then with wonderment and finally with awe. The tendons were moving! Maybe God really *was* going to miraculously heal the damaged knee and its tendons. Laughter burst from John. He laughed until the tears came. "I'm not sure what's going on Lord, but I'm sure glad You are in control. I have to admit though, I am a tad bit worried."

The third day, I again knelt and prayed over John's knee. Thirty minutes after I finished praying, the tendons started moving, stopping when they reached the top of the kneecap. We were beginning to harbor the hope that God was up to something miraculous. By the fourth day, the tendons had inched downward over the front of the knee itself. This same pattern continued the next day as well; prayer, thirty minutes of waiting, then several minutes of movement.

On the sixth day, I had just begun to pray when John started to feel discomfort in his knee. At first it came as a tingling sensation, but soon it turned to a burning which got hotter by the second. Sitting upright as the heat became unbearable, John started fanning his knee with the magazine he'd been reading. This didn't make sense—something was wrong! Feelings of disappointment choked me as I ran to get a cold wash towel, placing it on his knee in an attempt to take away the burning heat.

Kneeling next to the bed, I placed my hand on the hot flesh of John's knee and cried out, "Lord what happened? I really believed You were going to heal his knee, but now . . . I don't understand what is going on. Should I call the doctor? Please tell me what to do!" Unexpectedly, after praying for just these few seconds, I felt more than heard, a voice in my ear, "*I have already healed him. Stop praying.*" Shocked over the words in my head, I stopped praying for just a second and pondered what I'd heard. Deciding to continue praying, I began again. Instantly, I heard the voice again say, "*I said I have healed him. Stop praying!*" This time the voice seemed so loud, so commanding, I was positive John had also heard. Glancing at my husband just lying there with his eyes closed, I knew he was not aware of what was happening. Immediately, I got up from my kneeling position and walked across the room.

I did not say anything to my husband; I just walked away. I was shaken. I wasn't sure I understood what had just happened. Did God really heal the knee? And what was that burning sensation? The doctor said the surgeon would have to fuse the tendons. Could this be *God* fusing the tendons in their rightful place? I didn't know. I did know that I was *not* going to pray anymore. At least not that night. Noticing my quick movement and short prayer, John commented, "That has to be the shortest prayer in history." I didn't say anything in return. What could I say? I wanted to share with John what I thought I heard, but I didn't know how to explain it. I was not used to hearing words pop into my head as clearly as if they were spoken out loud. Was this God speaking to me? Or was it my imagination and hopes jumbled together, playing tricks? Not sure, I decided to ponder these thoughts for awhile before I said anything to my husband.

The next night, seven days after the accident, I toyed with whether I should pray over John's knee. Deciding I should, I again knelt next to the bed, laid my hand on the injured knee and begin to pray. The exact moment the first words came out of my mouth, I was startled by the same voice I'd sensed the day before. *"I told you I have healed him. Do not pray anymore. You need to learn to trust Me."* In a flash I shot up from the floor. My quick action, startled John causing him to question what was wrong. "Oh, nothing," I replied. "I just don't feel like praying right now."

"Some wife you are," remarked John. Even though he said this with humor in his voice, I heard the sarcasm as well. I felt really confused. I should have shared this strange experience with John, but I didn't. When I heard the words "he is healed," part of me believed it was so. Yet there was that one part that doubted. I think I didn't trust my own hearing; so I kept the hope of the tendon's restoration safe within my heart. If God had healed the knee, John would know about it soon enough.

The appointment with the orthopedic surgeon was ten days after the accident—three days away. After supper for each of the next three evenings, John would ask me if I was going to pray for his knee. "Not now; maybe later," I would reply. There was no movement of the tendons during those three days; no burning, no moving, nothing. On one hand, I wanted to pray for John. On the other, I felt certain that God had healed his knee. Where before, I had been praying in hope, if I kept praying now I would be praying out of doubt. However small, there was still a tiny shadow of doubt with which I struggled. I did not want John to get his hopes up and then have them dashed if the healing had not taken place. So I remained silent. At least in front of John I was silent. Privately I prayed for my faith to be made strong.

The day of the appointment with Dr. Black (not his real name), the visiting surgeon from Honolulu, dawned bright and clear. John and I nervously waited for our turn with the doctor. "Let's see what we have here," the specialist said as he began a thorough examination. After an hour of poking, prodding, stretching, as well as taking new X-rays, the doctor finished the exam. First he looked at John, glanced down at the knee, and then back again to his patient. He scratched his head for a moment, then commented, "I am not sure why I was called in all the way from Honolulu. The chart clearly states that you have a severe case of torn patella tendons. I completely trust my associate and his judgement. There is no gray area; either the tendons are torn or they aren't. I have never known him to make a mistake about that. I'm not sure I know what's going on, but John, your tendons are right where they belong. I can see no damage or scarring, absolutely nothing whatsoever is wrong with your knee. Now tell me again what happened."

Carefully, I watched John for his reaction as he heard the news. He closed his eyes for a few moments. As he slowly opened them, it was like looking at a new man; his entire countenance was different. It was as if a fresh awareness of God's presence spread across his face as tears made pools in his eyes, threatening to spill over. John started to share about the power of God and how, when He chooses, He can and does heal. But the surgeon just waved away the explanation. Picking us the chart he marched out of the office with the sarcastic comment, "In case you ever *think* about getting hurt again, I will *think* about coming to take care of you. In the meantime, use the crutches and take it easy on that leg for a few days—for precaution's sake."

Still using the crutches for support, John and I walked outside and silently made our way to the van we'd borrowed. Goose bumps traveled up and down my arms as we tried to take in the implication of the doctor's diagnosis. The knee was healed! Never before had we seen anything like this; it was almost more than we could absorb. Did this mean we would be going to Ukraine as originally planned? Behind us we heard the sound of running feet. Turning to see who it was, we saw Dr. Simon, the orthopedic sports doctor, jogging down the sidewalk straight toward us.

Stopping when he reached us, Dr. Simon panted out of breath, "Dr. Black says that there is nothing wrong with your knee. I know what I saw when I examined you ten days ago. Black also said that you believe God healed you. Do you really believe that?"

"Yes," John replied.

"May I see?" Kneeling down, Dr. Simon examined John's knee right there on the sidewalk in front of the clinic. With a shake of his head he stood and asked John, "You really think God did this, don't you?"

"I know He did!" John assured him. "There is no doubt what God did for me."

With a reflective look, Dr. Simon stood and walked back to his office. I am sure he was as full of awe at that moment as we were.

Five minutes later we were back on the campus. Still using the crutches for support, John and I walked back into the classroom trying not to disturb the guest speaker who was giving a lecture. All eyes however turned on John as we walked into the room. Noticing he had just lost the class, the speaker also turned to see what was catching the students' attention. John didn't say a word but lifted his crutches above his head, waved them in the air, going in a circle as if dancing in slow motion. A great roar went up along with clapping, whistling, and cheering. Some of our classmates started yelling "Yes, Jesus," while others began to weep. Emotions were running high as one after another the students recognized that a miracle had just taken place in front of their very eyes.

Although God had shown us an aspect of Himself by the healing of John's knee, it was not just for our family's benefit that He had healed. The miracle spoke volumes in answering some of the students' questions of who God is and reassured many of their doubts. The power of God's healing took all of us in that Crossroads class into a deeper, more intense degree of understanding of God. For the rest of our stay in Hawaii and on into our outreach time in Ukraine, a new awareness of God's love, His intimate care, and His deep abiding presence was felt by us all. We started a fresh walk with the Lord from a new faith born not only from the healing of John's knee, but also from a healing within our hearts.

Lord, I believe; help thou mine unbelief. (Mark 9:24)

6

Grind, Whine, Rattle, and Clunk

Angels

The trip from Hawaii to Ukraine with an overnight stay in Los Angeles and in Amsterdam was an exciting, fun-filled trip. Seeing all the wonders, especially through the eyes of the children, made the traveling that much more enjoyable. Amsterdam was emotionally touching for me as I am half Dutch; my grandparents had immigrated from Holland. I was thrilled when I learned we would be in Amsterdam; I had a list of the places I wanted to visit while there. As it turned out though, we arrived late in the day and left at sunrise with no time for sightseeing. I was disappointed, yet grateful for the chance to be there for even a few short hours.

At long last we arrived in Ukraine, part of the former Soviet Union. Kiev, its capital, was filled with people peddling their wares in a never-ending effort to make enough money to feed their families that day. With a thirteen-hour time difference, it took the first two days to adjust our bodies' time clock to Ukrainian time. The second night in Kiev we would have "the meeting,"where our school leader, Dr. Doug Kinne, would tell each family in which of the three cities they would be living and working for the next eight weeks. Dr. Kinne and his wife, Jan, a nurse, would open a clinic in Ternopil near the Polish border. The other two teams, whose main objective was to share the love of Jesus, would go to Kharkov, on the eastern coast of Ukraine, and to Crimea, on the southern tip by the Black Sea.

Medical personnel and their families already knew they would be on the team in Ternopil, so Doug read only the names for the other two teams. Our name was not on the Cremia list, which meant we would head for Kharkov in the morning. Out of formality, Doug read the names from the second list, finishing with, "Of course, any name I have not read is going to Ternopil."

John and I looked at each with a shrug; our name had not been on either list. John called to Doug, "You forgot us. Are we going to Cremia or to Kharkov?" Dr. Kinne replied matter of factly, "That must mean you're going with us to Ternopil." That statement does not sound so earth shattering, but to us it was. We paid nearly $10,000 to come to Ukraine to share the gospel, and we just heard we were going with the medical team. The only thing I know about medicine is how to apply a bandage on a paper cut, and my husband is a mechanic by trade, so why go to Ternopil? What possible use could we be to a medical team?

Then it hit me. They wanted me to be a babysitter! On the medical team alone, there were six children; someone needed to watch them while their parents worked in the clinic. I was *sure* this was the reason we were being sent to Ternopil instead of Kharkov or Cremia. I marched up to Dr.

Kinne and politely, but quite sternly, told him there was no way we were going to Ternopil, there was nothing for me to do there other than babysit and babysitting was *not* why we came to Ukraine. With arms folded, I continued with my little tirade of why I came to Ukraine, what I wanted to accomplish, and all the reasons my goals could not be achieved by going to Ternopil. Patiently, Doug listened. When I was satisfied that I had laid out a clear, precise argument for Doug, I smugly looked him straight in the eye as if to say, well, what do you have to say about that?

Doug, being a laid-back man of few words, merely gave me a half-laugh and replied, "We prayed and felt the Lord led us to put your family on the Ternopil team. God didn't say why, He just said where." With that, he dismissed me by turning to talk to someone else. I was left with my mouth hanging open and wondering, *What happened?*

To say I graciously accepted Doug's decision would be a far stretch of the truth. I was truly upset. But more than that, I was hurt. Struggling with my feelings, I started to pray, though I must admit it was not one that was open to hearing what the Lord had to say about the whole situation. In fact, I don't think I even asked God where *He* wanted my family. My prayer ran more down the line of "I'm mad God, and I want you to fix this. After all, I came here to tell people about you, not babysit." I slept very little that night as discontent mixed with a strong need to have my own way began to settle within my heart.

The next day, about to board the bus for Ternopil, I looked over to Doug and merely said, "Are you sure?" "Yep!" he answered, so I climbed on the bus still positive our family was headed the wrong direction. Little did I know that our going to Ternopil would set our family in motion to witness even more of God's miraculous deeds.

Sitting on the old dilapidated bus and ignoring the excited chatter of the other eighteen team members, I did some thinking, questioning myself and my motives for being in Ukraine. Five or six hours passed as I stared at the acres of wheat fields, which is why Ukraine is commonly called the "breadbasket of the world". I thought about the people who lived in this country that appeared to be so different from my own. It took quite some time before I began to feel the Lord's correction over my attitude during the past twenty-four hours. I was still mad, but now instead of fuming I was more or less just pouting. I didn't like not having my own way, *especially* when I thought I was right. As conviction moved in, bitterness moved out. The Lord began to make me realize He was not concerned with what town I lived in, but with my attitude and my willingness to be used—wherever He sent me. I again prayed, only this time with a much more contrite heart.

"Jesus, You love the people of Ukraine; I know they are so very precious to You. I don't know why You have called my family here, but I do know it was for a specific reason. If You say we are to be in Ternopil, then Ternopil is where I want to be. Forgive me, Lord, for my wrong attitude and for always striving to have my own way. You alone are God. You know where we need to be, I don't. Whatever You ask me to do, even if it is to babysit for the next two months, I will. I'll be the best babysitter these kids have ever had. Thank You, Jesus, for bringing us here. Allow me—allow us—to be used by You in Ternopil. More than anything else, even in spite of me, I want our time in Ukraine to give glory to You."

Mile after mile I continued to pray, while little by little my unsettled heart begin to surrender to God and to His will for me and for this trip. I wanted to serve with what YWAM calls the "two-handed gospel." That is, serving the needs of people with one hand, while presenting them with the gospel of Jesus with the other. It took some honest looking at my heart to realize that it really did not matter where I was, so long as I was where God wanted me to be, doing what He has asked me to do.

For me, the ten-hour bus ride from Kiev to Ternopil was tiresome. The other team members were happily "oohing" and "ahing" over every new thing they saw. For the most part, I neither joined in the conversation nor enjoyed the sights. My rebellion, along with a tremendous sense of wanting my own way, spoiled the new sights for me. But at the same time God was working with my attitude *on* the bus, He was also working His miraculous ways *with* our bus.

In the midst of my grumbling prayers a loud rattling sound started coming from the rear end of the bus. Everyone's attention was instantly drawn to the direction of the commotion. Several men, my husband included, quickly went to the back of the bus to see if they could discover the source of the racket. What sounded like large rocks tumbling in a tin can were coming from the undercarriage of the bus.

John went to the front and, with the help of an interpreter, explained to the bus driver about the noise he was hearing. With a shrug, the driver turned his attention back to his task of driving. Assuming the driver did not understand what was said, John explained a second time, but his efforts were awarded with a wave of the hand, dismissing any concerns he had.

Soon, adding to the rattle, came a whining. As the whining grew louder and the pitch higher, we began to get really worried. The whining continued for some time when, with a loud clatter, something from underneath the bus fell to the ground. Racing to the front of the bus, John again tried to make the bus driver understand. As before, he waved his hand, ignoring John. After an hour of listening to the nerve-wracking noises, the driver pulled to the side of the road and announced a potty break.

For the guys this was not a problem—and the young boys were thrilled that they could actually "go" outside and not get in trouble with their mothers. For the women and girls this woodsy potty break was not met with a smile. But what else was there to do? Up to this point of the trip, after nearly eight hours on the road, we hadn't seen a town, only a scattering of adobe houses; only occasionally was there even a passing automobile. Needless to say, when nature calls there is no place to stop except the woods along the highway. This was the second time that day the bus pulled off to the side of the road, we'd disembark with girls heading right and boys heading left. The prickly bushes, the snakes in the grass, and the poison weed in which we stood definitely made this part of our trip a memorable, although not too pleasant, experience.

On this stop, the bus driver, the interpreter, and John walked to the back of the bus where the bus' motor was housed. Raising the cover, the driver poked, prodded, banged, and then slammed the cover shut. John, using hand motions, asked if he could look at the motor, but the driver shook his head no and stomped away, muttering what we could not understand. John kneeling down took a peek under the bus. To his shock he discovered that the piece that had fallen out earlier came from the transmission. There was no earthly way this bus could slip into gear. Now that we had stopped, we were not going anywhere.

Acting as if he did not understand the severity of the problem, the driver motioned for everyone to get on board the bus. As John suspected, when the driver tried to put the bus in first gear, we heard not only the whining, but also a great grinding sound as well. Now it was obvious even to the women and older children that the bus was in trouble. A dozen times the driver tried to get into first gear, but the gear shift resisted. With no towns, telephones, or even a hint of rescue in sight, we were stranded. Realizing only a miracle could get this bus moving, we took turns praying out loud for the gears.

"Lord, we are 125 miles from Ternopil; there are no towns close by. There are no garages, no tools, and nothing that we can do. We have to depend on You. You have brought us here; now help us. Please don't leave us stranded. Hold the gears together in the right position so we can continue our trip to Ternopil."

Surprising even to those of us who prayed, after some loud grinding, the bus jerked into first gear. Second gear did not come much easier. We continued to pray as the bus went through its series of gears and slowly picked up its forward speed. As the grinding, whining, and rattling became louder, so did our prayers. By the time we were through all the gears, we were praying at the top of our voices. Lurching into last gear, we again heard a clattering of metal scraping against metal. Then *pop!* We feared the worse. One look at the face of the team member who was staring out the rear window and we knew our fears were justified. We'd lost another piece.

Every last one of us was acutely aware that we were in desperate need for this miracle to continue. One after the other we took turns praying out loud for the bus and its transmission. By the time the bus reached the cruising speed of 45 mph, we were fairly certain that as long as we didn't stop we'd probably be OK. Fortunately for us, the highway was flat with no towns to go through, which meant no need to shift gears. We hoped the Lord would continue to hold the gears together and no more pieces would fall out.

About the time we got comfortable with the fact that the bus would continue its forward journey, the driver began to yell above the loud noises at the interpreter. "We're almost out of petrol. There is no place to buy any," was the translated message. Immediately we started to pray again. Within minutes a station with petrol (gas) came into sight. At first we just laughed; here we were praying for gas when the station was only a mile away. However instead of stopping, the driver just continued right pass the station.

We all started hollering at the translator at once, "Why didn't he stop? We'll give him money for the gas. We have *kupons* (Ukrainian money)." Again the driver acted as if he could not hear us, as if running out of gas in the middle of nowhere was not anything to be concerned about. Within minutes, the bus started lurching, and we smelled the fumes of a near-empty tank. Doug Kinne approached the driver telling him to turn around and he would buy the gas himself.

"He does not like the man who runs the station. He will not buy from him," the interpreter replied. In America, where there is a station every few miles, this would be a satisfactory answer. But this was the first station we had seen since starting the trip nine-and-a-half hours earlier.

"How far until the next station?" Doug asked, leaning over the translator to be heard above the noise. Doug straightened up with a worried look on his face and we knew it was not good news; we still had at least twenty miles to go. We would never make it that far. Already the bus was discharging gas fumes, a sure sign of a tank that is approaching empty.

Our children had more faith then we did, as one of them said, "We prayed for God to hold together the gears and He did. Why not pray for Him to multiply the gas?" That is exactly what we did. Although the emitting fumes were getting stronger, meaning the tank was getting emptier, the bus continued to roll. Even though we prayed for the bus to keep going, we were actually surprised it did. Most of us were strong in the praying department but weak when it came to the faith to believe in our prayers. Sure enough, the bus rolled along for another twenty miles. The sickening fumes from the empty tank gagged everyone on the bus, including the driver. Cheers went up as another station came into sight and the driver pulled into the large, nearly empty parking lot. What a sight for sore, worried eyes.

Our natural assumption was that the driver would fill the tank. We were puzzled when he put in only two liters of gas, about a half gallon. Several of our team members reached in their pocket and handed the driver *kupons* so he could purchase more gas. Obviously, two liters would not get us far. John said that because the tank was so empty, that it may not even be enough to get the bus started. Stubbornly, the driver refused the *kupons* and motioned for us to get on the bus. We were a little afraid to get back on, but there was only one alternative to sitting there: to place our lives in the dubious hands of this Ukrainian bus driver. With great misgivings, we again boarded in preparation to continue our journey. Although we had only about thirteen miles to Ternopil, the driver had bought only enough petrol for about a mile or two, provided he could even get the bus started again . . . if the gears would cooperate. We knew we were in a jam.

As John feared, the bus wouldn't start because of the dry fuel lines. As we started to pray for the bus, the engine cranked with a roar but not without whining and clattering to go along with it. As before, it resisted sliding into gear and the grinding noise, as the driver tried to shift, was worse than before. Stubbornly the driver kept pushing on the gear-shift with both hands. Finally, he put his foot on the shift and tried to force its cooperation.

Then we heard *clunk*. Another piece fell out. This threw John into motion as he hopped off the bus, crawled under the carriage and brought back a mangled piece of metal that had once been part of the transmission. John tried to talk to the driver using hand motions and holding the piece up to him. But as before, the driver refused even to acknowledge John's presence; he kept pushing on the gear shift with all his strength. Holding the piece of metal, our prayers became more fervent. "God we need you more than ever. Help us!" The transmission slipped into first gear and we jerked our way onto the highway.

Within a few minutes we came to a more populated area. There were houses, people, and even a few small villages. The highway ran right through the middle of each of these rural villages, and because the majority of people walk in the streets, with few automobiles around, the speed of traffic is expected to be very slow. Unable to down shift, thus enabling the bus to slow, the driver simply laid the palm of his hand on the horn and blasted his way through the villages. One small village we came to had a ninety degree turn in the middle of the village; the driver took it going 40 mph, squealing around the corner on two wheels. Everything on the bus, luggage, food, pillows, and people flew off the racks and the seats. We were beginning to feel uneasy. The bus ride was definitely a bit more adventurous than we'd planned.

Grateful when we were out of the cluster of small villages, we proceeded into a hilly section of the area. Struggling to climb the steep grade, the bus went slower and slower. Everyone knew the bus would be unable to make the hill. Trying to go up such steep hills in high gear wouldn't work. The bus needed to down shift in order to obtain its maximum pull, but the gears refused to budge. We were almost to a stand-still and still had halfway to go. "Lord, You held our gears together, You multiplied the gas, now we are asking You to provide angels to push this bus the rest of the way up this hill."

Confidence, not in our prayers, but in God's faithful provision grew as the bus slowly but surely rolled to the top of the hill and then started its descent. There were no signs of angels, nothing visible, but there was no other explanation. We were moving. To conserve gas, the bus' motor was shut off and we coasted downhill. In front of us were several small hills and we easily coasted over each of them, down to the next one. The children thought this was loads of fun, and with their squeals of delight we rolled over one hill after the other.

Approaching the town of Ternopil, the driver was forced again to crank the motor as the hills were all behind us. Since the bus was out of gas it wouldn't start and was slowly coming to a halt. Even if it did start, with all the parts that had dropped onto the highway, we knew there was not enough of the transmission left to make the bus move forward. We would either have to walk the last few miles with our luggage or else God would again have to do something miraculous. Since none of us wanted to walk, we again called on God, asking Him to send His invisible angels to push the bus into town.

This was the moment of truth. With what sounded like a growl and a cough, the motor cranked. One hard push and the bus kicked into first gear. At a snail's pace it struggled to move. In front of us was a fairly steep hill; either this had all been a coincidence or God really had sent His special angels to push. Someone on the team started to yell in a sing-song way, "Push! Push! Angels push!" Soon everyone joined in the rhythmic cheer as the bus kept moving, slowly at first, but then with a little more speed. The gears were still a problem and would not shift, but the bus kept moving. Rounding corners without down shifting, and going through intersections without stopping should have been a frightful experience. But by now we were confident, whether or not it was angels, *something* was pushing this dilapidated old thing, and whatever it was would also provide safety.

"There it is. Hotel Ruta!" exclaimed the translator. Cheers went up as the bus choked, sputtered, and rolled to a halt directly in front of the hotel, where we would be staying. As if to say, *"There!"* with one last plunk, the bus spit out yet another part and died in front of the Hotel Ruta.

All of us were anxious to get off that deathtrap. Hurriedly we unloaded our luggage, grateful not only to be stretching and moving, but also to be doing so in front of our home for the next two months. After everything was taken into the hotel, some of us came back to clean out the bus, which was quite messy after traveling all day. When it was time to leave, try as he might, the bus driver could not get the old bus to restart. We knew what had to be done.

Surrounding the bus we laid our hands on its faded, rusty sides and prayed, "Thank You, Lord, for the safe trip. Thank You for the provision of a bus and its driver. We pray Your blessings over the driver and ask for Your perfect plan of salvation be revealed to him in Your timing. If You bring him back to us, we will share about Your wondrous love for him. If we do not see him again, we pray that You will bring someone else to tell him about You. But, Lord, we have one last favor. There are no such things as tow trucks in Ukraine, and this man needs to take his bus home. Would You allow this bus to start again? We know that with all the pieces on the ground it will not move forward of its own accord. So will You please have Your angels push one last time? Push this bus to the man's garage; not an inch more or an inch less. Let him see it is really You and not his bus or anything he has done that delivered us to Ternopil. We desire to have all the glory be given to You."

Just as we prayed the bus' engine roared to life, it slid into first gear and ever so slowly began to inch its way spitting and sputtering down the block and out of sight. We erupted into cheers and clapping as we knew God was again at work. There was no way on earth there was any gas in the tank, yet the motor was running. There were pieces of the transmission scattered over the highway for 125 miles; one lay right here in front of us, yet the bus was crawling forward, albeit at a snail's pace. This defied any and all human or mechanical explanation.

Two months later, we were ready to leave Ukraine and return to America. Out of curiosity, John inquired about the bus. Getting directions to the driver's house, he walked the few blocks to his home. Sure enough, there the bus sat. With the help of a translator, John discovered that it had gone as far as the driver's home, pressed its nose against the door of the garage, and with a loud protest backfired, gave a mighty shudder, and died. Just as we had prayed, it did not stop one inch short of its destination but *exactly* at the door of the garage. And the driver couldn't get the bus to roll into the garage. No amount of pushing would make it budge an inch. So there it sat like a rusty dinosaur, out of place, facing the garage.

Peering under the carriage of the bus, John found only piles of metal shavings in places where the transmission should have been. As a mechanic, John knew better than anyone that bus could not have been driven 1 mile let alone 125. Yet, here it sat.

No one on our team had the opportunity to share the gospel of Jesus Christ with the driver. Our assurance is in the hope that the Lord will deliver His love message to the driver when he is ready to hear. Maybe, just maybe, the miracle that took place on our bus will help in the preparation of the driver's heart. Although no one on our team actually *saw* any angels, we are confident they were there. God sent something or someone to push us. We have no other explanation than angels. And what a wonderful job they did of pushing that rusty old bus.

> Behold, I am going to send an angel before you to guard you along the way, and to bring you into the place which I have prepared. (Exod. 23:20)

7

The Jigsaw
Direction

Living in Ternopil, I was pleased by the numerous opportunities our team had to go into the different communities and share Jesus. The two doctors and four nurses took turns on their days off to join the rest of us as we went to schools, hospitals, orphanages, a train station, and even the bazaar, which is an open marketplace. Even more surprising was the realization of what a great joy I found in working with the children. I wasn't babysitting as I first thought, but instead was joyously part of a powerful team of eight children and three or four adults. As we went from town to town sharing the love of Jesus through drama, song, and testimonies, my heart became lighter and my appreciation for the Lord's guidance to Ternopil more complete.

Each Thursday night, we also held a Bible study in the lounge of the fifth floor of the Hotel Ruta. On the second such Thursday Bible study, a man working with the city administrator, by the name of Basil, asked if he could speak.

Through an interpreter he explained the situation the city found itself in:

"In January, a group of people from New York City, called the Ukrainian Relief Society, decided to purchase and ship to Ternopil two American ambulances. These are the first ambulances in Ukraine; we do not have any others. Even though we are very pleased to have them, this does cause a problem. Since the ambulances would not fit in the shipping crates, the Relief Society dismantled the ambulances before pushing them into the crates. We were so excited and happy when they arrived. But, they are Fords and they are American. I can find no one who knows how to put them together. I show them to everyone. Even if I find someone who knows American Fords, we do not have the proper tools. We are so proud to own them, but they are useless to us. For eight months they have sat in our garage collecting dirt. I know you are doctors and nurses. But I need to ask . . . do any of you know how to put together Ford ambulances? Are any of you a mechanic?"

As John motioned with his hand to catch Basil's attention, every head simultaneously turned toward him. A mechanic . . . John was the *only* person who could help Basil on our entire YWAM team. He was excited over this wonderful gift the Lord was giving to him. Coming into missions, John felt he would no longer use his talents as a mechanic. But God had not only given him the opportunity to use his mechanical skills, but also to put them to use while in Ukraine. Now we understood why God had placed us in Ternopil instead of Cremia or Kharkov!

The next day John went with Basil to the garage where the ambulances were housed, and started the tedious job of putting back together the first two known ambulances in the country. Albina, the interpreter, translated as John explained what he was doing and how the inner parts of a Ford works. The Ukrainian Relief Society did not stop to consider the vast difference between SAE standard tools (those used in America) and metric tools (which are used in Europe and in Ukraine). They did not send along the proper tools to assemble the ambulances. Basil had only a handful of useless, mostly broken, antique-like metal objects he proudly called his tools. I have always jokingly said my husband could fix anything that "ever even thought about moving." In Ukraine, he proved this to be true. John was challenged to improvise, at times making his own tools, in order to get the ambulances assembled and in perfect running order.

Each day after John finished working on the ambulances, he would arrange a time to be picked up the next day in front of the Hotel Ruta by Basil or by one of his friends. Several days into working on the ambulances, John and Albina waited outside the hotel as usual. After nearly an hour, it became obvious no one was coming. Disappointed, John slowly walked up the five flights of stairs to our room. Taking advantage of the extra free time, Albina decided to go shopping. To John's surprise, within a few minutes two men he had never seen before came looking for him. Using hand gestures to indicate driving a car and saying only one word in English, "Ford," John was sure this was his ride to the garage where Basil would be waiting, so he left with the two men.

Since Albina was not along, there was no way to communicate, so John just sat in the back seat of the car and listened as the men talked to each other. But something was amiss. The driver was going the wrong way. At first John thought they were going by another route to the garage, but after several turns, he was certain they were headed totally in the wrong direction. Tapping one of the men on the shoulder, John spoke words the men did not understand. Talking by hand gestures and pointing, he tried to make the men understand what he was saying. Nodding their heads saying, *"tak, tak"* (yes, yes), they kept driving.

A pang of fear started to grow within John's heart. The KGB and the Mafia were prominent figures in Ukraine, although more so in the capital of Kiev than in Ternopil. But they still often made their presence known. Several times in the past few weeks we saw suspicious-looking men following us or watching us from the crowd as we gave our testimonies and delivered a biblical message. Many times they carried an AK47 machine gun slung over their shoulders. There was reason to be cautious. Discreetly, John peered over the front seat trying to see if the men had guns tucked under their belts, but he could not see anything unusual. But this fact did not alleviate the mounting fear as they left Ternopil and headed toward a less populated area. Now, John is not a man whose mind takes off into flights of fancy; he seldom gets upset about unusual occurrences. But this time, his imagination took over and led him into a world filled with fear.

Flashing through his mind were all the silly things one thinks about when you fear your life is in danger: *Did I kiss the girls goodbye? Did I tell my wife I love her? I was warned about the passport black market; I should have left my money and passport with Valerie.* The more he thought, the higher his panic level became. He, John Clayton, was being kidnapped by the KGB, the Mafia, or maybe a black-market gang, and he was starting to panic. He had to think. But the more he tried to think, the more muddled his thoughts became. So he prayed, "OK God . . . I need You *right* now! I think I am being kidnapped and I don't know what to do. I need You to show me, tell me, what I am to do. How do I act? If it comes to it, help me not to show fear in the face of death. Be with Valerie, Cariane, and Marleigh. Take care of them for me. I came here to be a witness for You. Help me to be just that. Have glory in whatever happens. Protect me. I need You. I love You so much. I know You won't leave me or forsake me; help me in my actions not to forsake You."

Approaching what looked like an old abandoned ware-house, they drove into the open garage doors right to the middle and stopped. In front of them was a group of men who were lined up and obviously awaiting their arrival. The driver shut off the motor, walked back, and opened John's door and motioned for him to get out. Guardedly, John exited and stood a few feet away. Trying to appear casual, he looked around trying to get his bearings in case he had to attempt an escape. Approaching, the men surrounded John. Then several of them reached out and started patting John on the back while all talking at once. John closed his eyes, trying to make sense of his kidnapping, when he heard a soft, female voice in broken English.

Looking toward the voice, John saw a pretty little girl about the age of twelve or thirteen trying to communicate with her few words of English. John picked out the words, "Basil . . . Ford . . . fix . . . ok?" finishing with a broad smile. The trembling from fear had nearly made John giddy. When he realized that he was not being kidnapped, but had been brought to this warehouse to work on a Ford van of one of Basil's associates, John had to stifle a laugh. While on the one hand he was silently reprimanding himself for this journey with his over-active imagination, on the other hand he felt like laughing with relief! Lifting a silent *thank you* toward heaven, John followed the men to the van on the other side of the warehouse. With the help of sign language, pointing, and the limited English from the young girl, John had the van fixed and running in just a couple of hours.

With the van again running, the men motioned for John to get into the car and they drove back to the hotel. Relief along with a sense of comedy filled John as he reviewed his day's adventure with the YWAM team. Tomorrow he would again wait for his ride to the garage to work on the ambulances. John was not sure, though, if he would ever again get into a car driven by someone he did not already know. Even though he wasn't really kidnapped, the emotions John went through were alarming and quite exhausting!

At first John thought it was strange, but each day as he arrived at Basil's garage, there would be another man who had not been there the day before watching and listening as John explained the inner workings of the ambulance. The next day there would be another, and then another. Some days, there were three or four new men arriving to watch, listen, and learn from John. It wasn't long until there were well over thirty men in attendance each morning, waiting for his arrival. A relatively quiet man, John doesn't have much to say and *never* in front of a group. Yet here he found himself the center of attention in front of a gathering of men that kept growing by the day.

With thirty years' experience as a mechanic, putting the ambulances together would normally take John three, maybe four days. Yet, he took the better part of a month to complete his task. Even though Americans were a novelty in Ukraine, John knew there was something more than his being American that beckoned these men, something more than them wanting to know the mechanics of the ambulances. It was the power of the name of Jesus.

Ukraine had recently came out of decades of living with "There is no such thing as God" and still suffers greatly from ignorance in spiritual matters. But no matter what man said or tried to do, the knowledge of God stayed alive in the hearts of Ukrainians. Many believed in His existence, but few knew of Jesus and His sacrificial love for them. Between the turns of the wrench and the twist of the screwdriver, John shared from his own life experiences the love, compassion, and faithfulness of God. The men in the garage responded with great interest as they asked numerous questions. Many times John did not readily know the answers. But as he would tighten a bolt or fiddle with some part, an answer would suddenly pop into his head. The words would be so profound that John knew the Lord had supplied those specific words just for him and his group of spiritually hungry men. It was a wonderful time not only for John, but also for the Ukrainian men as well. Questions were answered, doubts laid to rest, and firm foundations of faith were established as the ambulances were completed and set on the streets for use.

Like working with a jigsaw puzzle, God put together His plan for not only those in Ternopil, but also for our family as well. And, as with a jigsaw puzzle, He brought the pieces together so we could see His hand at work. Sitting under a tree at a neighborhood park watching our girls play, John commented, "You know, God is really awesome. If we had insisted on going to Kharkov or Crimea, we'd be over 1,000 miles away; I would not have been available to work on these ambulances. More than the ambulances, though, there wouldn't have been the opportunity of sharing with that whole group of men the love and hope we can find only in Jesus. They had so many questions on how to be honest businessmen, while still being a Christian. You know, this made the whole trip worthwhile."

Hearing what John said, I began to understand the bigger picture of the ambulances, to realize the timing of the Master's plan. There was more than Doug Kinne hearing through prayer that we were to be with the Ternopil team. As dates and facts came into my mind, I could barely grasp the enormity of it all:

- The month God revealed He wanted our family to go to Hawaii and then to Ukraine
- The month He miraculously led Fred to drop the $100,000 lawsuit against John, thus clearing the way for us to come to Ukraine
- The month the Ukrainian Relief Society in New York felt led to ship two American Ford ambulances to Ternopil
- The month He began to see His perfect plan implemented
- The month . . . It had been last January.

Eye hath not seen, nor ear heard, neither have entered into the heart of man, the things which God hath prepared for them that love him. (1 Cor. 2:9)

8

The Prison, the Picture, the Promise

God Knows Best

Each day in Ukraine our team would spend several hours either in a school, hospital, orphanage, train station, or the bazaar. The place did not matter; if there were people, we were there sharing about the love of God. Our team had developed a regular program of presenting the gospel with singing in the Ukrainian language, followed by a presentation of drama through mime. Next, with the help of an interpreter, we shared testimonies and a biblical message of love and hope, ending with an invitation to accept Jesus. Afterward, those in the audience who had questions or wanted to pray would walk up to one of the team members and we would resume our discussion about Jesus.

The day came when we were invited to visit and share Jesus with the inmates at the local women's prison. I'd heard the prison was filthy and the women uncouth. I did not like the idea of our girls going into a place such as that. My offer to stay behind and watch the six youngest children was accepted. While the adults not working in the clinic spent the afternoon at the prison, the children and I spent the day in the park.

Two weeks later we were told that our team was invited to another prison; this one was full of young men ranging in age from fourteen to twenty-six. Quickly, I again volunteered to forgo the two-hour trip and stay behind to watch the children. For the second time, I expressed my fears and motherly concerns about our children not endangering their lives by going into the hazards of a prison. I was content to let Paul, our group leader, think this was the sole motive for my objection. I didn't feel I could tell the *real* reason I didn't want to go. Just thinking about it made me weepy, so speaking about it was nearly impossible. I felt confident Paul would understand and agree with my parental concerns, so I went to bed and slept peacefully.

Peace, however, was short-lived. Along with the early morning sun came the news: Not only was I going to the prison, but the children were as well. A bombshell couldn't have taken my breath away any quicker when I was informed that I was the one chosen to share an evangelistic message of hope and love with the young prisoners. Tears of anger and shame welled up as rebellion reared its ugly head within me. Silently, I screamed *no! No! NO!* As I dug in heels of determination, I proclaimed to anyone within earshot a half-dozen reasons why I could not, why I *would* not go to the prison that day or any other day. But my tears of protest fell on deaf ears. Why wouldn't they listen to me? I *couldn't* go to that prison! I *wouldn't!*

"Go back and pray," I begged my leaders. "I am sure that you are not hearing God correctly. I know He would not want me to speak to these boys. Anybody, *anybody* but me. Please . . . go back and pray!"

After again praying, the leadership returned to inform me God made Himself clear. I was to speak at the prison that day. I boarded the bus completely overcome with anger and frustration. As we drove through the Ukrainian countryside, I couldn't stop crying. I begged God to help me out of what was surely a mistake. Yet when I walked through the solid steel prison doors, heard the clang of the gate shut, the click of the lock being bolted, and the sound of the buzzer, I knew I couldn't escape my plight any more than these young prisoners could.

We made the long trek, winding our way through the courtyard between one old dilapidated building after another. I could smell the musty aroma of the dirty mattresses on the concrete floors. My bones felt the cold, unfriendliness of the steel bars. Dozens of half-dressed youth hung out barred windows, staring at me as I stared past them. Tears of desperation streamed down my face as I followed the feet in front of me. Like a robot with no feeling or awareness of its surroundings, I automatically put one foot in front of the other. Locked in my own thoughts, I no longer saw the deplorable conditions of the buildings or the hopelessness in the eyes of the prisoners. I cringed inside as I selfishly thought of myself and how I did not want to be here. The thought of my son, Marcus, invaded my mind.

"Oh God," I cried out. "How can I share Jesus with these boys? How can I stand here and tell them how much You love them, that You want to make a difference in their lives, when my own son is locked away in a prison in Texas? I failed Marcus, so how could I possibly reach these young men? I feel like a hypocrite, God. You know I don't belong here. Please get me out of here. Please?"

Quietly, yet distinctly, I heard a voice I was coming to recognize as the Lord's, *"Did you not say that you would go anywhere I asked?"*

Yes Lord I did. I'm here . . . in Ukraine.

"If I ask you to talk to these boys, will you?"

I can't. It's not possible, God. What about Marcus? Why would You even want me to talk to them? It wouldn't be right. I just can't.

"But will you?"

Yes, Lord. I don't understand why, but I'll do as You ask.

"If you take care of my boys here, I will take care of your boy back there."

Mechanically, I continued to follow the footsteps in front of me. Slowly, the dawning realization came that the Lord had just made a request and followed it with a promise. My fears, both those I had voiced over the children and those I had silently prayed over my son, disappeared from my once heavy heart. Just as surely as the sun's rays burst from behind rain clouds, I lost my doubts about what I would do. I would share from the perspective of a mother with these Ukrainian prisoners.

As I opened my mouth, a wealth of God's love, understanding, and compassion poured out. With the help of an interpreter, I shared from a mother's heart not only the pain of having a son in prison, but also the personal guilt and responsibility I carried for his imprisonment.

"I want to talk to you today as a mother, a mother of a young man the same age as many of you. A young man who sits behind prison bars back in America while his mother, that's me, cries tears that seem to never end. See, I was not a good mother when my son, Marcus, was growing up. I screamed at him, hit him, and called him names— when all he wanted was to be loved. I helped put my son behind bars just like the ones you sit behind. Yes, it was Marcus' choice to break the law, just like it was your choice, but I helped push him into a life of crime.

"Each of you has committed a crime of some sort or you wouldn't be here. Although you may each have committed a different crime, you all have one thing it common: sin. That same sin is in all people; no one is exempt. The sin, or the thoughts and actions that got you into trouble in the first place, is the same sin that will get you in trouble again and again. You will tell me that once you are out of here, no one will make you ever come back. But the truth of the matter is, you will probably find yourself in trouble and possibly right back here again—maybe even for the rest of your life. Prison is not where anyone desires to be; but we are all in a prison, whether we are behind steel bars or out in the world. We are locked in a prison of sin.

"It is only by experiencing the love of God, the love of the very One who created you, that sin can lessen its stronghold and allow peace and goodness to take over in your life. It is only the love of God that can free you from the never-ending prison of sin. Probably many of you have had your mothers disown you . . . say they did not want anything to do with you any longer. Maybe they even said they no longer loved you. They may have even thought they meant it. But I will let you in on a secret. Way down deep she loves you with the same fervent love I have for my son Marcus. Your mother may be hurt, crushed by the things you did or said; her love may be buried, but she still loves you. I can *almost* guarantee that.

"Now if you want a *real* guarantee, then you are talking about God's love. The God who knows everything you have ever done. The God who knows everything you ever even *thought* about doing or saying. The God who knows more about you than your own mother does—that is the God who loves you with a passion and will *never* turn away or forsake you—not even when you sin. His love does not falter one iota—not even while you are in prison. His love is so great, He sent His Son down to earth to die on the cross for your sin. How many of you would willingly place your mom or little brother—or your own child—on a cross to die for some person who isn't even born yet? God did. Because He knew you even before you were born . . . and He loved you. He has provided a way for you to be forgiven of the sin in your life. It will not magically get you out from behind these bars, but it will set you free on the inside, where it really counts. Peace and contentment will reside where hate, bitterness, and anger now live. You can trust me on this . . . because I know firsthand. Better yet . . . trust Jesus."

The truth of God's forgiveness and His endless grace was shared as many young men responded to the prompting of the Holy Spirit that day. A number of them prayed for the first time in their lives. A few admitted to asking Jesus into their hearts. Nearly all had tough, really hard questions to which they were seeking answers. The Spirit of God filled the entire team with His words of wisdom and knowledge as we sat on the hard wooden benches talking and praying with the boys for several hours.

Leaving the prison that afternoon, I was overjoyed at God's goodness to the prisoners, while at the same time filled with excitement and hope concerning His promise for my own son.

Three weeks later when we returned to the United States, I was confused to learn that Marcus had been transferred to a maximum security prison. My son, considered a nonviolent offender, had stolen television sets and VCRs. He did *not* belong with men convicted for rape, murder, and armed robbery. Was I mistaken about the promise I felt God gave me in Ukraine? Questions flew to heaven, but seemingly no answers came in return.

Prison, even those in the United States, are full of men who think nothing of jumping a fellow prisoner to commit rape. Marcus, who is a good-looking, blond, blue-eyed, six foot, well-built young man, was a prime target for this kind of crime. When a prisoner resists an attack of this nature, usually a beating follows, until submission comes.

Out of self-preservation and a fear of this danger, Marcus voluntarily kept himself in his cell, coming out for only meals. Loneliness, boredom, and endless days stretched before him. In an attempt to preserve his sanity, Marcus took the only things at his disposal—pencil and paper—and set his hand to drawing. Never having had lessons in art, he tentatively started to sketch, not knowing what would take shape. Marcus soon realized there was something special behind that pencil: a real artistic talent. As his drawings began to materialize into recognizable pictures, he became bolder and gained confidence.

More than a year and a half passed since God had so clearly spoken to me in the Ukrainian prison. It was now Christmas 1996. There in the mail, marked "Do Not Bend," was a large brown envelope from the prison. Excitement and curiosity over what Marcus had sent kept me from waiting until I got home to open it. Right there in the crowded campus mail room I peeled back the flap and peered inside. I cannot express the awe I felt, the deep well of amazement I experienced as I pulled out two sheets of paper. There in my hand were what seemed to me the two most beautiful pictures in the world.

One was an angel, a sweet cherub sitting on a cloud unwrapping a gift, waiting for something special. It peered out of the picture as if watching me. So innocent and peaceful with inquisitive eyes and full, kissable lips, the winsome face couldn't help but stir emotions in my heart. If someone asked me what a small child in heaven looks like, that angel face would be the picture most likely conjured up in my mind.

One glance at the other picture and you knew the little boy could be the son of the shepherd who visited baby Jesus at His birth. The little boy, not more than six or seven years old, seemed real as he looked over with awe to what you can only imagine is the manger scene. The song "Little Drummer Boy" came to mind as the young lad, complete with drum and precious newborn lambs at his feet, appeared to be singing with complete abandon.

This time the tears I shed were from sheer joy. My heart was overflowing with love, both for Marcus and for my heavenly Father who had not forgotten my boy. As a mother watching my son grow up, I knew Marcus had artistic abilities, but I never envisioned that he could draw anything *quite* like this!

God had not forgotten His promise to take care of my son. What appeared to be a forgotten promise was in actuality God's promise in the making. My interpretation of God's word was an early release for my son, or at least a safer, easier place for him to serve his time. What Marcus received instead was a place with more danger, making his time harder to serve, with release still several years away. At times, I felt like God had forgotten His promise. But that was not the case; God had a different plan than mine.

I begin to wonder: Without the change of prison, would Marcus have picked up his pencil to draw? Would he have realized the incredible talent with which God had blessed him? Could it be that his solitary confinement, mixed with his talent for drawing, was part of God's answer for my son regarding his earning a living after his sentence is completed?

Marcus' Christmas pictures are more than just a gift from my son . . . more than a couple of nicely drawn pictures. They are the beginning of the fulfillment of God's promise that as I took care of His boys, He takes care of mine.

> Do not waver through unbelief regarding the promise of God, but be strengthened in your faith and give glory to God. (Rom. 4:20)

9

Only One Word
Following a Promise

Time sure seemed to fly by quickly. I could not believe more than half our time in the country of Ukraine was over. I loved being there; I loved the people. I especially loved serving the Lord through missions; it was better than I ever imagined it could be.

Every day for five weeks our YWAM team, with the help of translators, ventured into neighboring communities, sharing the gospel of Jesus. The most rewarding feeling I have ever experienced was seeing scores of people, young and old alike, come to accept Jesus as their Savior. It was positively exhilarating.

Surprisingly, I found I love to stand up and share Jesus with others. I always thought standing in front of a crowd, sharing the gospel was for preachers or evangelists; at the very least it was for men, it certainly wasn't for me. I thought back to our mission training in Hawaii. We had had many different speakers; the last one being a man named Danny

Lehmann. For two days he enthusiastically shared how we as a team could successfully share Jesus.

However, my mind was not on Danny or what he was saying. Instead, it went over the list of all the preparations for our first trip to a foreign country. There were dozens of thoughts swirling through my mind, distracting me from Danny and what he was saying. But that is no excuse for not showing respect and giving him my complete attention.

"Say you have been in Ukraine for a few days," Danny continued, despite my digressing mind, "and you decide to share about the love of God. How do you get someone to understand their spiritual need, and then successfully lead them to accept Jesus? What words should you use? I will walk you through a scenario. Since John is sitting in the front row, let's use him as an example. John meets a man. Let's say his name is . . . Vladamir, and John successfully leads him to the Lord. What did John have to do or say to make Vladamir realize his need of a personal Savior?"

That was all I heard, as I again lost my focus on Danny and his words of instruction. For a moment I felt remorse, but only briefly as my mind again turned to the upcoming trip and all the preparations for which I was responsible. With a shake of my head, I was brought back to the present.

I still chuckle as I think of the first time our team went out to share the gospel. It was our first week in Ternopil, and our team leader asked me to be the one to share the message, or in essence, preach. This surprised me, as I did not have intentions of being the main speaker on this trip, or any other trip. Talking with people one-on-one I could do, but speaking in front of hundreds of people was not for me. I tried to argue my way out of it, but my leaders were adamant—I was to give the message. As I stood up that day to share in the bazaar, I was completely amazed at the people who were interested in spiritual matters and what I had to share. Then I wished I had listened better to Danny Lehmann!

But this did not stand in the way of God obtaining His purpose, as the Holy Spirit faithfully brought many into His Kingdom that day. Seeing the number of people who prayed, asking Jesus into their hearts, was wonderful. But something else happened as well; I found I absolutely loved sharing the gospel! From then on, I took every opportunity I could to stand in front of a group and share the love of Jesus. I was surprised to realize how completely at home I was speaking in front of a crowd—as if I was made for this.

My husband and I are complete opposites. Whereas I am talkative and outgoing, he leans toward being more quiet; John is a mechanic by trade and shy by nature. Talking with his customers while he works under the hood of their car is natural to him, but talking to crowds is another matter. John does not even like to be *in* a crowd; he could never envision himself speaking in front of one. That is completely out of character for him. At each outing we took, the adults on the team rotated sharing their testimony. John also was called upon to take his turn. I could tell by the quick blinking of his eyes and the shifting of his feet that he was quite nervous. This was by far the hardest thing he had ever been asked to do. I was so proud of my husband, when in obedience he stepped forward to share from his heart his own experiences and how God is always there for him.

Time after time John shared with men and women individually about Jesus. Each time he asked, "Would you like to ask Jesus into your heart?" But the answers would always be, "No" or "Not now, maybe some other time." Yet, as other team members and I counseled and prayed with individuals and groups of people, the answer was almost always, "Yes!" After weeks of this, John told me of his feelings of inadequacy when it came to sharing his faith. He wondered if maybe he was doing something wrong. Was he even cut out for this sort of thing? Could it be having a *desire* to serve God was not enough? Yet in obedience, despite what he was feeling, John continued to share the love and faithfulness of Jesus everywhere he went.

Our team had developed a regular program of presenting the gospel that included singing, drama through mime, testimonies, and a biblical message completed with an invitation to accept Jesus. Afterward, those in the audience who had questions or wanted to pray would walk up to one of the team members and we would speak to them about the saving power of Jesus. Of course, there were always those in a crowd who, for whatever reason, would not come forward to ask questions but stood back and just watched. We took this as a good indication that they had a desire to know more. After the crowd diminished, it was our custom to approach the few left and take the initiative by asking them if we could answer any questions they might have about what had been said.

About the sixth week in Ukraine, our team spent eight days in the small country town of Stukes. There we visited a sanatorium, a large hospital-like building where the elderly or those recovering from surgery lived. We presented our program as usual and then prayed with those in the audience. Toward the back of the auditorium, sitting by himself, was a man in his mid-eighties who we discovered was blind. I walked up to the man and asked if he would like to talk about Jesus. "*Znāt!*" he snapped, which means "no" in Ukrainian. Twice more, other team members approached asking if

they could speak with him, only to hear the same curt "*Znāt.*"
Since he did not have a cane, and his wife was busy talking
to someone from the team, we figured he was simply waiting
for her to guide him back to their room and not interested in
talking about the things of God.

Finished with our work, we gathered our Bibles and
backpacks in preparation to leave. The residents filed out
of the auditorium along with us, but the elderly blind man
remained. Something inside pulled at John, something tell-
ing him to stay and talk with the man. Those of us who
tried to speak to him earlier told John just to leave the old
guy alone; he did not want anyone bothering him. We had
just started the thirty-minute hike back to the church where
we were staying, when John announced he was going back;
he wanted to see if the man was still there. If this pull, this
nudging, was from the Lord, then John wanted to be obedi-
ent. He would go back and try again to speak with the man.

John and Inna, his translator, walked the several blocks
back to the sanatorium. There they found the sightless old
man still sitting in the semi-dark auditorium, staring blankly
ahead. John was sensitive to the fact that this man, who
had lived all but a dozen of his eighty-plus years under
Communism, would have strong opinions about the non-
existence of God. Praying for the right words, John asked if
he had any questions about Jesus. Taking him by surprise,
the man answered, "*tak*"—yes.

At first his questions were carefully asked, with much
thought given to the way they were worded. But as John
gave honest answers, along with personal examples, the
man's questions came faster and with more urgency. Thirty
minutes passed; then an hour. Now it was the end of the
second hour and the man still fired questions, with Inna

translating John's answers. Getting hoarse from all the talk-
ing, both John and Inna were relieved when the questions
dwindled and finally stopped all together, giving their
parched throats a much-needed rest. For a few moments
the three sat in silence, each in their own thoughts.

Finally John asked, "Is there anything else I can ex-
plain to you? Do you have any other questions?" The eyes
of Inna were shining as she interpreted his reply. "*Tak*. Tell
me how to pray. What do I need to say to have Jesus in my
heart, just like you?"

John felt the goose bumps travel from head to toe. This
man, who spent nearly his entire life believing God did not
exist, now believed! Not only did he believe, but he also
wanted to pray that wondrous prayer leading him to eter-
nal life. John now knew without a doubt that it was the
Lord who had given him the nudge to return and speak to
this precious man. He was glad he had obeyed. His feelings
of inadequacy vanished. John's memory momentarily
flashed back to the example Danny Lehmann gave, "Let's
say John meets a man named Vladamir and leads him to
the Lord. What words should he use?" John slowly said
those special words Danny taught him, which when hon-
estly said would assure eternal life.

With tears rolling down his weathered face, in a shaky
voice the man repeated the words after John said them in
English and Inna in Ukrainian. At the end of his prayer, the
man opened his tear-filled eyes and smiled a toothless but
(to John) a beautiful smile. A glowing replaced the sadness
that previously lived on his wrinkled face. Whereas before
there ws a "deadness" in his eyes, now you could almost
"feel" the new life. Wanting to say a personal congratula-
tions, John started to speak and realized that after more

than two hours of talking he still did not know the man's name.

"Sir, I never asked you your name. Can you tell me what it is?"

Although only one word was said, it was one word that forever cemented John's trust and faith in God. It is the one word that always comes back to him when he doubts himself or when he questions his own faith. It was only one word, but it instantly brought tears to John's eyes.

When asked his name, the eighty-three-year-old man replied, "Vladamir."

> I tell you . . . there will be more joy in heaven over one sinner who repents than over ninety-nine righteous persons who need no repentance. (Luke 15:7)

10

The Attacker Brought Popcorn?

He's Never Late

Our entire team was full of anticipation as we boarded the bus for the three-hour drive to Chortkiv to work alongside the Crippled Children's Society. In exchange for opening a week-long clinic for children, the Society would provide families for us to stay with for the duration of our work. We were excited as we had been praying for an opportunity to learn firsthand the culture and to understand the people of Ukraine; living in their homes would provide that for us. Only three translators came, which meant that while in the homes most of our team would rely on hand gestures and smiles to communicate. We welcomed the change of scenery and looked forward to working in this small Ukrainian town several hours outside Ternopil.

The YWAM office in Ternopil called the Children's Society to double-check our accommodations the morning we left. Assured everything was in perfect order, full of high spirits and expectations, we boarded the bus. We were more or less left to our own devices as our team leaders, Doug and Jan, were not coming with us. With the help of our interpreters, we were confident everything would go smoothly. Were we in for a surprise!

On the outskirts of Chortkiv, the sky opened, dropping blinding sheets of rain, making visibility almost nil. Fortunately, the driver knew exactly where the clinic was located and delivered us to the Crippled Children's Society doorstep. Our team doctor, Amanda, and one of the translators, volunteered to dash through the rain to find the location of our accommodations. After we waited nearly a half-hour, Amanda came running back to the bus, out of breath. "You won't believe this," she said between gulps of air. "But they do not have anyplace for us to stay. Apparently no one here followed through with the arrangements. I explained that we called this morning and were told everything was in order—but it's not. I am going back in to see what I can find for us. I think you better pray!"

Amanda, along with the other two translators, rushed back through the rain as we tried to keep the restless children quietly entertained. Within minutes the bus driver stood and made an announcement. Although none of us understood the words, we read his gestures—get off my bus, because I'm leaving! No amount of shaking our heads and pointing to the clinic or handing him *kupons* could dissuade him; he was going to leave and we better get ourselves and our belongings off his bus. Thankfully, as we were gathering our luggage from the back of the bus Amanda arrived back waving a key in the air.

A nurse from the society had access to an old abandoned schoolhouse which had been used for orphans. We had permission to stay there. How does one live in an abandoned schoolhouse for orphans? Anxiety was replaced by dread as ten minutes later we were dropped in front of an old, ugly, sprawling building. No sooner did we step off the bus than the driver pulled away, leaving us standing there wondering what we'd gotten ourselves into.

A damp, musty smell greeted us as we cautiously stepped into the large, empty hall. Exploring a little, we found large classrooms, locked doors that led to other wings, a boiler room, and an auditorium, but no place to sleep. There were light fixtures on the high ceiling but only one had a bulb. The semi-darkness, along with the echoes when we spoke, lent an eerie feeling to the entire ground floor. As we circled to the left, a set of stairs was discovered. We felt our way up the pitch-dark staircase and were pleased to find the second and third floors were dormitories with eight to ten beds in each room. To the children gripping onto our shirttails, this was becoming better than a treasure hunt, albeit a scary one. Each family chose a dormitory as their private sleeping quarters for the next week.

The rooms had large eight-foot windows across one wall, but most were either rusted or nailed shut. The few we could pry open provided us with much needed light and fresh air. I couldn't help but laugh as Marleigh walked into the room we chose. She reminded me of Pigpen in the "Peanuts" cartoon, with dust circling around her as she walked. Being a typical nine-year-old, she immediately bounced on the bed causing great puffs of dust to engulf her and anyone else in the immediate vicinity. Layer upon layer of dust, dirt, and grime from years of disuse were in every corner of the old orphanage.

I didn't want to create trouble, but I was afraid I would not be able to stay in this dismal place because of my allergies. With this amount of dust, I knew my eyes would itch and swell shut and I would not be able to easily breathe. Without any medication or a place to purchase any, I knew I was in trouble. Although my allergies were serious and quite painful, it was not life threatening. Paul, on the other hand, had asthma, which could be fatal from breathing in the dust in the building. To further the complications, Paul left his inhaler in Ternopil. Without transportation, telephone, or a pharmacy, Paul could be in deep trouble if an attack flared up.

"God, You knew where we would stay before You led us to Chortkiv. You know Paul has asthma and I am allergic to dust. Theoretically, neither one of us can stay here; yet here is where You have brought us. So we are calling on You, Jehovah Rhapha, the God who Heals, to be our medication for us. Keep us from getting sick. We want to do what You brought us here to do. We are in Your hands. It is up to You to keep us well."

God did just that. We spent eight days and nights in that grime-filled building. Neither Paul nor I became ill, or even sneezed. We looked for brooms, buckets, and rags to clean with, but never found any. So we continued to pray for health, and God granted us our prayer.

There were doors on each room, but the latches were broken and most were off at least one of its hinges. This meant that the doors would swing open, affording little privacy. Desperate times call for desperate measures! The ends of our sheets were ripped and tied in knots around old nails for makeshift doors.

Almost immediately we discovered there was no running water—other than what was in the toilets. On an excursion John found that the closest place to get fairly uncontaminated water was from a cemetery about a mile away. We were grateful, that even when John was told it would not be necessary, he still brought our metal buckets and coils so we could boil water for drinking and have hot water for sponge baths. That was, of course, if we were willing to walk a mile each way for our water.

Finding suitable toilet facilities was another matter altogether. Right across from our dormitory room was a most unusual sight. There in the middle of this closet-sized room was a set of five or six steps leading up to a concrete platform. On the platform was what we referred to as a "squatty potty." As its name suggests, when nature called one squatted over a hole in the cement. From lack of use, mice had made this hole in the platform a nesting place for their family. Trust me when I say no one came to this room with much enthusiasm!

Using a flashlight to guide us, we made our way back down the stairs, around a corner, and along the very black hallway, to the (almost American style) toilet. Entering that dark, dank room sent little critters scurrying, but not before our children saw them, which sent them running and screaming as well. Our Cariane cried, begging us to find another place, but nothing was available other than the bushes outside. So the adults would find themselves banging on the walls, waving the flashlights in circles, while making enough noise to raise the dead, thus causing any creature in the near vicinity to run for its very life.

Despite the toilets, the dirt, the lack of water, and the twenty-minute walk to and from the cafe three times a day, we loved this peaceful little town. Each day during the lunch hour, we would stand in the middle of the town's shopping square, sharing the love of Jesus with whomever would stop and listen. Many people in those eight days gave their hearts to the Lord. We were thrilled. We had a roof over our heads, food to eat, people were getting saved, the clinic was going smoothly, and we were safe. Or so we thought.

Toward the end of our eight-day stay, our team was invited to attend a prayer meeting about a forty-five minute walk from the schoolhouse. Knowing that Ukrainian prayer meetings usually last until eleven or twelve o'clock at night, and as there was no public transportation, it was decided I would stay behind with the younger children while the rest of the team walked to the meeting. I had no fears of staying alone and was actually glad not to have to walk so far.

After everyone left, I heated water in a bucket with our coil to help the kids wash up. Helping active, fun-loving children take a sponge bath and brush their teeth without running water takes quite a bit of time and is somewhat of a challenge. Of course everytime one had to use the restroom, I had to go along, hold the flashlight and bang on the pipes while hollering to scare away the creepy things—then rewash their black-bottomed little feet. Finally, tucking the younger children, Christopher and Sherisa, into bed, I told stories until their little eyelids closed in slumber. Rachel decided to stay in their room until everyone came back in case the younger children woke up and were frightened.

Toward ten o'clock, with Cariane and Marleigh tucked in but still awake, I decided to take a sponge bath. Heating the last bucket of water, I gathered my toiletries and pulled my shirt over my head. Almost instantaneously, the sheet covering the door to our room opened and two men stood in its opening. Shock mesmerized me for a moment as the two men stood there staring at my half-naked body. I struggled to put on my T-shirt while screaming, "What do you want? Get out of here! Leave, now! I'll call the police. Get out!" Call the police? Who was I kidding? The men seemed completely unaffected by my screaming. My assumption was they did not understand English, but my volume and tone of voice made the message clear . . . get out!

Reaching over, I picked up an umbrella I had left drip-drying against the wall. Using it as a sword, I poked the men in the stomach, chest, and arms, prodding them backwards down the stairs the whole time yelling at them. I continued my poking until the men exited the only un-chained door to the building. I bolted the lock, waved my fist and shouted at them through the glass not to come back. They just stood smiling at me in an eerie sort of way. I turned and slowly but confidently walked away. Once out of their sight, I bolted like a rabbit back down the unlit hallway and up the darkened staircase two stairs at a time.

My whole body was shaking as I rushed over to Cariane and Marleigh, who at this point seemed uneffected by the whole scene. Had I overreacted? I reassured my girls (or was it me I was reassuring?) that we were safely locked in and the men wouldn't be coming back. Deciding to check to make sure the other children were still asleep, I was almost across our room, when the sheet was ripped aside and the two men boldly marched right into our room, grinning from ear to ear. Fear flashed through my whole being. Almost immediately it was overridden by a great sense of anger—how *dare* they come into this building let alone into our room again!

Startled, Cariane and Marleigh screamed as I jumped to grab the umbrella. Realizing what I was about to do, one of the men snatched the umbrella first and held my would-be weapon behind his back. My instinct was to run to the corner and hide with my children, but I felt our very lives were in danger and would depend on a strength I didn't know if I possessed.

Keeping my distance from the men, I again started hollering at them, "What do you want? Get out of here! Come back tomorrow. I'll get my husband—he'll call the police. Get out!" Still grinning, one man brought out from behind his back a large bag of what looked like the white Styrofoam curls used when packing breakables. The bag was at least three feet tall and about eighteen or twenty inches wide. "Popcorn!" was all they said as they opened the bag and put a handful of these Styrofoam-looking curls in their mouths. My mind, nearly paralyzed from the fear of being raped, maybe even killed, could not grasp the scene unfolding in front of me. These men who intruded our peaceful evening wanted to share a bag of snacks with us! My heart was racing, my body was quivering, yet I had to stifle a nervous giggle.

Feeling a little foolish for assuming these men were up to no good, I sighed with relief. Yet the mother in me, the natural instinct, was screaming "Danger!" *"D'ya koo you"* (thank you), I said while pointing the way back down the stairs. Again I walked down the dark staircase, through the hallway and out the door fully aware of how vulnerable I was. Although I was feeling a little like a lunatic for my outburst a few minutes ago, I still felt invaded by these men. "Stay out!" I shouted with as much authority I could muster. This time when I locked the door, I gave my best fiery stare as I turned and stomped away. Just before rounding the corner, I gave one last glare at these intruders. To my utter horror, one of the men dangled a set of keys in front of him with—and this time there was no doubt—an evil grin. My instinct had been right; we were in grave danger. My body shuddered as the hair stood up on the back of my neck. They were going to come back and this time it wasn't to deliver a neighborly bag of popcorn.

Running for all my might, I flew up the stairs and to the room where the younger children were sleeping. Yanking the covers off the bed, I laid the kids on the floor between the bed and the wall. This way if the men peeked into the room, it would appear to be empty, and hopefully the children would be safe. Racing back to our room, I quickly tried to think of what would be safest for Cariane and Marleigh. Knowing I was racing against time, I grabbed blankets and pillows and literally shoved the girls down the hallway while giving instructions.

"I want you to stay in this room and don't come out! Keep your heads down. If Christopher or Sherisa wake up, you keep them quiet and don't let them make any noise. If you have to, cover their mouth with your hand—just don't let them make any sound. *Do not* under any circumstances come out of this room. I don't care what you hear, don't come out until you hear your daddy come back. Understand? Promise me. Don't come out no matter what!"

Bolting to our room, I looked for something, anything, I could use as a weapon. I couldn't find anything promising, so grabbing an old wobbly chair, I broke it over the metal beds. It wasn't much in the way of protection, but it was better than nothing; I could only hope I wouldn't have to use it. "God protect us! If something has to happen, let it happen to me. Don't let any harm come to these kids. Please God, I beg You . . . protect these babies of ours. I know John won't be back for a couple more hours . . . but please God, send help! We are in Your hands."

Yanking the sheet off the doorway so the men could not sneak up on me, I stood with legs braced for battle, broken chair leg in hand, frantically praying.

Unbeknownst to me, there were now three men instead of two using the key to enter the building. Each had a near-empty whiskey bottle in their hand, which they had just guzzled. This time, there was no bag of friendly popcorn they wanted to share.

John had quickly become used to the long prayer meetings in Ukraine. It was considered impolite to have the words translated, thus making the three-hour meeting seem more like five or six hours long. Both in the church services and in the prayer meetings, no one wiggles, speaks out, or even looks around the room. This would be disrespectful. Yet John could not sit still; he was becoming fidgety. He went outside and began to pace back and forth. Something in his spirit felt wrong. Several times he walked back into the prayer meeting sitting in the back as to not disturb anyone. Within minutes, he was back outside pacing. Without reason he felt panic rising, as if he could not breathe. What was causing this agitation?

Michael, the father of Christopher and Sherisa, knew John well enough to realize that something was terribly wrong for John to behave this way. Slipping out of the prayer meeting, he joined John outside. After only a few minutes in conversation, Michael too felt there was something amiss. The team had worked long and hard to get in the good graces of these church leaders, yet Michael knew that John's feeling needed to be acted upon. Risking an offense, Michael went back inside, interrupted the prayer meeting with the announcement that he and John would be leaving immediately to return to the schoolhouse. The rest could either join them now or walk later. Tension from Michael's words was felt as everyone quickly gathered their Bibles and backpacks in preparation to leave.

For the most part, cars are a rare luxury in Ukraine and not owned by the average man. But God in His provision sent two men who had automobiles that night to the prayer meeting. Sensing the urgency, both Ukrainians offered to leave the meeting and drive whomever wanted back to the schoolhouse.

❖ ❖ ❖ ❖

Trembling, I stood ready for whatever was to come. I did not know if I should stay upstairs or if I should face my attackers on the bottom floor. Neither was a good idea. The only sound I heard was me hyperventilating, which added a spookiness to my wait. Then I heard it . . .

. . . yelling . . .

. . . beating on the door . . .

. . . the door bursting open . . .

. . . feet pounding up the stairs . . .

By now, tears of terror streamed down as I called out, "God help me!"

Suddenly . . . in stormed John, Michael, and Paul.

"Thank God you're back! I was so frightened!" I exclaimed as I threw myself into my husband's arms. From his trembling I knew at that moment he needed to be held and reassured as much as I did.

Our team had returned at the same instant the blurry-eyed men succeeded in opening the door to the schoolhouse. Immediately, our men assessed what was happening and wrestled the keys away while tossing the would-be attackers out the door. The Ukrainian drivers summoned help from the overseer of the building while a makeshift blockade was erected to keep us all safe the rest of our stay in Chortkiv. Later we heard the men had been relieved of their duties at the orphanage.

I shudder at what the three men had on their minds when they entered the building for the third time. Yet I rejoice at the absolute perfect timing of the answer to my prayer, "God protect us!"

> Be strong and of good courage; do not fear nor be afraid of them; for the Lord your God, He is the One who goes with you. He will not leave you nor forsake you. (Deut. 31:6)

11

A Tropical Answer

Exact Answer

Our time in Ukraine was finished. It was amazing how everyone on the team had made fast, hard friendships that we were reluctant to leave. As we said our final goodbyes outside the Hotel Ruta in Ternopil, hugs, kisses, and many tears were shared between our team members and the Ukranians who came to bid us farewell. Although it had been only two months, we had invested a big part of our lives in these Ukrainians; we had fallen in love with the country and its people. It would be hard to say goodbye. As we boarded the bus to return to Kiev, promises were made in the hopes we could return, mixed with tears in case we never did. From Kiev, we flew the reverse trip to Amserdam, Los Angeles, and then Kailua-Kona, Hawaii. Tears and sadness stayed with us through our entire two day flight and into our landing in Hawaii.

Hawaii! It felt good to be back on American soil again. Our team spent three days for debriefing at a five-star hotel with a pool overlooking the ocean, hammocks swinging between the palm trees, and sunsets that defy any and all description. We would spend three days relaxing in beautiful Hawaii then my family would catch an early morning flight back to Texas. We could hardly wait to get home!

Our daughters, Cariane and Marleigh missed their grandparents and their sister Robin and her two-year-old, Nikki. We were all especially anxious to meet our newest granddaughter, Kaitlyn Reneé, who was only a few weeks old.

But there was one flaw with these fabulous three days in Hawaii—you could call it a technicality. My body's time clock was still on Ukrainian time, a thirteen-hour difference. Cariane and Marleigh, being children, quickly adjusted. Their days were spent running around the hotel grounds, visiting friends, playing hard, and swimming countless hours. John, who had not slept a wink on the 9,000-mile flight from Amsterdam, was also having no problem sleeping soundly.

I, on the other hand, could not sleep a wink, no matter how exhausted I felt. I was beginning to feel like a zombie. During the day I had clothes to wash and repack, meetings to attend, plane reservations to check, and numerous other obligations to meet. Logic dictated I should be too tired to do anything other than crash at the sight of a bed; yet there I lay for the third night in a row with my eyes wide open. Strangely instead of relaxing, a new surge of energy welled up within. Lying in the darkened room, I begin to feel like a caged tiger with the need to get up and move about. Quietly dressing so as to not wake John and the girls, I slipped out the door and down to the ocean front of the hotel in the hopes of walking off some of this newfound, unwanted energy.

Midnight was a peaceful time, with all the other guests soundly tucked away in their rooms. I loved walking along the ocean side of the hotel, listening as the waves made a lovely symphony of sound as they rhythmically crashed against the lava rock. The salty taste of the air, the rustling of the palm trees, the sounds magnified by the night spoke volumes of its Creator. God's hand could almost be felt as well as seen in every corner of this lovely island paradise. By far, this place ranked among the most enticing places I have ever found for praying.

That is exactly what I did as I wandered aimlessly back and forth along the hotel grounds. There is something magical about solitude. After a period of being totally alone, tension begins to slowly melt away and is replaced with a fresh, new calmness. I had not realized I was so uptight, but as the minutes ticked away into hours, I felt my body being drained of its stress. I began taking deep breaths, and with the expelling of the old air, new life began to move through my veins.

My prayers began to progress from general praying to a more personal prayer and finally into an incredibly close and intimate fellowship with my *Abba*, my heavenly daddy. Hour after hour, I meandered around the hotel grounds. My favorite spot was the two-person hammock that was anchored between giant palm trees. The hammock was low to the ground, so I could reach over and push, making the hammock rock slowly. The sound of the rustling palm leaves mixed with the crashing of the waves and the beauty of watching the millions of twinkling stars brought a new, deeper level of awareness of God's presence in my life. I alternated between walking, swinging in the hammock, and just standing still while I prayed. Hours passed as I relished the inner peace and joy I was experiencing as I spent time in prayer.

I prayed over a lot of different things that night, but my main target was our next step in missions. John and I did not have a clear sense of direction. When God made it apparent He wanted us to serve Him full-time in missions, we thought He was directing us to work on the Mercy Ship, which is a branch of YWAM. Strangely, though, with our Crossroads training now completed, we did not feel He was leading us in that direction after all.

YWAM has a catalogue called the GO manual that lists all the different areas in the world mission work is being done with the organization. While still in Ukraine, I had randomly picked Salem, Oregon, as good a place as any for us to move while serving in missions because we knew it was not to be the Mercy Ships. Disappointing to us, we also felt it was not to be overseas. Since Salem needed a mechanic and our girls had never seen snow before, why not Salem? Although John did not sense a special desire to go there, we sent for an application for staff positions in Oregon. If this was not where God wanted us, I felt sure He would let us know.

My strongest desire was to go where God wanted us to go. I was confused why He did not lead us to the Mercy Ship. But was Salem the right place? How was I to be sure? As I prayed, I thought back to other times when I had received instruction from the Lord; how did I know then what He was saying? I needed to hear God's voice again. I decided to use what worked for me in the past. I would just lay it all out to God and allow Him to show me His plans.

"Lord, I do not know what You have planned for our family. I need to hear clearly from You what Your plans are.

So I am going to ask You to show me. I know it is only 4:15 in the morning, but I want You to wake up John, have him walk down here to where I am. Have him say just one thing: no "good morning," no "hello," nothing but the place that You want our family to serve You. In this way, I will know it is from You. Just one other thing. Could You get John up in the next five to ten minutes? I think I need to try to get some sleep tonight."

About ten minutes passed as I continued to wander the grounds near the pool. Hearing a noise, I looked up to see someone approaching. There, walking out from behind the shadow of the trees came my sleepy-eyed husband. By the mussed hair and the inside-out T-shirt, I could tell he had just gotten out of bed and dressed in the dark.

Ambling over to where I was standing, John walked up, looked me straight in the eye and said, "We are not to go to Salem. We need to stay right here in Kona." With that statement, he turned around and headed back to the hotel.

For some *totally* unexplainable reason, I raced after John, hollering, "Wait a minute! You can't just make a statement like that and then walk away. I have a right to help in this decision too, you know. Besides, we already agreed that we weren't coming back here; neither one of us want to live in Hawaii, remember?"

My prayer of request so recently said, just seemed to slip into the forgotten recesses of my mind. Poor John did not know what hit him as for the next seven hours I hounded his steps with demands for explanations . . . all the while giving excuses and alternatives. John did not remember getting up and walking down and looking for me. He said he never really considered moving to Hawaii to work; he wasn't even sure where the thought came from.

But suddenly, when he said it, he knew that this was where we were to stay.

By noon, we were packed, checked out of the hotel, and waiting for our ride to the airport. Cariane and Marleigh were saying their final goodbyes to their friends. Together John and I sat on the curb, each consumed in our own thoughts, trying to make sense of John's sudden desire to move our family to Hawaii. My mind was in a jumble of mixed-up thoughts. How I longed for the quiet solitude of last night; the welcoming sound of the crashing waves, the peacefulness of the deserted hotel, and the acute awareness of God's presence.

Trying to recapture those precious moments at the hotel, I was brought up short by my own prayer so recently said: "I want You to wake John up out of his deep sleep. Have him walk down here to me and say just one thing—the place where You would have us to serve." In an instant, it all became clear; God had answered my prayer *exactly* as I had asked. But I was too blinded by my own wants and desires to hear the very answer I had asked for. That all-consuming need to control every situation and be the decision maker was trying its best to surface again.

"God, I want to obey. Help me to let go and allow You to guide us."

With a great sense of amazement, John listened as I shared with him my prayer at 4:15 A.M. and the subsequent answer. At first John just sat there thinking. Then he started laughing with such joy; it felt so good to know for sure that his sudden desire for Hawaii was not some stray thought from out of the blue, but was actually God making His plan for us known. It was a welcome feeling.

Looking down at his watch, John jumped up from our curbside seat and said, "Doug is suppose to be here in forty-five minutes to pick us up. There is just enough time to go to Campus Services and see what they think about our coming back. The luggage will be fine right here." Quickly, we crossed the campus to the building that housed Campus Services. In the office sat Don, the man who was in charge. As we walked into his office, he said the strangest thing, "It's about time you got here. I was beginning to worry." With that, Don picked up two manila folders, which contained our personnel files. My husband and I looked at each other with a questioning shrug; this really was strange. I knew that the files are stored at the personnel office, which was clear across campus, so why were our files on Don's desk? I did not see any of our other classmates' files there. And what did he mean by "It's about time"? Was Don expecting us?

Ignoring Don's odd remark and our questions of what he meant, John begin by telling Don what had transpired over the past eight hours. Don just sat there smiling like the Cheshire cat, letting out little chuckles of laughter from time to time while nodding his head. Neither one of us knew what to make of him.

"What do we need to do to apply as staff? I don't know what you have available for Valerie, but I want to apply for the position of base mechanic," John explained.

Opening our files that were in front of him, Don replied, "Just fill out these applications before you leave. You see, the Lord told us several days ago that He wanted you here. That is why your folders are on my desk. The staff has already starting praying about you coming to be part of the Kona family. My wife said that I should have set up a meeting with you to ask if you would like to serve here. I did not want to influence you in any way, so I have been praying that the Lord Himself would bring you to us. Really the only thing you have to do is fill out the application and then tell us when you think you can return and start work."

God had done it again! Without our realizing it, He orchestrated the answer to our prayers and had them ready and waiting for us. All we had to do was be still, listen, and be willing to be obedient. This time as we crossed the campus, we walked slowly as we shared our feelings of how God had again blessed us by leading us on the path we should follow. Knowing God was actively involved with our lives, that He was diligently working on our behalf, overwhelmed us with the feeling of being loved and cherished beyond anything we had ever experienced before.

Rounding the corner, our luggage came into sight and we were jerked back to the present. In just fifteen minutes, Doug would be there to take us to the airport. Personally, I could not see dragging all our stuff to Texas, only to turn around and come back to Hawaii with the same suitcase of clothes. A plan was set in motion to store our belonging under the Plaza Building (which just happened to be right in front of us) and which had a small storage space beneath the building. As John raced to the kitchen dock to find cardboard boxes, I proceeded to unpack our four trunks and four large suitcases. Knowing I had only minutes to complete my task, I moved quickly, sending clothes flying through the air every which way. John returned to a shocking mess with clothes strewn across the driveway. "Just grab a pile and stuff," I instructed. That is just what we did; we grabbed whatever I'd tossed out and stuffed it into the large boxes. As I picked up the last of the articles and clicked shut the nearly empty trunks to take back to Texas, John went into the Plaza Building to borrow tape to seal the boxes and a marker to write our name on them.

Robert, a staff member who works in the Plaza Building, came outside and, in his very proper Australian accent, informed us that we could not leave our personal belongings in Kona. What if we were not accepted as staff? Suppose we changed our mind and decided to go elsewhere? Did I realize what it would cost to mail those huge boxes back to Texas? Neither he, nor anyone else could be held responsible for our unclaimed boxes should we not come back. I understood what Robert was saying, but I also *knew* what the Lord had said. Before I could explain, Doug pulled up in the van. A confused look crossed his face as he saw what we were doing. "We're coming back as staff," John explained. "Grab a box and help me shove."

Laughing, Doug grabbed a box and headed for the storage door. "I knew you'd would be back," Doug stated. We wondered what Doug meant, but with only a few minutes remaining until we had to leave for the airport, all conversation halted while we quickly stored our belongings and tried to assure the worried Robert that everything would be just fine.

With the last box stored, Doug continued to explain. "Last month in Ukraine, while I was praying for all the students and their futures with YWAM, I had a feeling about you guys. I knew you were considering going to Salem. But I felt the Lord would tell you all to stay in Kona and join the staff right here in Hawaii."

Shaking our heads in wonder at the Lord's planning, we loaded the near-empty suitcases into the back of the van. I was exhausted. I still had not gotten any sleep, but at this moment, sleep was the furthest thought from my mind. God had again made His way known. I felt a great sense of peace concerning our decision. Surprising to me, although I did not think I wanted to come back, I suddenly realized I was anxiously looking forward to living here . . . to the very place God wanted us. Others call Hawaii an island paradise. We would now be calling it home.

It will also come to pass that before they call, I will answer; and while they are still speaking, I will hear. (Isa. 65:24)

12

God Loves Me

Child's Faith

Walking off the Boeing 747 that August night was like stepping into the hush of a library. The hustle and bustle I expected from Houston's Hobby Airport was a stark contrast to the terminal's eerie quietness that greeted us; of course, it was 1:30 in the morning. The squeak of our tennis shoes on the freshly polished floor seemed ridiculously loud as we walked down the long corridor, dragging our carry-on luggage toward the main terminal. It felt good to be back in Texas again after being away for five months. We were especially anticipating meeting our new granddaughter, Kaitlyn, who had been born while we were in Ukraine. The only tough part was returning home with less than $100 in our pockets. Thankfully, we would be staying rent-free with my parents.

The terminal was strangely empty as we rounded the corner of the corridor. I saw a small group of people at one end waiting for passengers to deplane. I scanned the area looking for my son-in-law, Dell, who was to pick us up, and I was puzzled when I didn't see him. Robin decided that with a newborn and a two-year-old, it would be too difficult to come, so she would stay home and let her husband pick us up.

A small commotion from that group at the end of the corridor caught my attention. There, a small child was trying to get past the guard at the corridor entrance. As the little girl tried to go under the barricade, the guard reached out to grab her arm. Squirming from side to side to free herself, she wiggled free from the confines of the guard, slipped under the barricade and, with miniature pony tails bouncing, bolted our direction as fast as her short little legs could carry her.

We all chuckled as the little girl ran with the guard trying to stop her. Out of curiosity, I turned around to see who the little girl was running to, but the corridor behind us was vacant of passengers. When the little girl was almost to us, she stopped short and just looked at us. Stretching out her little arms toward us she loudly squealed, "It's me—Nikki!" Nikki? I had not even recognized my own granddaughter.

Dropping our carry-on luggage, each of us in turn swooped Nikki into our arms and smothered her with kisses. Through teary eyes, I marveled at the beauty of my wide-eyed granddaughter. I could not get over her sweet cherub face and how pretty her blond curls had become. Except for the curly hair she reminded me of Robin when she was a toddler. Nikki excitedly chattered with no time in between for us to say a word. Such childish enthusiasm was refreshing to our tired bones.

Hurrying ahead, I saw that our daughter Robin had accompanied Dell and Nikki to the airport after all. There in

Robin's arms was our newest grandchild, Kaitlyn Reneé. Although she was barely a month old, I could tell that she was going to be a beautiful child. Tears of joy slid down my cheeks, as I held my tiny grandbaby and whispered sweet nothings in her ear. What a group of chatterboxes we were as we made our way through baggage pickup. It was fun listening to Nikki jabbering, while Cariane and Marleigh animatedly gave a running commentary of all the details of the past several months all jammed together. In the car on the way home, Robin shared with me the details of her pregnancy, Kaitlyn's birth, and how much the baby had grown in her short thirty-two days of life. It truly was great to be home.

But Nikki and Kaitlyn were not the only ones who had grown since we had been away those past five months. Our girls were going through a growing spurt as well—especially Cariane. During the past few weeks, we noticed that all of her clothes were becoming too small. Her shorts would barely snap and her tops were too tight. Even her feet had grown. Cariane had to fold the back of her shoes over and walk on the flattened heels because her toes were pinched otherwise. Marleigh also had grown taller, but had not seen the sudden growth that her sister had.

Naturally, being an eleven-year-old girl, the first day home Cariane was ready to go shopping at the new mall that had conveniently opened only three miles away. Unfortunately, after buying milk, bread, shampoo, toothpaste, and other essentials, there was not enough money to go shopping. We did take the girls out for new shoes, but told them the rest would have to wait. Their daddy would spread the word that he would resume working on cars during our stay in Texas. In this way, we would have enough to support us during this transition period between Ukraine and our move to Hawaii. I assured the girls we would go shopping for new clothes soon, probably not at the mall, but we would go shopping.

For Cariane, this announcement went over like a lead balloon. Normally, Cariane is a quiet, agreeable child, but not this time. Being somewhat dramatic, she flipped her hair over her shoulder, turned, and stomped out of the room. In the doorway, she turned back and declared, "Fine. I will just ask God to get me some clothes. He'll get them for me. *He* loves me."

No matter what I tried to say to Cariane that night, I could tell that she had tuned me out and was not listening. She was so convinced God would miraculously provide her with clothes that nothing I said made any difference. That night I earnestly prayed asking God to protect her little heart and the faith she had in Him. I prayed not for clothes to suddenly appear, but for customers to quickly come in so John could earn enough money to take his daughters shopping. I was confident in God's provision—He never lets us down—so I did not mention to anyone our immediate need of new clothes for our daughters.

Our second day home was Friday. There in the driveway, lugging a two-and-one-half foot tall, plastic bank in the shape of a Coke bottle, came my oldest brother Randy. The weight of the bank was such that Randy could barely carry it; he more or less half-carried, half-rolled this heavy bank from his pickup to the house. Straightening his aching back, Randy merely said, "Welcome back. Did you all have a good time?" Then he said, "Last night I was sitting at home when I had this thought. Maybe you girls would like to have these pennies to buy some new clothes. I don't know what is in there, but it is probably over a hundred dollars."

I know I shouldn't have been, but I was surprised at how quickly God answered my daughter's prayer. Cariane was thrilled. Turning to me, she smugly remarked, "See. I told you God loved me."

Rolling pennies by hand is no simple task when there are over 15,000 of them. Each one had to be examined to check the date. Mixed in the bank were the older wheat pennies, which my dad likes to collect. But even more exciting was the discovery of coins dating as far back as 1901! Day in and day out for the next several weeks, the four of us rolled dirty pennies; I even rolled pennies in my dreams. Each time we obtained $20 or $30 worth, off to the bank we'd traipse to convert them to "real" money, so we could go to Wal-Mart for a new outfit. Cariane and Marleigh enjoyed rolling pennies but loved spending them even more. Knowing all the pennies were theirs to do with as they wanted added fun to the sometimes mundane task of looking for antique coins, counting, rolling, and marking bank account numbers on the wrappers. All told there were $156 of pennies (not counting over $30 of nickels, dimes, and quarters) stuffed in the plastic bank from their Uncle Randy.

Saturday, the day after Randy's surprise bottle of pennies. Tessie, a woman I'm not even sure I knew at this point, called and said the oddest thing—she wanted to take Cariane shopping at the new mall. During her prayer time that morning, she felt the Lord instruct her to do this—not both of the girls, just Cariane. He even gave her an amount to spend. Naturally I objected, but she was adamant since the directions came from the Lord. And who am I to argue with God? Needless to say, the two of them went shopping and had a blast. Cariane came home with several of the cutest name-brand shirts, jeans, and a jumper, which she picked out herself. Best of all, they shopped at the new, coveted, Woodlands Mall.

That Sunday in church, Cariane strutted like a peacock with her new clothes. I was grateful and thanked the Lord for this precious lady, who willingly obeyed what the Lord asked of her and provided Cariane with new clothes, as well as Randy and his bottle of pennies. I must admit though, that I was somewhat surprised at the way God provided them. It certainly did not match my own idea of how *I* would provide for my children.

That morning just before the service started, I was approached by a lady in the church foyer. Apparently, her daughter had gone shopping over the summer for new school clothes. However, now that school was starting, the daughter decided that not everything was to her liking after all. Instead of running around town trying to return the clothes, they wondered, since Cariane wore the same size, would she like the new outfits? Cariane's wardrobe was being added to nicely.

That night at church a third lady and her daughter walked up to us. "We were hoping to see you tonight. In the trunk of our car are several boxes of really nice clothes that my daughter would like to give to Cariane. I believe they will fit. Would you like to meet me after church in the front parking lot to get them?"

Cariane's prayer for clothes extended its blessings to Marleigh as well. Marilyn, a friend of Marleigh's came by with several bags of new or nearly new clothes. Apparently her grandma had gone shopping and bought Marilyn lots of cute shirts, shorts, and several pair of long pants. The problem was that Marilyn had grown more than her grandma realized; the clothes were too small. Some of the clothes still had their tags on but rather than return them, Marilyn wanted to share them with Marleigh—that is if she wanted them.

Our nine-year-old Marleigh was thrilled with all the new clothes her sister was getting. Just weeks prior to leaving for Ukraine, both girls had gone shopping for new clothes. Since Cariane had outgrown nearly everything, this meant Cariane's other clothes would now belong to Marleigh. For Marleigh, this was Christmas in August.

We had been home less than a week. I thought the Lord had provided quite well for my daughters in the clothing department. On that first Thursday night I joined a women's craft class. John's sister-in-law, Jenell, walked up to me before we started the crafts, saying she felt the Lord told her to give Cariane and Marleigh $50 for new clothes. She mailed us the check the next day.

By the end of the first week back in Texas, we had boxes piled high with clothes, many still with tags on them. I asked Cariane to pray, thanking God for His generosity and to ask Him to stop the clothes and money from coming in, as we had enough clothes to last for some time to come. "Are you crazy?" Cariane repied. She didn't agree at all with my request, but together we bowed our heads while I prayed. After that prayer, not another outfit was given or another dime donated for new clothes. The flow dried up.

Do I believe God sits in heaven with the sole purpose to do nothing more than answer our prayers? No. But I do believe that no prayer is too small for Him to hear and no request is too large for Him to answer. A child's simple prayer for clothes is as significant to God's heart as any "important" prayer we adults earnestly—sometimes frantically—plead.

What about Cariane? She knew all along that God loved her and that in some way He would provide her with the new clothes she so desperately needed. It was through the answering of her very own prayer that Cariane received affirmation of God's intimate care for her as His child. For many months God had shown Himself to our family in numerous ways, but this time it was different. This time it was Cariane who was doing the praying. Most importantly, Cariane witnessed the Lord working on her behalf, not for the family as a whole. Cariane believed God would answer her need. She was rewarded with her very own personal miracle . . . accompanied with a giant boost of faith.

> For this reason I say to you, do not be anxious for your life, as to what you shall eat, or what you shall drink nor . . . what you shall put on. Is not life more than food, and the body more than clothing? Look at the birds of the air . . . your Heavenly Father feeds them. Are you not worth much more than they? (Matt. 6:25–26)

13

The Security Blanket

Lack of Faith

G od had given us His answer: We were moving to
Kailua-Kona, Hawaii. The move would begin our first
staff positions with Youth With a Mission. Excitement, anxi-
ety, great expectations, along with sadness over leaving home,
were blended together; it was hard to distinguish one feeling
from the other. At times it seemed like a dream; we were
actually going to live in Hawaii for the next two years!

But under the seemingly endless task of sorting, throw-
ing away, giving away, packing, and repacking, the reality
of moving begin to set in. I enjoy planning, organizing, and
making lists. This brings a much needed order to my life.
Yet with all the lists I made, there was one small detail that
had the biggest impact on everything else: the date we were
to leave.

I agonized over this minute detail. On the one hand, we
were anxious to start our new life in missions. On the other
hand, we wanted to stay until after New Year's, which was

only a few months away. I had airline tickets to purchase, reservations with the shipping company to make, and a dozen other last-minute items to attend to. Problem was, I did not know when the last minute would be. The sooner I made reservations, the smoother our move would be. It seemed every other week someone from Kona was calling, checking to see if we had an arrival date. The Housing department in Kona had held our room for us for two months already; could we tell them how much longer it would be until we arrived?

Youth With a Mission does not have paid employees. Instead, everyone who works in YWAM is a volunteer, raising their own support. We had been counseled by our soon-to-be leaders to have the necessary amount of support money raised before we left Texas. They were talking about monthly support, where individuals pledge to send a specified amount each month for our living expenses. This requires a lot of faith in both the Lord and in the individuals making the pledges.

Although my faith was strong enough to believe God would supply the money we needed to live, my own need to be in control was overriding my faith. Before we left I wanted *in my hand* the money to live on for an entire year. Why? Lack of faith. A weakness in me to trust God with what I could not see. A need to be in control of my life. I don't know. I just know for me, it was of the utmost importance that I have the money!

Many friends had blessed us by giving one-time gifts of money. By putting them all in the bank, we had acquired quite a sum—over $10,000. This money soon became my personal security blanket. Although it was a substantial amount, after subtracting the moving expenses, it still would not be enough to support us for a full year in Hawaii.

Each night I spent an hour or more praying while I took solitary walks down the lonely country road where we were living with my parents. Each day I waited for the phone to ring or the mail to come, informing us more money had arrived. Not knowing our departure date caused me stress, so I decided to pray and this time leave the departure date up to God. I needed to quit losing sleep over this one detail. All we really needed was about $300 more a month ($3,600 total) and we'd have enough. As soon as the money came in we would leave. I did not tell anyone the specifics of how much we needed. I wanted God to be completely in control of our lives, which included control of our money and our departure date. I continued my sorting and packing and tried not to think about the calendar too much.

A few days after Thanksgiving, John and I were visiting with Gordon, our pastor. We did not give the specific amount of money needed, but said only that we were relatively close to our target amount. Gordon leaned back in his chair and said, "I don't know how much more you need, but our finance committee met last Wednesday. We made the decision to support you for $300 a month starting January first. I hope this will help bring you closer to what you need."

Help? This was *exactly* what I figured we needed to be able to leave! God is so awesome. We did not expect Oak Ridge Baptist Church to support us financially, and we had not asked them to. We were elated as we told Gordon that we now had enough to leave for Hawaii. It looked like we would be in our new home for Christmas.

Since airlines prefer a seven-day notice, a date was set to leave the following Tuesday. We decided to drive from Houston to Los Angeles, pulling a small trailer with our personal possessions. The car and our belongings would be shipped via two different moving companies from Los Angeles while we flew. Our lives were a whirlwind as the final preparations were made, checking accounts closed, tickets bought, and the long-awaited call to Hawaii: "We're on our way!"

We arrived in Hawaii on Wednesday, December 13th, 1995. It felt strange and wonderful all at the same time. Christmas was soon approaching. Our boxes and the Christmas presents for the girls would arrive on Christmas Eve; the car on New Year's Eve. Our housing was small, just one hotel-sized room, but the view of the ocean and its sunset was incredible. Although it would be hard to be away from home at Christmastime, we were relieved finally to arrive and begin our life in Hawaii.

On our first Tuesday, six days after we arrived in Hawaii, I worked on a budget, hoping I could stick to it. Never before had I lived on a budget, but now with a limited amount of money, it was inevitable that I would have to learn how. Something was amiss though. I figured our money twice, three times, then again. Each time it came out the same; I had miscalculated my previous figures from Texas. I was actually $2,700 short of the amount needed to live for the next twelve months. My security blanket had a hole in it!

Crying, I stared out the window as I prayed, "God please help me. I made a mistake. I left before we had enough money. How could anyone misfigure by $2,700? I feel so dumb! I know that You promise to supply our needs, but I feel this overwhelming need to have money already in my possession, in the bank. I say I trust You, but my actions show I don't. You already know what I am feeling inside. Help me to learn to trust You more."

For the rest of the morning and early afternoon I spent much time praying while staring out the window at the ocean. I knew I could trust God for enough money to live on. What I didn't trust was my own faith. One would think by then I would have learned to trust God. But my need to always be in control of every situation was surfacing again, interfering with my believing for His provision.

That afternoon John and I attended our first staff meeting. Even though I had never been to a staff meeting, I assumed it would deal with business from the campus. Instead, Vice Chancellor Gene Early made the entire meeting about personal finances. Gene said, "As you all know, the base is under major reconstruction financially. We are working on becoming debt-free within the next five years. The leadership feels the Lord desires the same freedom for us as individuals as He does for us as a mission. The leaders, including myself, have made the commitment to become debt-free. We feel that many of you have financial problems or worries as well. We desire to pray for you. If you will stand up, we will seek the Lord on your behalf for your finances, or the lack thereof."

Numerous people stood, giving opportunity for others in the room to pray for them. This went on for over an hour as, one after another, individuals shared their monetary needs, and then someone prayed specifically for them. Thinking of our own financial plight, I had the strangest urge to stand and tell my mournful story. But I didn't know these people. I certainly wasn't going to make my debut into life on the campus by standing in front of a room full of strangers and telling them my most personal money problem. What would they think? If we knew everyone that might be different, but we knew no one. So I made the decision to keep our money shortage to myself. After everyone had been prayed for, Gene was about to bring the meeting to a close. In mid-sentence he stopped and said he felt there was at least one other person who needed to have prayer for their finances. A long silence followed.

Again I felt the prompting to stand and confess my bank shortage. Again I reminded myself that I could trust God to provide the money; I just needed to be patient and watch Him work. In the middle of my arguments with myself, I heard Gene once more say he was waiting for someone to come forward and that there was no need to be shy or embarrassed. Inside, I felt as if someone was pushing me from behind, but resolving not to stand up or to say anything, I burrowed down further in my chair. Everyone in the room sat waiting.

I felt a strange sensation as if someone else was moving my arms and legs for me. Soon I found myself standing with a whole room full of eyes staring at me, waiting to hear what I had to say. I haltingly introduced myself and confessed my financial miscalculations. Maybe because I was nervous, or maybe it was just the way it popped out of my mouth, but instead of saying we needed $2,700, I gave the amount as only $2,400. Those sitting near us surrounded John and me and started to pray. John could not believe that I actually stood up and made such an announcement. Although he did not say anything to me, I could tell by the scowl on his brow that he was not too pleased with what I had just done.

I never wrote back to my friends, family, or to my church about the money we needed. But within that next week, support pledges for $20 a month ($240 a year) were made, along with a cash donation for $60; that equaled the sum of $300 for the year. Now all we needed was $2,400, the amount that was prayed for. Since Christmas was only a few days away, I more or less forgot about the $2,400 and focused all my attention on making the holiday special for the girls.

Walking to the mailbox a few days after Christmas, I was rewarded with a whole stack of Christmas cards and letters. Hurrying to our room, I started to rip them open; I was homesick and hungry for news from Texas. In the pile of cards was also an envelope from our home church. Around the end of each month, they would be sending us $300 for that month, but that was not to start until the end of January. I was curious to see what was in the envelope. Tearing it open, out fell a check from Oak Ridge Baptist, along with a note from the church secretary.

Larry and Pat Barker, a family from our church had made a donation to our ministry. We knew the Barkers somewhat, but were not personally close to them. Pat and Larry felt the Lord encourage them to share part of their savings/inheritance with us. Out of obedience they sent a check for the amount the Lord had prompted. The amount of the check: $2,400!

That first year has passed and my "security blanket" account has long been empty. Our church family still sends us a check each month, but that is not nearly enough to live on. God says He will supply all our needs and He is doing just that. Last year, I needed a security blanket in the form of cash in the bank, and God supplied it for me. Now, our savings is empty but my faith is full. No longer do I require money in advance to feel secure. I sometimes still worry about money and where it will come from. But when that happens, I know *exactly* what to do. I just exercise my faith in the Lord and it comes in His perfect provision. God is the ultimate security-blanket account for me—an account that can *never* be emptied!

> Each man should give what he has decided in his heart to give, not reluctantly or under compulsion, for God loves a cheerful giver. And God is able to make all grace abound to you, so that in all things at all times, having all that you need, you will abound in every good work. (2 Cor. 9:7–8)

14

A Little Self-Grandeur
Feeling Insignificant

The American dream: living on the fabulous tropical island of Hawaii. I spent hours on the beach, walking along the sea wall or relaxing with a good book under a palm tree.

Cariane and Marleigh were usually swimming in the pool, while I watched the incredible sunsets on the horizon of the ocean. Every so often, I would get a pang of guilt. I came to Hawaii to work yet all I was doing was relaxing or playing with our daughters. I would quickly dismiss my guilty feelings because after all, the staff here in Kona told me to enjoy myself for the next couple of months. I guess you could say, I was just obeying orders.

Actually, I was waiting for just the right staff position to open. John was already approved as base mechanic, but I did not have the foggiest idea what I would be doing. Of course, I felt it would be something of great importance and hopefully something with a little grandeur. I knew I had talents that the base would be anxious to tap in to. There were positions on base that desperately needed filling, and I was certain I would be just the right person to fill some of that void.

I thought back to our three months in Texas, the time between Ukraine, and our arrival in Hawaii. Each night after the girls were asleep, I went for long walks down the country road on which we lived. Blackness was my companion; the only light was at the end of the gravel road. On moonless nights the darkness was eerie, while the quietness invited long walks and provided a great time for prayer. Even the noises from the crickets and bullfrogs were diminished by the thick weeds and tall grasses.

As I slowly wandered down the road, I would pray in a soft whisper so as not to disrupt the natural hush of the night. At the top of the list of things to pray about was the timing of the move to Hawaii and the position I would fill once there. Even though John and I both prayed daily, we did not receive any specifics about my role in Kona. I knew that answer would come soon, so I continued to pray.

Being somewhat of a theatrical person, I often become dramatic. This even spills over into my prayer times with the Lord. One night, while going for my nightly prayer walk, I became emotional and again went into my dramatic mode. "Lord, I have asked You over and over what I am to do when I arrive in Hawaii. But I haven't heard from You. Are You speaking and I am just not hearing? You know that I will do anything You ask me to do, because I love You so. I really didn't want to move to Hawaii, but when You directed us here it became what I wanted as well. This is how I feel about my staff position. Wherever You direct, that is what I want. I will do the best job any person can do. I love You so much I would take even the lowliest position there on the base. If You want . . . I will even be willing to clean toilets! Lead me where You would have me. Prepare my heart and my mind for the task ahead." Although my prayers did not bring me an answer, I was content to wait until we moved to Hawaii.

December 13th was the date we arrived in Hawaii. After a good night's sleep, John and I went to see the Campus Services' director to check in and report for work. Only minutes into our conversation the phone rang. The call was for John. The caller did not know who the new mechanic was, but she heard he was coming and her car was having trouble. John was taken back as he certainly did not expect customers to hunt him down quite so soon. Stammering for words, he took her phone number and told her he would call back. A half-hour later John and the Campus Services' director were walking to the top of the hill where the mechanic shop was located. As they were unlocking the door to the shop, the phone began to ring. Answering it, John heard a voice at the other end, "Can you tell me if my car is finished yet? I didn't know what day you were coming in, so I left it last week with a note on the front seat."

Needless to say, John was in popular demand. This was reinforced when, at the staff meeting where we were officially introduced, John received a standing ovation. There had not been a regular mechanic for four years. John and his talents were sorely needed.

Then there was me—riding the waves, lounging under the palm trees, enjoying my time in Hawaii. I wasn't sure where I was suppose to fit. Finally, Campus Services asked me to work in their department as manager of Housekeeping. This wasn't *exactly* what I had in mind. I was thinking more in line of working with the "top brass" on base. But I figured no one knew me yet, because I was new. If I worked in Housekeeping a few months, the leadership would get to know me, realize I was in the wrong department, and move me to my rightful place. So I agreed to manage Housekeeping. The position would be open February 20th. Until then, I could relax and enjoy myself.

All too soon February came and I was busy at work. One particular afternoon, I found myself singing while I worked; almost enjoying myself. Midstanza, like a jolt, it hit me: I was cleaning toilets! I remembered my theatrical prayer back in Texas, *I love You so much, I would even be willing to clean toilets for You.* For a moment, I did not know whether to laugh or cry. Was God testing me? Or was this His sense of humor being displayed? Was this some sort of discipline for my prideful attitude? I did a lot of thinking as I finished the work on that restroom and started on the next one.

By the time I finished and put the mop out to dry, the singing in my heart returned. It could be God testing me to see if I really would be willing to do anything for Him and do a good job as I declared. And partly, it could be His great sense of humor. And yes, I did have a prideful attitude that needed correcting. Whatever the reason, I was in Housekeeping, and I was grateful for the Lord's gentle care and leading. Unfortunately, the issue of being the manager of Housekeeping and cleaning restrooms was far from over.

All our married life, John and I attended Oak Ridge Baptist Church; in fact, we met and married there. Although John faithfully attended Sunday School and church, he did not actively participate when it came to teaching, singing in the choir, committees, etc. On the other hand, I was involved in everything. I taught Sunday School, sang in the adult choir, taught in the children's choir, was director during Vacation Bible School, was a camp counselor, worked in numerous children's programs, and the list goes on. I was quite active and well-known to almost everybody at our church.

Then came the move to Hawaii. I became the silent unknown, and John became one of the most popular men on campus. With YWAM, John is known by his initials, J. W. Whenever I was introduced, it was always as "J.W.'s wife." This really irritated me; I wanted to shout, "I do have a name of my own, you know!"

I felt people could at least say, "This is J.W.'s wife, Valerie." But they didn't, probably because nobody even knew my name. I was just J. W.'s wife. The more well-known and loved John became, the more I struggled through what was quickly becoming an identity crisis. When I met someone new they inevitably asked what I did on base. When I told them I was the manager of Housekeeping, almost without fail, the return comment would be something like, "Oh yeah, you're J.W.'s wife. Listen, I need to get some toilet paper. Are you the one I need to see?"

I came to Hawaii to serve God. Yet in my heart, I had been reduced to cleaning toilets and handing out cleaning supplies and toilet paper. I worked at doing a good job, but my heart was not in what I was asked to do. My attitude remained outwardly pleasant, but deep inside, there was a tiny root of bitterness that grew larger as each week passed.

No one came to recognize any of my other talents or the benefit I could be working elsewhere. I was stuck in the Housekeeping Department. It was as if . . . I had lost my identity between Texas and Hawaii. Yet, wasn't my identity suppose to be *in* Jesus, not engulfed in what I *do*? Did full-time ministry include cleaning public restrooms? How was this making a contribution to further His Kingdom?

It was slow in coming, but many times God brought up my heart's attitude concerning my position, and little by little it changed. I ran across an old article written by Dean Sherman, the International Dean of the College of Christian Ministries in YWAM.

> God wants you to know it's OK to be where you are. It's OK to not be out in some remote jungle or some other place trying to be significant for God. Unless we're living in known disobedience, we all need to allow the favor of God, which is directed toward us, to bring us to a sense of security and well-being. There is a subtle attack of the enemy upon Christians that makes us feel we need to be doing more in order to please God. There is something totally fulfilling for you and for the Kingdom through you, in your present circumstances. This time is not being wasted. What pleases God is not what you do or where you are, but your willingness to receive the grace He extends toward you. (YWAM Associates International *In Touch,* 20th ed., April–September 1995).

Although reading this article did not immediately change my attitude toward my job, it made a profound dent in my understanding that God was not using this time in Housekeeping to punish me or to test me. He had a higher purpose, even though I did not have a clue what that purpose was. Whatever time I did spend in Housekeeping, I was certain it would not be wasted time. I worked diligently on making the Housekeeping Department run more smoothly, while having a servant's heart toward those I came in contact with each day.

The longer I stayed in Housekeeping, the more I came to realize the importance of that position. Our base runs in quarters—three month increments. There were literally hundreds of people each quarter relying on me to perform my duties to facilitate them. Students could not stay on the base unless the rooms were first prepared for their arrival. Each family, school, and student had special needs. My job was to fill those needs, if possible. With over 300 staff, there are many offices that need cleaning. Without my services the office staff could very well drown in its own trash and dirty floors. Although almost anyone could do what I was doing, I knew my particular organizational skills were being utilized and I *was* making a difference. I still did not feel I was filling my potential as a person, that there was something more for me, but I became satisfied in my job and with what was asked of me.

About a year after I started Housekeeping, our girls, who attended Kona Christian Academy, brought home a weekly newsletter for the parents from their principal, Mrs. Pitts. Cariane walked in and the first thing out of her mouth was, "Mom, I read this newsletter and it has the perfect thing for you. Look." The newsletter read:

> Help! We need one parent to volunteer his/her time to daily give a good cleaning to the restrooms at school. This would be a real blessing to the students and teachers as well. Please contact Thaddeau Pitts if you would be willing to help.

At first I was nearly devastated by Cariane's remark that this would be perfect for me. Is this what my daughter thought of me? Am I only good for cleaning other people's dirty, smelly toilets? I thought the issue of my own self-worth and importance had been settled in my heart, but my emotional reaction to Cariane's remark proved I was mistaken.

Later that afternoon I asked Cariane why she thought cleaning the restrooms at school was perfect for me. Her answer took me by surprise: "Because you like to help other people. It doesn't matter to you what they need help with, you will do it. You already clean the restrooms on the base. You like what you do, and that makes you do a good job. So why not clean the restrooms at school as well? Besides, you always volunteer for things anyway. Plus, you are at school everyday to pick us up. I read the notice and I just thought about you. I think you should do it."

Cariane's comment that I liked my job shocked me at first. All that night I thought about what she had said. If Mrs. Pitts had asked for a volunteer to help in the office, I would not have hesitated a moment. I also knew that if I had read the notice myself about the restrooms, I probably would not have thought about it twice but just thrown it in the trash. Did I really have a heart ready to serve the Lord, no matter what was asked? Or was it tainted by my own wants, desires, and thought of self-grandeur?

There seemed to be a struggle going on inside. As I prayed, I knew Cariane was right. I had grown to like my job on the base, and I *was* good at managing the House-keeping Department.

Now, I not only clean the restrooms on base, but I also scrub the ten toilets at Kona Christian Academy every Monday through Friday. I can honestly say I enjoy what God has called me to do at this time. I no longer wait for the "great promotion" to work with those who run the base. I realize that what I do on the Kona campus is not only important but also vital to the smooth running of the base, both on the academic side and on the side of operations.

When the time comes to move on, God will let me know when and where I am to go, all in His timing, not mine. Never before have I sat by quietly and allowed God to be God in my life. Now I am learning to do just that. I love watching John shine through his automotive ministry with the staff on the base. Most importantly I realize that it is OK to be where I am. To be significant for God does not depend on what I am doing or where I am. What does matter is fulfilling my calling for God from my present circumstances—the circumstances where He has purposely placed me. If I am where He has sent me, then I am in the perfect position—under His loving care.

> But you, are you seeking great things for yourself? Do not seek them. (Jer. 45:5a)

15

Exceeding Expectations

Discontent

Our new life in full-time ministry was definitely different than I imagined. When I heard the word *missionary*, it automatically conjured up pictures in my mind of sacrifice, rough conditions, hardships, and doing without modern conveniences. Yet, we did not have any of these. While in Ukraine, we had gone without conveniences such as regular toilets, running water, and sanitary conditions. And I am sure that as we serve abroad in the future, we will again experience these hardships and more. But for now: tropical island, view of the ocean, palm trees, perfect weather, flowers galore, and a university campus that provides a safe environment for our children. Tough life! At times I even felt guilty. We desired to serve in a developing country, working and living among those less fortunate. Yet, the Lord had led us to live for a season on the island of Hawaii.

As wonderful as our new life was, it was not without its difficulties. Living on the YWAM base was somewhat different than what we were used to. In Texas we owned one and one-half acres and a large five-bedroom home nestled in the midst of tall pines and giant oaks. Even with nine of us in the house, everyone had their own corner or special spot they could call their own.

Not so in Hawaii. The base where we lived is a converted vacation rental. The rooms are lined up hotel-style upstairs and down. They are slightly larger than the average hotel, but still just a room. Each family had only one room in which to eat, sleep, and live. The bathroom is made up of only a shower and a toilet. The furnishings consist of twin beds, dresser, desk, and a lamp. The closet for all four of us was only 28 inches in width. The kitchen area was a microwave and one sink, where we brushed our teeth. Needless to say, one must keep personal belongings to a minimum, otherwise we could easily drown in "things" with nowhere to put them.

There is a slight difference between the rooms downstairs and the ones upstairs. The rooms on the upper floor have a loft for the children to sleep. The ladder leads to an open-ended loft area that is three-and-a-half feet tall. That doesn't sound bad, until I mention that it quickly slopes to eighteen inches. The loft has room for only a couple of mattresses on the floor; there's no closet space or room for a dresser and almost no airflow. Children who were delighted at the prospect of loft-sleeping quickly lost their enthusiasm as they found the difficulty of sleeping in what amounted to not much more than a low-ceilinged cave. With poor lighting, the heat from lack of airflow, and the bruises from sitting up in bed and cracking their heads on the ceiling, the adventure of the loft soon lost its appeal.

The hardest part, though, is that the base is old. The carpet is the gold and green shag from the 70s. The shower is peeling, the fixtures rusted, and the building is too run-down to make it into a charming little home. Termites are permanent residents; mice and an occasional rat use the rooms for a hunting ground for scraps for their babies (which they sometimes bring with them). Geckos (a type of lizard) are everywhere. Because they do eat the mosquitoes, flies, and roaches, they are accepted as part of the room's decor.

This, however, was our new life. The upside was the view. The rooms have three regular walls, with the fourth wall being a screen from floor to ceiling. This allowed for breezes (there is no air conditioning) and brought in the fabulous fragrances from the abundance of flowered trees. There was also the spectacular view of the ocean and its magnificent sunsets. Just the constant view of the beautiful grounds, with its flowering trees and the ocean as a backdrop, made life a whole lot more pleasant.

We had just purchased our first computer and I was having a great time leaning the intricacies of using it. Cariane was fascinated with it as well, and we spent hours experimenting with all the icons, trying to figure out what they were used for. I discovered I could write my weekly letters to our parents and older children much quicker using the computer. I found great delight in my newest toy. Life seemed so wonderful. Not at all as I imagined.

There is a saying that every cloud has a silver lining. Well, I found the opposite to be true—a cloud in our silver lining. After six months, I began to feel claustrophobic. With only one room for all four of us to live, I was finding it increasingly difficult to find a corner that was all mine, a place to retreat when I wanted to think or needed to work.

Since we all slept in the same room, the light from my computer would keep the girls or John awake if I wanted to stay up late. The three of them retire early; I like to stay up until 10:00 or 11:00 each night. John and the girls would complain about the light and the clicking noises I made on the computer, so I would join them by going to bed early.

Problem was, I would just lie there by the hour, not able to fall asleep. As the weeks went by, I began allowing dissatisfaction to take root in my heart. It wasn't long until discontent made itself at home; no amount of praying seemed to help. Instead of tossing and turning in bed when I was unable to sleep, I went for long walks. During these walks, I gave myself many a good scolding, but to no avail. My disgruntled attitude grew.

Logic told me if we had a larger place, a place that had privacy and a corner I could call my own, then I wouldn't feel so unhappy. So the search began. Every night before going to bed, I scoured the newspaper, circling places for rent. Each morning I spent considerable time calling, making appointments, or going to take a look. For nearly a month, this was my daily ritual. Although I found several promising apartments and one that in my opinion was perfect, John vetoed every place without even going to see them. I began to wonder if we would *ever* move. My focus shifted from my family and our ministry, to my selfish desire to have more than God had provided. I became obsessed with finding a house or a condo. I seemed to have lost my peace and could no longer find it.

Unable to bear the incredible unsettled feelings any longer, I went for my usual midnight walk and prayed. Even though I had been praying all along, this time it was different. I realized I had not been sharing my feelings with the

Lord or asking Him to help me with my discontent. Nor had I asked for help in finding another place to live. What I was doing was whining and complaining. So I laid it all out—feelings, desires, financial abilities—all of it.

I asked forgiveness for my self-centered, ungrateful attitude. As a foreign missionary, I would gladly have endured hardships. But here I was, living on a gorgeous island in the middle of the Pacific without any hardships, and I was suffering. Suffering? All I was doing was going without a little space to call my own. I knew I was being all emotional and purely selfish. But putting a name to my feelings did not help me one iota. I was still dissatisfied. The prospect of getting another place to live was consuming my life, and I did not like the feelings it produced.

"Lord, You already know how I am feeling. I am not sure I know how to express what it is, other than to say I feel disgruntled and unhappy. You have given so much to us. I know the way I am feeling is not pleasing to You. Will You forgive me? I do not want to feel like this anymore. I give to You my discontent, my selfishness, and my ungodly attitude, and I don't want them back. I want You to give me Your peace and contentment.

"You say I have not because I ask not. I am not asking for another place to live. I only want that perfect peace that comes from You. Help me to be content where You have placed us. I am not going to look any longer. I will let You decide if and when we move from here. When that time comes, I want You to bring the place to us and plop it in our laps. Until that time, I will no longer search for something else. Take away my desire to move and replace it with gratitude for the room we have. I sure am glad You are always here when I need a listening ear."

I went back to our room and was asleep the second my head hit the pillow. Out of habit, the next morning I reached for the daily newspaper to start my search. Immediately, I remembered my prayer from the night before. I threw the paper away; I didn't need it anymore. I started cleaning the piles I always seemed to collect. I cleaned the cupboards, the closet, and under the bed. If I was going to stay here, then I needed to be free from the clutter that seemed to grow of its own accord. My heart was no longer in a turmoil. I had placed my wants and desires in the hands of the Lord; I knew they would be safe with Him.

As was my habit, I prayed as I went about my day. For the most part, my prayers resemble a conversation with my best friend. I talk about everything and anything that comes to mind. As I cleaned the girls' clothes closet, I reaffirmed that I wanted to find peace staying on the base until maybe, someday, He brought the perfect place to us.

Then I ended with, "Let me tell You what would be perfect in my eyes. To live at the Royal Kailuan Condominium because it is adjacent to the base. I would want the second or third floor because the first floor does not get a breeze. Two bedrooms. I'd want to face the ocean, not the mountain. I'd especially want to be on the sunset side because I so love the incredible sunsets and desire to watch them each night. And if I had a choice, I would pick the end unit because it would be the coolest and have the best view. Oh yes, it would also need to be under $800 a month. To me that is about as perfect as one can get. But I will wait for Your best, even if that best is right where we are. I will learn to be satisfied with wherever we are, so long as it is where You have us."

Several days passed and I finished with the spring cleaning. The room was spotless. (Well, as spotless as any room of mine ever is.) I was feeling good about myself and my new feeling of peace. Sitting down to dinner at the community dining area, we were joined by a man named Paul Pittendrigh and Asher Motola, the Vice-Chancellor of Academic Affairs. John had worked some with Paul up at the heavy mechanic shop, but I didn't know him at all. I knew Asher by name and sight only. Sharing a meal was a good chance to get to know each of them a little better.

The four of us made idle chit-chat while we ate. I mentioned that I had been looking for housing off base but decided to stay where we were for the time being. "I know several places that are soon to be available over at the Royal Kailuan, if you are interested," Asher said. "In fact, just today Paul told me he and Naomi will have a one-bedroom available in a few weeks." At this point, I really was not interested in going to look at any place. I felt the peace I was feeling was the Lord telling me that we were to stay where we were for right now. But out of courtesy and curiosity, John and I agreed to go look at the condo Asher mentioned and the one Paul was going to have available.

Cockroaches, no furniture, large stains on the floor, cigarette smells, no view, horrendous bathroom, and an all over stink greeted us when we walked into the condo Asher spoke about. It was on the sunset side, but it was also on the first floor, with a large hill right in front of the window. We could see nothing but dirt. Worse yet, no breeze was able to get through. And it was only one bedroom. No thanks! There was no way I would live like that and still pay $700 a month. Even if it had been only $200 a month,

I would have done some serious thinking before I ever lived there. For us, what we had on base was much better.

The next day, we had an appointment to see Paul and Naomi's one-bedroom condo, but I was skeptical about going to look at it. The sky had opened its doors, and the rain was coming down in sheets. Neither one of us wanted to venture out on such a night, but I didn't want to drag this out. I wanted to get this over with so I could quit thinking about it and go on being satisfied where I was. John and I decided we would walk through the condo, say "Thank you very much," and then go back to our little room on base.

Paul said they had two condos, one they lived in and one they rented. We were going to see the one-bedroom that he rented, the one that did not face the sunset. Paul said that he would be in his apartment, 215. Finding the right condo we knocked. Shaking the water off, we stepped in and met Naomi. Almost instantly Naomi and I bonded. Even though she is close to the age of my parents, as we sat there and talked, I felt more like we were best friends than women of two different generations. That kind of bonding doesn't happen often, so we found ourselves talking about everything under the sun, except the condo.

After an hour had passed, Paul reminded us why we were there. As he was talking about the condo, I began to realize that he was talking about the very one we were sitting in. The mother and daughter renting the one-bedroom would be moving out Paul explained. He and Naomi would be moving into the one-bedroom unit and they were offering us their two-bedroom to live in. I do not remember half of what Naomi was saying; I was in a daze and was having trouble focusing on Naomi and Paul's words. They wanted us to live in this condo! They were renting it turnkey, which meant all we needed to do was bring our clothes and hang them up. Not only was there furniture, but also sheets, towels, dishes—everything one needed to keep house. We would not have to buy anything, just move in and be all set.

It may have taken a few minutes, but finally it all started to sink in. This was the Royal Kailuan. Second floor. Facing the ocean. Sunset side. Two bedrooms. It was even the end unit. To top it off, it was only $750—$50 more than the dirty one we'd looked at the day before.

I thought the peace I had been feeling the past few days was the Lord telling me to stay where we were and be content. Now I knew that He had a special gift for us all along and was waiting for me to focus on Him instead of myself, so I could receive what He had. My list of the perfect place fit this very unit to a tee. Until an hour before, I did not know who owned this unit, and now it was going to be ours!

I had to struggle to pull myself out of my thoughts and listen to what Naomi was excitedly chattering about. "Paul and I do not like to rent to people we aren't familiar with. Even though Paul and John are fairly good friends, I wanted to know you and what kind of person you are. This past Wednesday I went to the ladies tea where you were the guest speaker. I feel now I know your heart. We would love to have you all live here. Isn't God so good? I asked Him to help us find renters for this place by the twenty-first. Today is the twenty-first. God loves to answer our prayers doesn't He?"

Living in the Royal Kailuan condo 215 far exceeded my expectations of the perfect place I had dreamed. Any one of the other places I found would have been good. Yet for some reason, even unknown to John, he did not want any of them. The old me would have pushed, finagled, and nagged until I got my own way. But I was learning that God directs us in

His perfect way when I let go of my demands. I did not agree with John when he said "no" to the other condos. I thought he was being insensitive, selfish, and a jerk. But for a change, I allowed John to be the head of our little one-room household. Then I went to God and gave the whole situation to Him to handle. By letting God be God in my life, by not pushing through what I wanted, I received a far better place then anything I could have found on my own—and all adjacent to the base.

In just a few weeks we will have lived at the Royal Kailuan for one year. John now feels that we are to move back on base again to that one small room. Why would I want to go from a lovely two bedrooms, two baths, two *bathtubs*, a full kitchen, wonderful breezes, and cable TV to a hotel-size room, with no bathtub, no kitchen, no TV, 28 inch closet space, and no privacy? I wouldn't. Why are we moving? I haven't the foggiest idea. Since John does not really know either, I am trusting that God is behind this move.

I feel something wonderful is around the corner, which will be revealed only when we surrender to His leading. God knows and sees what I cannot. It is always to my advantage to allow God to direct us even when I do not agree or understand.

John and I know that when we are obedient—even when it is not what we think we want—God's special floodgates of goodness open and flow downward, filling even the deepest crevices of our wants, needs, and desires.

> Let your character be free from the love of things; being content with what you have; for He Himself has said, "I will never desert you, nor, will I ever forsake you." (Heb. 13:5)

16

God Deserves an "A"

In My Own Strength

M y sudden burst of emotion at the simple notice I was reading really had me puzzled.

> There is still room in the school of "Communications and the Biblical View of Man" for any student or staff interested. Develop effective communication skills through the written and spoken word. Call Jean Hartley at ext. 4012.

What was so touching that I would be moved to tears? This was strange; I'd never even heard of the school of "Communications and the Biblical View of Man." So why this reaction?

The next week, sitting in a staff meeting, I listened about the different schools that would soon be starting. Again when the Core Course—the school's nickname—was mentioned, tears started to spill over and down my cheeks. Quietly I left the room and walked over to lean on the banister of the stairs. From this vantage point I had an unobstructed view of the ocean, a perfect place to reflectively pray.

"Lord, I don't understand. Why am I crying over a school? You know my heart longs to be a speaker and a writer. Is that why I am crying—my desires are coming out of the place where I have buried them? Help me to see and understand."

A few days later, while in the registrar's office I came across a brochure for the Core Course. The brochure stated the goal of the communications school was to develop the student's potential as an effective communicator through the tools of writing and speaking. It used the expression, "venture into your future." Instantly, I felt a great stirring, almost like a churning, rising up from deep within. I knew something was going on that I needed to heed.

Walking to my favorite spot by the row of palm trees, I sat on a large boulder. "Lord what are You trying to tell me? Do You want me to take that school? You know that I have made a two-year commitment to be on staff. I don't think it would be right to quit in the middle of my time here. Besides, the school starts in only a few weeks. Who would take my place in Housekeeping? And then there is the issue of money. I need to have You show me what You want. I think I know who Jean Hartley is, but I have never been introduced to her; she probably doesn't even know me. If You are trying to tell me to take this school, then You need to bring Ms. Hartley to me so we can discuss it. If not, take away these feelings I have."

That afternoon a student from "Introduction to Biblical Counseling" (IBC) invited me to her classroom to take part in one of her assignments. Walking into the classroom, I stopped short as there sat this week's instructor—Jean

Hartley! The students were studying the projection of their voice, making eye contact, and presenting an interesting speech to their audience. As students took their turn giving their speeches, the audience, which I was a part of, would grade the speaker on presentation.

During the morning break, I approached Jean and we fell into conversation. Jean was all too glad to give me information about the Core Course. Surprisingly, she knew exactly who I was and even a little about me. She felt certain that the communications school was the perfect next step for me and felt it would be to my advantage to take the three-month course. Walking slowly back home, I wondered if this school was God's plan to help prepare me for my future walk with Him? Stopping by the registrar's office, I picked up a packet with all the information about the school and its fees. Whew! Nearly $2,800! This would *have* to be from God in order for me to attend.

That night John reminded me that just two months ago, while visiting in Texas, someone from our church handed us a check for $300, while a pastor friend had given us $1,000. This was a good start, but I still had a long way to go. After John and I prayed, we began to believe the school was the direction I was to follow. I filled out the registration forms and turned them into the office.

"Father, if it is You who is leading me to take this school, then You have to make this known to me without any doubts. Right now I have $1,300, but that will not cover the cost of the school. I do not want to walk into the school owing money. Next Tuesday is the day we receive our support checks. If You want me in this school, I want the balance of the money by then; school starts the following Monday. If not, then I will withdraw my application and know that this school is not for me at this time."

My mind flashed back to 1992 in Shreveport, Louisiana, where I attended the Christian Leaders, Authors, and Speakers Seminar (CLASS) led by Fred and Florence Littauer. The seminar was a major turning point in my life. For several days I was trained in effective methods of gathering material, making outlines, and presenting an interesting, informative speech.

Recognizing God's voice was not my strong point, yet I knew He planted this thought in my mind: I would be a speaker. This thought I kept hidden in my heart, hoping and dreaming that one day it would become a reality. With the dream came the fear that I never would. Speakers were these wonderful people who had their lives all neat and clean—and mine had been a mess. Still, I clung to that dream . . .

The old Valerie would have run around the campus telling everyone who would listen that I wanted to take the Communication Core Course. I might even have called Texas to make sure that everyone there knew of my plans (and my shortage of money). But not now. I wanted to be sure it was God who was leading me, so I told no one. No one except my husband and Davis, my immediate supervisor in Campus Services. Instead, I concentrated on praying for the Lord's plans to be made clear.

Ten days before the school was to start, I received a phone call from Ms. Hartley letting me know that I had been accepted as a student for the school. Wanting this to be completely from God, and not something that I tried to push through, I only told Jean that I was waiting for final confirmation from the Lord before I could attend. I was sure I would know something by the next Tuesday. I spoke with Davis, and he cleared me to take the school. Now I only had to wait on an answer from the Lord.

Monday before school, I received written notice of my acceptance to the school of "Communications and the Biblical View of Man". With great joy I noticed the amount due: $1,550! Because we did not live on base, the school had subtracted for food and lodging. Subtract from this the $1,300 I already had and the balance needed was only $250. I could just write a check for that amount; $250 was not a barrier for me. However, I felt for right now I needed just to be still and wait—see what God said. Throughout my life I have always achieved my goals by clawing, scratching, and forcing things to becoming reality. Now I wanted God to provide for me *without* my interference.

Tuesday morning Peggy, my friend from the Accounting Department, whizzed by on her little moped on the way to deliver our support checks to the mailroom. When she saw me, she stopped. Peggy is very conscientious about her job and normally would never dream of discussing support checks outside the office, let alone blurt out the amount across a parking lot. But that day she was being the Lord's messenger to me when she said, "Val, you got a really big check today. Want to know how much it is?" With that, she pulled out of the stack of checks the one belonging to my family. There was our normal support, plus a bonus from a friend in Texas. The amount of that bonus? $250! I had the confirmation I'd asked for. Our friends, Ken and JoAnne York, had sent us surprise checks several times in the past few years. Each time the check was for the same amount—$300. This time though, only $250 came. Coincidence?

Going to school with young university students was a challenge for me. Where they were full of energy, sharp wit, and spunk, I struggled from years of being out of a school situation. I felt I was fairly talented in my writing and speaking skills, yet my grades proved differently. I worked hard on my speeches and spent hours on the writing assignments. My reward was a grade in the low seventies. Some speaker I was turning out to be! I even had the nerve to ask the school leader to review my work, certain she would agree with me that I needed an *A*, not a *C*; she didn't. The grade of *C* stayed and my hopes of making an *A* in the course dwindled.

One night while the girls and John were playing basketball, I threw my school papers across the room out of frustration. Stomping back and forth while I prayed (actually I was hollering), I vented the disappointment I felt with myself and my lousy grades. The majority of the twenty-five students were from other countries with English as their second language; they were making better grades than I. My little tirade was full of self-pity.

It wasn't until I stopped long enough to catch my breath that I heard what I had come to recognize as the Lord speaking to me: *"Are you working in My strength or in your own?"*

Such a simple question, yet it stopped me dead in my tracks. I pondered that question for some time. Who's strength was I relying on for my speaking and writing? The answer of course was my own. God is the perfect communicator. He ranked higher than the grade of a *C*.

My first instinct was to immediately pray and ask for the Lord's words, for His wisdom in my schoolwork. But I didn't. I knew that way down deep, I was hoping God would zap me with instantaneous genius, and that was wrong. God is not a puppet I can play with. Neither can I say "forgive me" with one hand while the other is outstretched, saying "gimme." For a long time I sat there thinking about what was really in my heart. I saw some not-so-pleasing areas.

"Father, I need to ask Your forgiveness for the way I sometimes act, as if the whole world revolves around me. I'm forty-five years old. I don't have the energy level of some of the other students, but You have given me a sharp mind. Help me to hear what is being taught and then apply it to the best of my ability. I am not perfect, but I desire to live in Your perfect will. Lead me in the right path. If a C is all I am capable of and it is my best work, then so be it. It is not the grade that matters as much as what I learn and the openness of my heart to follow You. You led me to this course; now lead me through it."

Wednesday night rolled around; it is the only time in the week that we had evening class. This particular Wednesday, our school leader handed us a list of paraphrased Bible verses from the New Testament, such as "I am liberated," "I am accepted," "I am a new creature," etc. We each had to randomly choose a verse and then write it on a small piece of tissue paper. I chose Romans 6:6 which paraphrased reads "My old self is dead." I chose this one because I desired more than anything in the world to have this be true. I desired to have my old ways, my self-centered thoughts and deeds, the shame from my abusive past to be dead, so I could successfully live a new, victorious life. I was tired of my past haunting me, tired of always not feeling good enough. I wanted these life-long feelings to be put to rest—permanently.

Jean read part of Ezekiel 3:1, which read in essence, "You shall eat My words and they will become a part of you." Then we did just that; put the tissue paper with the words in our mouths and ate them.

Jean prayed, "Father, as each of Your children eat what they have written from Your Word, I ask that the words would come alive within them. I pray they will believe and accept this as Your special word for them."

As I ate the words "My old self is dead," I felt a great stirring down in the depths of my soul. Although I did not hear anything, I knew the Spirit was confirming the words I had just eaten. *My old self was dead.* My past was just that—my past. I had this incredible feeling, which I knew was God sharing His love with me. I cried—great sobs of relief mixed with unfathomable joy. Part of me wanted to stop the display of emotions in front of my classmates, but the other part of me knew this was a cleansing time that needed to run its course. Truly the words I ate became part of me as I became aware that I no longer had to hang my head in shame over my past. I could walk boldly in the person God always intended me to be. He was setting the captive free!

Within the next few weeks, two major assignments were due, which would determine my final grade. The first was a fifteen-page research paper on a group of people from a country who as a whole did not know the true God. The other assignment was an eight-minute speech on the people group I chose. Both assignments contained very specific details on what and how they were to be presented. I knew this would be a real challenge for me.

"Lord, I want to rely on Your strength in these projects. I read in the Bible that my talent comes from the Spirit within me; I choose to give Him free reign. The grades are no longer the most important thing to me. Teach me what I need to learn through these assignments."

Surprising even to me, I brought in a grade of 99.5 percent on the written research paper. The speech was a little more difficult, as I not only had a list of specifics to present, but I also only had an eight-minute time allotment. I finished the speech in eight minutes five seconds and was rewarded with a grade of 99. Final grade in the school, an *A*.

New Year's Day, a week after the Core Course was completed, I was invited to a friend's open house. There I fell into conversation with Norm Frame and Colby Slavmaker. We got on the subject of all the things the Lord had done for my family during the past two years, including our experiences in Ukraine. Both Norm and Colby challenged me to write a book. We prayed and I could feel the desire to write this book begin to grow. Norm stopped during the prayer and said he felt I should make a vow. When the Lord said it was time to write, then I should not hesitate but begin to write. Two weeks later I started *Answering My Heart's Cry*.

I was actually fearful of telling anyone about the manuscript I was working on. I have always struggled with procrastination and I feared this project would be no different than anything else I had ever started—shelved before completed. Yet each day found me joyfully clicking away at my computer, diligently writing.

The last chapter I wrote was Chapter One. Writing it brought up memories of the life-saving help the Lord provided through Fred and Florence Littauer and Janet Sylar. Realizing I had never written to thank them for all the help they had been to me, I decided I needed to do just that. To the Littaurs, I wrote a quick synopsis of my life, along with the changes the Lord had made in me from reading their books and attending their seminars. I expressed my gratitude for their willingness to be vulnerable and open with their lives for the benefit of others.

Not so with Janet Sylar. My procrastination, a constant struggle to me, won out and I never wrote to her. Janet was the first person the Lord specially used to begin my long journey of healing and restoration. The path my feet are now on is a direct result of Janet's perseverance in getting John and me to the Littauer seminar. The thought was always right there: write to Janet. But I didn't. Now I never can. Just recently I heard that Janet died suddenly. Obedience has its rewards, just as procrastination has its pain. I can never tell Janet how her acting on the Lord's prompting had changed my life. Through tears, I have asked the Lord to tell her for me. The Sylar family has received the letter that should have been written to Janet.

The honing of my skills and encouragement to write my book was not all I gained from the Communication Core Course. My desire to be a speaker was also rekindled; I am now praying over the timing of launching into my speaking ministry. My prayers are said with the confidence that it will be brought to pass and the knowledge that in *His* perfect timing, I will speak for Him.

In retrospect, I know why I was placed as the manager of Housekeeping. God knew what I could not foresee. Although there were hectic times in Housekeeping, for the majority of each day, I had the freedom to be home writing. Any other position on this base would have required six to eight hours a day in the office, with no time to write. This manuscript was finished in June. In July I resigned from Housekeeping. I flew to Atlanta to the Christian Booksellers Convention where I found the publisher for this book. After flying back to Hawaii, I joined Jean Hartely on staff with the school of "Communication and the Biblical View of Man", which I dearly loved.

Writing this book, working with Ms. Hartley, having a free spirit on the *inside* to be a speaker, being led by God into my future—what more could I ask. Obedience and a willing heart, even when mixed with a little fear, makes it all possible. My future is in front of me. My present is full of questions whose answers lay in the hands of the Lord. I no longer push, shove, and try to make things happen. Instead, I am content to pray, ask the Father for what He knows is best for me, and then wait . . . and watch His best take shape in my life.

> Do not call to mind the former things, or ponder things of the past, Behold, I will do something new. . . . (Isa. 43:18–19*a*)

17

Yes? No! Wait . . .

Unanswered Prayer

I could fill volumes of books about the times I have prayed for something and then . . . nothing. Absolutely nothing happened. I used to wonder if God heard me? Did He care? Was He too busy? Or was the prayer just not important enough for Him to bother with answering? I can hear you now saying. "How absurd." Yet, I am sure that even the strongest, most faithful Christians sometimes wonder where their prayers disappeared.

Usually when this happened I took matters in my own hands, and then suffered because of it. At times I decided to help God along, to make it happen by pushing and manipulating circumstances and people because God did not answer me in the way I wanted. At times I have acted like a spoiled two-year-old and threw a tantrum because God was not quick enough with His answer. I have even had the gall to announce smugly how great God was to "do this for me." Of course that was not God working, but me.

The results of my manipulation have ranged from mediocre to tragic. Things would appear to be perfect but then down the road they always fell apart. Oh, I lived through those hard times, but not without plenty of battle scars and many wasted years. There were years where I had chased the pot of gold to the end of the rainbow only to find nothing more than a pit of mud that I had to climb out of. During these past two years, I have learned the most valuable lesson: When it seems God is not sending His answer right away, or even when He tells me "no," it is still OK. God is God and He doesn't need me to help Him be God. I need only to pray then leave it in the hands of the One who has the perfect solution and answer. Praying does not guarantee I will get my way. Sometimes God is silent and says nothing at all. Sometimes He even tells me "no." Sometimes I have not liked the answers I have received from Him.

A Time When God Said No

The incredible struggles I go through as a mother with a son in prison defies description. Learning to understand my past behavior, the way I raised my older children, realizing the fact that I was not a good mom—that I share in the responsibility of Marcus being in prison—is almost more than I can bear.

I have cried, prayed, begged, pleaded, and demanded of God that my son be released. Foremost, though, I pray for a miraculous turnaround in Marcus. From his letters, I am aware of subtle changes in his attitude, but I wonder if there should be more? Has God been helping him to change and am I too blinded by fear to see it? Fear that he won't change enough; fear that if I totally believe he's transformed, I'll be disappointed later and hurt all over again? I feel that as his mother, I should fight tooth and nail for his release, yet I haven't.

In 1995 we sold our house for a profit of $34,000. When the check was handed to me, I turned white. John noticed but thought it was because I'd never held so much money before. This was true, but that wasn't why I was so shaken. I held within my hands the means for Marcus to be released. Twenty thousand dollars would pay an attorney's fee for my son. Marcus is a victim of a lousy system and does not deserve the severity of the punishment he received. Stealing TVs and VCRs should not hold more time than armed robbery or rape. Marcus needed a good lawyer to fight for justice and his release. It felt like my son was lost in the system and $20,000 and a good lawyer could help him find his way out.

The desire to hire an attorney for my son was strong. I knew John would not agree with this so I prayed, asking God to soften John's heart when I approached him for the money.

I never asked my husband. My answer came back to me not as words, but as a feeling: No! I was not to pay for an attorney. How can a mother who loves her children more than life turn and walk away from her only son when he needs her? It wasn't easy.

The second opportunity to help Marcus came during the summer of 1997. I have a wonderful friend and Sunday School teacher who personally knows Texas Governor Bush and his wife. Jan encouraged me several times to write to the governor about the severity of the punishment my son received and seek his release by a special governor's parole. I always meant to write that letter but never did; I kept putting it off.

Imagine the horror I felt when I received a letter from the prison hospital. Marcus had been attacked from behind and knocked unconscious. His assailant proceeded to kick his face with steel-toed boots until the guards realized Marcus was not fighting back and pulled his attacker off. My son was dragged to the infirmary, where he lay unconscious for several hours. When he came to, he was given an aspirin and locked back in his cell—to suffer. This was on a Thursday.

By Monday Marcus still had not moved out of bed; the guards took notice and asked if he needed the doctor again. Marcus mumbled that a tooth was cracked in half, but his jaw would not open to get it out. Within minutes of arriving at the dentist, it was decided that Marcus needed to be hospitalized. It took until Wednesday to get him transferred. Along with the excruciating pain, Marcus suffered cuts, bruises, a broken tooth, and his jaw was snapped in half by the brutal kicks. A surgeon pulled his split tooth and wired his jaw together. Then for six weeks Marcus was locked in a hospital room with no television, no radio, no pencil or pen—sipping his meals through a straw, staring at the four white walls while in a world of pain.

Sitting in Hawaii, I felt as if I was going to explode. How much more can my son take? How much more can I as his mother sit and allow him to be hurt? Then I remembered Jan Pierce. Of course, I will write the governor, mail it to Jan, and ask her to hand deliver it herself. Fully expecting God to approve of my plan, I started composing my letter.

As an afterthought, I remembered to pray. "If I should write Governor Bush via Jan, then let me know. I will e-mail my Sunday School class about Marcus. If Jan writes, calls, or e-mails me back within the next two weeks, I know that I am to write that letter. If I do not hear from Jan, then I will know that You do not want me to get involved."

Naturally, I drafted a dozen different letters trying to evoke enough empathy toward Marcus so the governor would take affirmative action. I cried out for my son's recovery and for a call from Jan. One week went by. Then two. Then a month. Prayers of anguish went up to heaven, but no word from Jan. *Maybe God did not hear. Maybe I needed to give God longer than just two weeks. Maybe Jan didn't get the message. A little help wouldn't hurt; I could write Jan personally to make sure she has a wide-open door of opportunity to respond.*

Sounded good until I asked, "Is this me pushing again?" God doesn't need my help to get a message to Jan Pierce!

Although I did not *hear* anything, the answer was loud and clear, *"No."* Disappointment lay heavy in my heart. What I did not hear was just as clear a no as a contact from Jan would have been a yes. I did not write the letter to the governor. I did not communicate with Jan. I just soaked my pillow each night as I cried myself to sleep over my boy, who was still locked behind those prison walls. I clung to God's beautiful promise made while I was at the Ukrainian prison: *"If you will take care of my boys here, I will take care of your boy back there."* In that promise alone I place my trust.

> Oh, the depth of the riches both of the wisdom and knowledge of God! How unsearchable are His judgments and unfathomable His ways. (Rom. 11:33)

A Time When God Seemed Not to Hear

Julia and Ralph were beside themselves with worry. Raising six children on a farm during the Depression had not been easy. But a strong back, tenacity, and a faithful prayer life saw them through. As tough as their farm life had been, this had to be harder. Their youngest daughter wanted to marry a truck driver. He believed *in* God, but he was not a Christian. Talking, pleading, forbidding, and dozens of heart-to-heart talks did no good. Marie was determined, with or without her parents' blessing, to marry her love, Cary Baker.

Ralph and Julia realized they could either accepted Cary into their tight-knit Dutch family or they could lose their daughter. Hours of prayer covered with tears saw them through those first few rough months. It helped tremendously that Cary was a good man, took wonderful care of their daughter, and loved her passionately. Charm went a long way to win his way into their hearts and into their lives. Cary was there to stay.

My grandparents, Ralph and Julia, being devout Christians began to pray for the salvation of their son-in-law. They prayed day after day, year after year. Ralph died in 1977 at the age of eighty just a few months shy of their sixtieth wedding anniversary. Julia died in 1992 at the age of ninety-three. I visited my grandma in South Chicago just a few weeks before she passed away. She told me that she never missed a day praying for Dad. I too had prayed, but not everyday. How can one pray for so many years without seeing positive results yet still have the faith to keep praying? I have trouble waiting even a few weeks for my prayers to be answered. There are just times that God seems to not hear. This appeared to be one of those times.

In January 1997, I was praying for our family's future in full-time ministry. Our desire was again to have the privilege of working in a developing country, working alongside the people while sharing the gospel. This was our dream and our goal. Suddenly I was struck with the horrendous thought, *What if Daddy dies while I am in some remote place and I cannot get back in time to pray with him if he wants to get saved? What if I can't even make it back for the funeral?* Morbid, I know, but Satan has a way of twisting the guilt-knife right where we are the most vulnerable. My dad is one of those vulnerable spots in my heart.

Standing in my living room I prayed, pouring my heart and fears out to God. On and on I went about what "I" wanted, what "I" desired, and the great hopes "I" had concerning my dad. "Father, You know the great love I have for my parents. I cannot imagine the pain of not knowing if Dad is with You or not. Even though my desire is to serve You wherever You send us, how can I go and tell perfect strangers of Your love and sacrifice while leaving my own father here not knowing You? What if I got a letter saying, 'Your father is dead, and we had to bury him because we couldn't wait for you.' Oh, God, what do I do? I am so torn! I want to follow You, but I am afraid."

I wept until I was too exhausted to do anything but be still.

Ever so softly, a gentle voice whispered, *"Will it be all right with you if you know that he is safe in My arms?"*

I recognized it as God's voice speaking to me. Instantly, my fears disappeared. There was not a *specific* promise made that my dad would someday become a Christian, but the peace that voice brought was unmistakable.

About this same time, my dad, who only came to church for special programs or musicals, started to attend my mom's little mission church. He went every Sunday morning for over a month. Then one cold January morning, Mom was down with an attack of the flu and could not go to church. What a surprise when Dad went without her. Soon my dad was going both Sunday morning and evening. Later, when Needham Road Baptist Mission was looking for a place to hold Wednesday night prayer meetings, Dad invited them to meet in their living room each week. When the mission started having Sunday School, my dad was the first one in the door . . . carrying his own Bible.

Sunday, May 11th, 1997, Mother's Day, my only nephew, Zacary James Baker, was dedicated at the mission church. A baby dedication is a promise made by Zacary's parents, Rodney and Amy, to raise Zacary in a Christian home with Christian values. This was a special time for our entire family. At the finish of the sermon, during the final song, Daddy felt what was becoming a familiar tugging on his heart. He knew it was God wooing him—calling him to accept His Son's sacrifice for him. At first Dad did not move but let the last stanza of the song be sung. Then, as if someone else were moving his legs, Dad found himself at the front of the church. The time was now. The angels in heaven rejoiced as Cary Baker said yes to Jesus and invited Him into his heart and life. For Mom it had been fifty years doused in thousands of prayer. For Dad it was the glorious promise of eternal life.

Later that same year on November 13th, my parents celebrated their fiftieth wedding anniversary. Fifty years is a long time to be married. It is even a longer time to pray the same prayer. Although God did not immediately answer the prayers for my dad, answer us He did. The changes we see in Dad are wonderful and well worth the wait. Obedience reaps rewards. Randy, by older brother, was impacted by watching our dad and seeing the genuine changes in his life. Eight months after Dad said yes to Jesus, Randy invited Jesus into his own heart and life. We all rejoice . . . especially Daddy.

Sometimes I close my eyes and try to picture heaven. I dream what it will be like to walk the Streets of Gold. I cry when I realize that my grandpa will be there, no longer bent over from old age and Grandma will not stumble when she walks; they will be vibrantly young and full of life. I smile when I see that John's mother does not have to use her walker and her fingers and toes are not all crippled from arthritis, but straight and strong. My own mother's aches and pains will not exist. I see myself walking in the Garden of Heaven hand-in-hand with Jesus. He is leading me to the Throne to visit my Abba — my heavenly Daddy. Jesus is smiling at me as we walk. He is telling me He knows . . . everything . . . and He loves me. He looks straight into my eyes with such incredible understanding. I feel feelings that have no earthly words to describe them. We walk past a crystal-clear lake which reflects our images perfectly. There I am, radiant from the pure joy of His presence . . . walking . . . holding Jesus' hand. But that is not all. As I look more closely I see I am holding hands with two men; Jesus on the one side . . . and my own daddy on the other.

This dream will now someday be a reality. For all eternity.

For the vision is yet for the appointed time; it hastens toward the goal, and it will not fail. Though it tarries, wait for it; For it will certainly come, it will not delay. (Hab. 2:3)

Epilogue

Update #1

Marcus . . . my only son and my first-born child. Several times in this book, I have referred to my son and my own struggles while he was in prison. What a glorious day February 17, 1998 was as together my parents, daughters and I stood and watched Marcus walk out those prison doors! The reception my whole family gave him was heartwarming and genuine. Like the prodical son's father, we were all ready for him to be home and be a part of our family again. Within a month of his release, he received a partial grant from the state of Texas and is now attending the Art Institute of Houston.

Best of all he is going to church every Sunday. The other young people in his Sunday School class have accepted Marcus for who he is—a wonderful, talented young man, full of charisma and charm. The have blessed him with their trust. He is invited to "hang out" with them and is welcomed into their inner circle. They are living a godly life . . . leading the way for my son to follow.

I realize now that if Marcus would have gotten out of prison earlier, he might not have been ready to face the outside world. But more importantly, Marcus' family, his sister, cousins, grandparents, aunts and uncles would not have been ready either. God had to do a work in their hearts as well preparing them to again make Marcus a welcomed, trusted part of their family and life.

God kept His word. He was and still is . . . taking care of my boy.

Update #2

Then there is Charlean. Our precious, alburn-headed daughter. Smart. Likeable. Courageous. A love of laughter. My years as a wife and mother out of control stole Charlean's childhood and replaced it with pain and unhappiness. Because of this, at age seventeen she escaped our house in an effort to free herself from the life she hated. Eight years went by. The grapevine whispered that Charlean was a mother of a beautiful baby daughter ; my heart yearned to be a part of Miranda's life. I wanted the priviledge of knowing Charlean as an adult and the chance to meet and know her husband Scott. I desperately prayed for the opportunity to try to make amends, to explain to Charlean, to seek her forgiveness. But knowing the strong personality and inner strength of Charlean, the faith in my prayers were weak.

Imagine how thrilled I was when in February of 1998, I received a letter from our Charlean inviting us to her home for a visit and to meet three year old Miranda. What a beautiful, precious, child she is. Even though we are not related by blood, I am as proud of Miranda and love her as if she were my own granddaughter. During that short visit, John asked his daughter to make the four-hour trip down to Conroe to have a four-generation picture taken. Two weeks later they did. The picture with Grandma Clayton, John, Charlean and Miranda is priceless. The three days we spent together was heaven for me. Although we did not discuss the past, we agreed that someday we would talk.

Today, I am allowed to write to Miranda and send her little things in the mail like all grandmas do. She in turn sends me the pictures she scribbles. I have them hanging on my wall; a constant reminder that God is more powerful than a strong personality and mightier than my own weak faith.

Valerie's Comments

Answering My Heart's Cry is full of God's miracles. Personally, I only planned to write chapters 2–17; never did I intend to write the first one. But when the Spirit directed, I obeyed. I couldn't write without becoming vulnerable or revealing my shame. I Corinthians says God chose the lowly things of this world and the despised things to show that He is our righteousness, holiness and redemption. Revelation of my past could very well cause you to despise me; if not me, then certainly my actions. Chapter 2 of I Corinthians continues as if it was written by me: "I came to you in weakness and fear and with much trembling. My message is not with wise and persuasive words but is with a demonstration of the Spirit's power—power so that your faith might not rest on my words or wisdom but on God's power."

Jeremiah 29:11 says, "For I know the plans I have for you," declares the Lord. "Plan to prosper and not for harm. Plans for a future and a hope."

If you get nothing else from this book, I want you to understand this, to rest in the assurance and confidence of this knowledge. In fact, say it out loud to help it sink in. Go ahead, say it right now, out loud: God really and truly loves me. He desires an intimate, personal relationship with me. There is no such thing as an insignificant prayer or one that is too astronimical for God. He does not neglect, ignore or forget about me even when it seems as if He has. He is ever-present in my life, guiding me with His wisdom, His unending love and through His unimaginable power. God loves me no matter what I have said, thought or done. And

because of His incredible, unfathomable love for me, He
really and truly does sets about

Answering My Heart's Cry

Do not fear, for I am with you;
do not anxiously look about you, for I am your God.
I will strengthen you, surely I will help you,
surely I will uphold you with My righteous right hand.
—Isaiah 41:10

**May the promises of God
lead you all the days of your life.**

Bibliography

Littauer, Fred and Florence. *Freeing Your Mind From Memories That Bind,* 4th printing, San Bernardino, CA: Here's Life Publishers, 1990.

Littauer, Fred. *The Promise of Restoration.* San Bernardino, CA: Here's Life Publishers, 1990.

Blackaby, Henry T. and King, Claude V. *Experiencing God.* Nashville, TN: LifeWay Press, 1990.

To order additional copies of

Answering My Heart's Cry

send $10.95 plus $3.95 shipping and handling to

Valerie L. Baker Clayton

Valerie Lee Baker Clayton
% Oak Ridge Baptist Church
26569 Hanna Road
Oak Ridge North, Texas 77385
U.S.A.

Cool
Recipes
&
Camping
Hacks

FOR VW CAMPERS

THE BAREFOOT CHEF

Also from Veloce Publishing –

An Austin Anthology (Stringer)
An Austin Anthology II (Stringer)
An English Car Designer Abroad (Birtwhistle)
An Incredible Journey (Falls & Reisch)
Armstrong-Siddeley (Smith)
Art Deco and British Car Design (Down)
Autodrome (Collins & Ireland)
Automotive A-Z, Lane's Dictionary of Automotive Terms (Lane)
Automotive Mascots (Kay & Springate)
Bentley Continental, Corniche and Azure (Bennett)
Bentley MkVI, Rolls-Royce Silver Wraith, Dawn & Cloud/Bentley R & S-Series (Nutland)
Bluebird CN7 (Stevens)
BMW 5-Series (Cranswick)
BMW Z-Cars (Taylor)
Bonjour – Is this Italy? (Turner)
British Cars, The Complete Catalogue of, 1895-1975 (Culshaw & Horrobin)
BRM – A Mechanic's Tale (Salmon)
BRM V16 (Ludvigsen)
Caravan, Improve & Modify Your (Porter)
Caravans, The Illustrated History 1919-1959 (Jenkinson)
Caravans, The Illustrated History From 1960 (Jenkinson)
Car-tastrophes – 80 automotive atrocities from the past 20 years (Honest John, Fowler)
Citroën DS (Bobbitt)
Classic Engines, Modern Fuel: The Problems, the Solutions (Ireland)
Cobra – The Real Thing! (Legate)
Cobra, The last Shelby – My times with Carroll Shelby (Theodore)
Concept Cars, How to illustrate and design – New 2nd Edition (Dewey)
Cortina – Ford's Bestseller (Robson)
Cosworth – The Search for Power (6th edition) (Robson)
Cranswick on Porsche (Cranswick)
Dodge Challenger & Plymouth Barracuda (Grist)
Dodge Charger – Enduring Thunder (Ackerson)
Dodge Dynamite! (Grist)
Dodge Viper (Zatz)
Dorset from the Sea – The Jurassic Coast from Lyme Regis to Old Harry Rocks photographed from its best viewpoint (also Souvenir Edition) (Belasco)
Draw & Paint Cars – How to (Gardiner)
Driven – An Elegy to Cars, Roads & Motorsport (Aston)
Dune Buggy Files (Hale)
Dune Buggy Handbook (Hale)
East German Motor Vehicles in Pictures (Suhr/Weinreich)
Essential Guide to Driving in Europe, The (Parish)
Fate of the Sleeping Beauties, The (op de Weegh/Hottendorff/op de Weegh)
Fiat & Abarth 124 Spider & Coupé (Tipler)
Fiat & Abarth 500 & 600 – 2nd Edition (Bobbitt)
Fiats, Great Small (Ward)
Ford F100/F150 Pick-up 1948-1996 (Ackerson)
Ford F150 Pick-up 1997-2005 (Ackerson)
Ford Focus WRC (Robson)
Ford GT – Then, and Now (Streather)
Ford GT40 (Legate)
Ford Midsize Muscle – Fairlane, Torino & Ranchero (Cranswick)

Ford Model Y (Roberts)
Ford Mustang II & Pinto 1970 to 80 (Cranswick)
Ford Thunderbird From 1954, The Book of the (Long)
Ford versus Ferrari – The battle for supremacy at Le Mans 1966 (Starkey)
Forza Minardi! (Vigar)
France: the essential guide for car enthusiasts – 200 things for the car enthusiast to see and do (Parish)
From Crystal Palace to Red Square – A Hapless Biker's Road to Russia (Turner)
The Good, the Mad and the Ugly … not to mention Jeremy Clarkson (Dron)
GT – The World's Best GT Cars 1953-73 (Dawson)
Immortal Austin Seven (Morgan)
India - The Shimmering Dream (Reisch/Falls (translator))
Intermeccanica – The Story of the Prancing Bull (McCredie & Reisner)
Jaguar - All the Cars (4th Edition) (Thorley)
Jaguar from the shop floor (Martin)
Jaguar E-type Factory and Private Competition Cars (Griffiths)
Jaguar, The Rise of (Price)
Jaguar XJ 220 – The Inside Story (Moreton)
Jaguar XJ-S, The Book of the (Long)
Jeep CJ (Ackerson)
Jeep Wrangler (Ackerson)
The Jowett Jupiter – The car that leaped to fame (Nankivell)
Karmann-Ghia Coupé & Convertible (Bobbitt)
KTM X-Bow (Pathmanathan)
Lamborghini Miura Bible, The (Sackey)
Lamborghini Murciélago, The book of the (Pathmanathan)
Lamborghini Urraco, The Book of the (Landsem)
Lancia Delta Integrale (Collins)
Land Rover Design - 70 years of success (Hull)
Land Rover Emergency Vehicles (Taylor)
Land Rover Series III Reborn (Porter)
Land Rover, The Half-ton Military (Cook)
Land Rovers in British Military Service – coil sprung models 1970 to 2007 (Taylor)
Lea-Francis Story, The (Price)
Lexus Story, The (Long)
Little book of microcars, the (Quellin)
Little book of smart, the – New Edition (Jackson)
Little book of trikes, the (Quellin)
Lotus 18 Colin Chapman's U-turn (Whitelock)
Lotus 49 (Oliver)
Lotus Elan and +2 Source Book (Vale)
Making a Morgan (Hensing)
Marketingmobiles, The Wonderful Wacky World of (Hale)
Mazda MX-5 Miata, The book of the – The 'Mk1' NA-series 1988 to 1997 (Long)
Mazda MX-5 Miata, The book of the – The 'Mk2' NB-series 1997 to 2004 (Long)
Mazda MX-5 Miata Roadster (Long)
Maximum Mini (Booij)
Meet the English (Bowie)
Mercedes-Benz SL – R230 series 2001 to 2011 (Long)
Mercedes-Benz SL – W113-series 1963-1971 (Long)

Mercedes-Benz SL & SLC – 107-series 1971-1989 (Long)
Mercedes-Benz SLK – R170 series 1996-2004 (Long)
Mercedes-Benz SLK – R171 series 2004-2011 (Long)
Mercedes-Benz W123-series – All models 1976 to 1986 (Long)
Mercedes G-Wagen (Long)
MG, Made in Abingdon (Frampton)
MGA (Price Williams)
MGB – The Illustrated History, Updated Fourth Edition (Wood & Burrell)
The MGC GTS Lightweights (Morys)
Micro Caravans (Jenkinson)
Micro Trucks (Mort)
Microcars at Large! (Quellin)
Mini Cooper – The Real Thing! (Tipler)
Mini Minor to Asia Minor (West)
MOPAR Muscle – Barracuda, Dart & Valiant 1960-1980 (Cranswick)
Morris Minor, 70 Years on the Road (Newell)
Motor Movies – The Posters! (Veysey)
Motorhomes, The Illustrated History (Jenkinson)
Motorsport In colour, 1950s (Wainwright)
Nissan 300ZX & 350Z – The Z-Car Story (Long)
Nissan GT-R Supercar: Born to race (Gorodji)]
Nothing Runs – Misadventures in the Classic, Collectable & Exotic Car Biz (Slutsky)
Patina Volkswagen, How to Build a (Walker)
Patina Volkswagens (Walker)
Peking to Paris 2007 (Young)
Pontiac Firebird – New 3rd Edition (Cranswick)
Porsche 356 (2nd Edition) (Long)
Porsche 356, The Ultimate Book of the (Long)
Porsche 908 (Födisch, Neßhöver, Roßbach, Schwarz & Roßbach)
Porsche 911 Carrera – The Last of the Evolution (Corlett)
Porsche 911R, RS & RSR, 4th Edition (Starkey)
Porsche 911 SC, Clusker
Porsche 911, The Book of the (Long)
Porsche 911 – The Definitive History 1963-1971 (Long)
Porsche 911 – The Definitive History 1971-1977 (Long)
Porsche 911 – The Definitive History 1977-1987 (Long)
Porsche 911 – The Definitive History 1987-1997 (Long)
Porsche 911 – The Definitive History 1997-2004 (Long)
Porsche 911 – The Definitive History 2004-2012 (Long)
Porsche 911, The Ultimate Book of the Air-cooled (Long)
Porsche – The Racing 914s (Smith)
Porsche 924 (Long)
The Porsche 924 Carreras – evolution to excellence (Smith)
Porsche 928 (Long)
Porsche 930 to 935: The Turbo Porsches (Starkey)
Porsche 944 (Long)
Porsche 993 'King Of Porsche' – The Essential Companion (Streather)
Porsche 996 'Supreme Porsche' – The Essential Companion (Streather)
Porsche 997 2004-2012 'Porsche Excellence' – The Essential Companion (Streather)

Porsche Boxster – The 986 series 1996-2004 (Long)
Porsche Boxster & Cayman – The 987 series (2004-2013) (Long)
Porsche - Silver Steeds (Smith)
Porsche: Three Generations of Genius (Meredith)
Powered by Porsche (Smith)
Preston Tucker & Others (Linde)
Renewable Energy Home Handbook, The (Porter)
Roads with a View – England's greatest views and how to find them by road (Corfield)
Rolls-Royce Silver Shadow/Bentley T Series Corniche & Camargue – Revised & Enlarged Edition (Bobbitt)
Rolls-Royce Silver Spirit, Silver Spur & Bentley Mulsanne 2nd Edition (Bobbitt)
Rover P4 (Bobbitt)
Russian Motor Vehicles – Soviet Limousines 1930-2003 (Kelly)
Russian Motor Vehicles – The Czarist Period 1784 to 1917 (Kelly)
RX-7 – Mazda's Rotary Engine Sportscar (Updated & Revised New Edition) (Long)
Schlumpf – The intrigue behind the most beautiful car collection in the world (Op de Weegh & Op de Weegh)
Singer Story: Cars, Commercial Vehicles, Bicycles & Motorcycle (Atkinson)
Sleeping Beauties USA – abandoned classic cars & trucks (Marek)
SM – Citroën's Maserati-engined Supercar (Long & Claverol)
Speedway – Auto racing's ghost tracks (Collins & Ireland)
Sprite Caravans, The Story of (Jenkinson)
Standard Motor Company, The Book of the (Robson)
Tatra – The Legacy of Hans Ledwinka, Updated & Enlarged Collector's Edition of 1500 copies (Margolius & Henry)
This Day in Automotive History (Corey)
To Boldly Go – twenty six vehicle designs that dared to be different (Hull)
Toyota Celica & Supra, The Book of Toyota's Sports Coupés (Long)
Toyota MR2 Coupés & Spyders (Long)
Triumph & Standard Cars 1945 to 1984 (Warrington)
Triumph Cars – The Complete Story (new 3rd edition) (Robson)
Triumph TR6 (Kimberley)
Volkswagen Bus Book, The (Bobbitt)
Volkswagen Bus or Van to Camper, How to Convert (Porter)
Volkswagen Type 4, 411 and 412 (Cranswick)
Volkswagens of the World (Glen)
VW Beetle Cabriolet – The full story of the convertible Beetle (Bobbitt)
VW Beetle – The Car of the 20th Century (Copping)
VW Bus – 40 Years of Splitties, Bays & Wedges (Copping)
VW Bus Book, The (Bobbitt)
VW Golf: Five Generations of Fun (Copping & Cservenka)
VW – The Air-cooled Era (Copping)
VW T5 Camper Conversion Manual (Porter)
VW Campers (Copping)
Volkswagen Type 3, The book of the – Concept, Design, International Production Models & Development (Glen)

www.veloce.co.uk

First published in May 2021 by Veloce Publishing Limited, Veloce House, Parkway Farm Business Park, Middle Farm Way, Poundbury, Dorchester DT1 3AR, England.
Tel +44 (0)1305 260068 / Fax 01305 250479 / e-mail info@veloce.co.uk / web www.veloce.co.uk or www.velocebooks.com.
ISBN: 978-1-787117-45-7; UPC: 6-36847-01745-3.

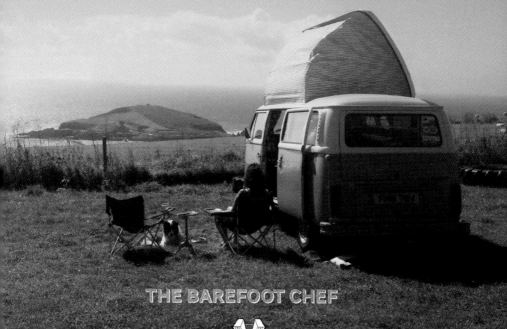

Cool Recipes & Camping Hacks

FOR VW CAMPERS

THE BAREFOOT CHEF

V
VELOCE PUBLISHING
THE PUBLISHER OF FINE AUTOMOTIVE BOOKS

Contents

Camping hacks & anecdotes

Introduction...6
About the author 7
Flexibility is the key 8
Suspension 10
Levelling blocks 12
Camp rules & cartwheels 14
Fairy lights...16
Looe Bay Farm 18
Fun with colour coordination 20
Camping myths & legends debunked!...........22
More camping myths............................24
Less is sometimes more, so very
        much more 26
Packing 28
Packing list..29
Porta Potti 30
Fun with tent pegs...............................32
The fridge 34
Kelly Kettle meets COBB 36
How to fasten down a sunshade
        – properly!.................................38
The best awning is no awning at all..............40
Equipment..42
Smashed roof.......................................44
Miscellaneous tips...............................46

'These old Volkswagens go on for
        ever, you know'............................48
'Fun weekends with wild friends'....................50
A suggestion for a full weekend
        of easy food. 51
Brighton...52
All the gear, no idea 54
Sun visor..56
Weekend hippies: a good thing, or bad? 58
Green Hill Farm 60
The definitive picnic............................62
Picnicking for absolute beginners...................63
Dealing with children...........................66
France 68
The Barefoot Bishop's knob!.............70
Three-in-one coffee sachets...............72
It seemed like a good idea at the time 74
Notebook 76
Campsite etiquette...............................78
Glamping..80
Takeaway..82
Disposable barbies are great! 84
Another weekend festival, and lots
        more fun with a sunshade...........86
Breakdown ... .88

Windbreaks...90
Bikes..92
Be scene, be safe......................................94
Fuel gauge...96
Chips...97
Heater...98
The double skillet....................................100
Tiny awning...102
The good camping pitch paradox..............104

Beaten by the weather 106
More miscellaneous tips..........................108
Goyt Camping..110
Dogs in vans..112
Glastonbury...114
Volkswagen clubs: to join or not to join?....116
Flags..118
My man with the spanners........................120
Mull..122

❊ ❊ ❊ ❊ ❊

Recipes

Happy hash (GF)...9
Breakfast pancakes with
    bacon & maple syrup!......................11
Kay-sa-dee-yahs!......................................13
Squaring up to breakfast............................15
Crispy avocado melt (V).............................17
Venison stew...19
Orange(?) chicken fajitas...........................21
Cheat's chilli taco surprise!.......................23
Super easy camping omelettes...................23
Sunny chicken (GF)...................................25
Monte Cristo...27
Pulled pork (GF)..31
Chicken fusion tagine (GF).........................33
Lamb koftas..35
Barbecued Buffalo wings (GF)....................37
Barefoot biryani (GF*)...............................39
Spicy chicken picnic burritos......................41
Game, set & match (GF*)...........................43
Shish kebabs..45
Barefoot chicken & chorizo (GF)................47
Fat sausages, braised in cider &
    mustard (GF).....................................49
Oatcakes with bacon & cheese...................51
ABC: Avocado & blue cheese burger..........53
Cheat's tandoori chicken kebabs...............55
Welsh rarebit or VW rabbit? (V).................57
Sweet & sour chicken.................................59
Lamb shawarma (GF).................................61
Chicken & beer picnic................................63
Coronation chicken & Waldorf salad...........64
Shooter's picnic..64
Vegshooter's picnic (V).............................65

Hungry man's goulash (GF*).......................67
Mushroom burgers (V)................................69
The breakfast basket (V)............................71
Lemony Chicket! (GF*)...............................73
Beef stroganoff à la rock track (GF)............75
Loaded tortilla chips (GF)...........................77
Portobello blue! (V)....................................79
Mexican steak with queso
    fresco (GF)..81
Orange chicken casserole (GF)...................83
Pan haggerty (GF*)....................................85
Spam & baked beans (GF)..........................87
Barbecued rib of beef.................................89
Smoked salmon, barbecued on
    a wooden plank!................................91
Posh Pot Noodle..93
Diffuser frittata (GF)...................................95
Tournedos Rossini......................................99
Pork shoulder (GF)...................................101
Pizza on the COBB....................................103
Houmous & pea fritters (V & GF)...............105
Cheatin' chicken Kievs.............................107
Chorizo & tomato pasta............................109
Toad in the hole.......................................111
Char siu pork (GF)....................................113
Egg fried rice (GF)....................................113
Lamb tzatziki...115
Onkar's lamb..117
Rolled beef...119
Gammon, with broad beans &
    new potatoes (GF)...........................121
Deconstructed scrumper's
    crumble (V & GF)............................123

Introduction

If you have a camper van, this is the book you've been waiting for: the laid-back person's guide to camping!

Included are more than 50 recipes that you really can cook from start to finish in the middle of a field somewhere, using only the standard dual hob and grill combo, or on a barbecue. Some of them are elegant and fragrant, and will have campers coming from all over the site to see what glorious feast you are preparing. Others are far more functional, and although they taste great and are quick and easy to prepare, they may not look very pretty.

A food stylist was occasionally consulted, but sadly their enthusiasm for placing poached eggs on top of things to add "a splash of colour," led them to a sound kicking and an early exit from the project.

Much time was spent in arranging and re-arranging the recipes into the 'right' order, but ultimately I couldn't decide which of the options was correct, so I gave up. You'll see that they are still completely disorganised, but it shouldn't be a problem as there's a comprehensive index at the back.

All the recipes are made to serve two people. You'll also see that some recipes are marked with a **(V)** to indicate that they are suitable for vegetarians, or **(GF)** to signal that they're gluten-free. **(GF*)** means that the recipe could be made gluten-free simply by using an alternative stock cube! Not only did this book not have a stylist, it didn't have a nutritionist either – but the vegetarian recipes don't have any meat in them, and the gluten-free ones don't make my fair, coeliac wife ill.

Along with the cookery, there's also lots of camping hints, tips, ideas and camping tales, all of which come from 25 years of working things out the hard way at festivals, VW shows, and a memorable mixture of holidays, both glorious and dismal. In terms of things to do and things to avoid, it doesn't matter what type of camper you drive: old VWs may look the part, but a vehicle less than 40-odd-years-old can generally be relied upon to perform slightly better.

The whole point of this book is that everything can be done in a field, in a camper van. You will find no instructions here that involve ovens, microwaves, or draining rice under a stream of boiling water. It is perfectly possible to make the vast majority of these recipes inside the bus on

the original Fellows hob and grill, but space is very restricted, and there are an awful lot of people who don't want their expensive new upholstery to smell of onions for the next 20 years.

For that very reason, I spend a lot of time using a gas stove outside, on the table. I've had a few of those cheap and cheerful 'portable butane gas stoves' over the years – the pressed-steel devices that come in a plastic case, and run on what look like aerosol cans. They are okay: they're easy to use and pans sit on them with minimal risk of spillage, but for some reason they are incredibly slow – you can be waiting ten minutes just for a kettle to boil. So, I replaced mine with a cheap Chinese copy of something exotic. It's featherweight and small enough to put in a large pocket. You'll see it in the photographs, but you can't tell just by looking how incredibly stable it has turned out to be. To go with it, I have a very small anodised aluminium kettle and an ultra-lightweight windbreak. The three things working in combination enable me to boil up water in about a minute-and-a-half.

It was interesting that it took a huge leap of faith for me to buy something so small: "What happens if friends pop round?" It can only hold about half a litre, and has very flimsy heat exchanger fins on the bottom, yet it has stood up well to over five years of constant camping abuse, and has inevitably been dropped on several occasions. There's also a disposable barbecue tucked away in the camper van somewhere in case of emergency. If you've not used one, you might be surprised at how consistent they are.

About the author
The persona of the Barefoot Chef began life as nothing more than a fun photography project. From humble beginnings, it progressed to a series of comedy cookery videos on YouTube. Amazingly, the character captured someone's imagination, and sporadic appearances on local radio led, in turn, to a regular column in a popular Volkswagen camper van magazine – *Volkswagen Camper & Commercial* – that lasted for more than a decade.

Dave Richards lives with his wife and dog, not in a small orange camper van at a variety of locations around the UK, but in a house in the Midlands.

Hanging on for just an hour before taking his tent down would have brightened up this chap's entire day.

Flexibility is the key

This is one of the pivotal chapters in this book. To impress upon you how important it is to be flexible, I've paired it with the simplest recipe; one that you might otherwise ignore.

It's all well and good making plans: things to do at the festival, bands to see, stalls to visit, people to meet. Similarly, it's great to research your holiday destination, so you can look forward to visiting the pier on Monday, walking over the dunes on Tuesday … but the weather always conspires against you. And, when your base is a little tin van in the middle of a field, you have to accept that the weather will ultimately dictate exactly what you can and can't do. It's alright telling yourself that there's no such thing as bad weather – just wrong clothes – but there really is little point trying to fight it.

If you've planned a walk to the village in the next valley on Wednesday and you wake up to find it pouring down, be prepared to change plans. The village will still be there on Thursday. Instead, just walk a couple of hundred yards to the nearest pub* for a pie and a pint.

If you've disconnected from the virtual world, that book you've brought won't read itself – you can enjoy the glorious smell of ink and paper. Or you could update Facebook with photographs of the people pitched up next to you as they return, soaked to the skin, from the walk they insisted on taking.

Unless you are the sort of folk who insist on issuing a proclamation and chiselling your intentions into huge stone tablets – "We must walk over that hill despite the pouring rain, for I have this day issued a decree" – then just chill out. Go with the flow and do what you planned to do the following day, or do something else, or just do nothing. Sit and spend some quality time together.

*Well, you could go to the pub back in 2019 BC – 'Before Covid' – the golden age!

8

Happy hash   (GF)

This is great as festival food, when you simply don't have the time or the facilities to go to any trouble, and need everything cleaned and tidied away with minimal effort.

Ingredients

- Half a pack of defrosted potato rosti or hash browns (these are both the same, but rosti is a luxury item and costs more than twice as much as hash browns)
- About 10oz/4 pre-cooked thick sausages or bratwurst, thinly sliced
- Lots of Cheddar cheese, thinly sliced or grated
- A drop of oil

Method

This is a quick meal that can be made quite cheerfully inside the bus, without any fear of lingering smells or spitting oil and fat.

Heat a drop of oil in a large, heavy-bottomed pan. Add the rosti or hash browns and mash them up a bit using a wooden spatula. Add the sliced sausage, give it all a good stir, put a lid on the pan, and turn down the heat to the gentlest of gentle simmers.

Leave it for about five minutes, then remove the lid and give it all another good stir. Replace the lid again and leave it for another ten minutes or so. Once again, remove the lid, give it another good stir, and this time cover the mixture with lots of thinly sliced or grated cheese. Replace the lid and leave for a final five minutes to allow the cheese to melt into the sausage and potatoes.

Divide the mixture into two, scoop out of the pan and serve immediately. This stuff is proper wintry, chilly weather comfort food. We cheated and served up ours onto paper plates. I know it's a bit amateur hour, but there was simply no fuss; nothing to wash up. The cutlery only needed a quick wipe with kitchen towel, the plates were folded and thrown straight into the bin, and the pan was shoved back under the grill and left until next time.

Suspension

If the front suspension was much lower, I'd spend my life in fear of speed bumps!

I suspect that I have been spoiled by three years of running a very cheap and very battered old Jaguar XJ, but the once-fluid suspension on my bus has begun to irritate me. As you can see from the picture, it has been lowered … a bit. I try to convince myself that I wasn't just following fashion, but as the rear began to settle with age, I had the front lowered on dropped spindles in an effort to level things out. Clearly it didn't work out exactly as I'd planned, and I was left with what can best be described as rake, or possibly stance. Whatever you choose to call it, I've succeeded in making the ride harsh, jittery and comparatively unpleasant. When you consider other cars from the '70s that were suspended on torsion beams – the Renault 4, 5 and 6, the Simca 1100, the Chrysler Alpine/Horizon, and so on – and consider how softly they all used to ride, I appear to have done an especially ruinous job, and my patience with it is beginning to wear thin.

A couple of years ago I was obliged to replace the original, rotten, front beam, and the only thing available at the time was an adjustable item from Creative Engineering. I've recently begun to wonder if matters might be improved by replacing the dropped spindles with stock items, then lowering the front a bit less and making it ride correctly level by dialling in just a bit of drop on the beam? Or I could chuck away the shock absorbers, wind it down as far as it will go, and shove an expensive air-bag and pump under its nose.

I've driven and ridden in a number of lowered vehicles, and have yet to be impressed by any of them. Some have behaved far worse than others; a particular low spot was a '57 pick-up that looked cooler than cool, but seemed to find bumps and undulations on a road I travel daily and had previously thought of as billiard-table-smooth!

Breakfast pancakes with bacon & maple syrup!

This always looks such a great idea – I found myself constantly tripping over the recipe, and especially the pictures. It's all over the interweb, and now those same glorious images have found their way into the best camping cookbook. I've planned to make this multiple times, and have even had a couple of attempts, including one where I made up a squeezy bottle full of batter mix and took it with me, all ready to squirt into a pan. But it's all such a complete faff …

Who can really be bothered, when the bloke in the camper next door rattles up an easy bacon sandwich in half the time? It's time for a camping cheat!

Ingredients
- Bacon – I used streaky, because I love it
- Ready-made Scotch pancakes, or, as an alternative, the more glamorous-sounding American version
- Maple syrup
- Blueberries
- Natural yoghourt
- A knob of butter

Method
In a reasonable-sized dry pan, cook as much bacon as you fancy until it becomes just crispy. Remove it from the pan onto some sheets of kitchen towel, which will absorb much of the fat, and then wrap it tightly in kitchen foil to keep it warm whilst you tend to the pancakes. There should still be some bacon fat left in the pan, but add a big knob of butter as well and, when it begins to froth, add the pancakes. These cook surprisingly quickly so leave them no longer than about a minute on each side to warm through and to absorb the lovely bacon saltiness.

Remove them from the pan and stack on a couple of plates, cover with lots of rashers of bacon, and then smother the whole lot in maple syrup, yoghourt and blueberries to make it look exotic.

You should eat this with a mug of hot tea, but without any feelings of guilt, because breakfast is apparently still the most important meal of the day and this will set you up until lunchtime.

Levelling blocks

For all my grumbling about having a 'stanced' van, to the cognoscenti it does look reasonably cool, and I can camp in it facing uphill without having to use my levelling blocks.

Levelling blocks are an oddity; they are often seen as a bit nerdy and a relic of the past that's best left for the caravanners. They also seem to take up far more space than they should when you pack them, and they always have to go in last, so they can be first out!

If you can get over the negativity, however, you'll find that they are invaluable. They vastly increase the number of usable pitches at any site, and also take up no room when you are camped, as, even if you don't need them, you can chuck them under the bus and reverse up onto them, just enough to prevent them being nicked.

It's important to remember that you should always – always, without fail – reverse up onto your blocks: it's something to do with leading and trailing shoes in the back brakes. Whatever: if you reverse onto them, the handbrake will hold the bus; if you go up forwards it won't!

Armed with a pair of blocks, you can take the time to level the bus on even some of the more gentle inclines – the sort that you perhaps don't notice at first …

The sort that, after a night's sleep, lead you to you realise that you've just spent eight hours with the blood rushing down into your head, because you've woken with a blinding headache. To avoid long-term brain damage, or at the very least a grumpy morning, feeling like you were up and drinking long into the small hours, you should always sleep with your head higher than your feet.

The photograph shows one of the more inhospitable sites that we've camped on. Amazingly, that was the pitch that had been saved for me by the kindly(?) site owner. If it wasn't for the combination of lowered front suspension and a pair of blocks, we would have been forced to abandon and go home.

Kay-sa-dee-yahs!

Quesadillas are wheat or corn tortillas, filled with a savoury mixture containing cheese and other ingredients, and/or vegetables, then folded in half to form a half-moon shape. This dish originated in Mexico, and the name is derived from 'tortilla' and 'queso' – the Spanish word for cheese.

For minimal effort, these are incredibly filling … but unbelievably moreish!

Ingredients
- Flour tortillas
- Chorizo, sliced and cut into ½in cubes
- Cooked or tinned potato, cut to a similar size
- Onion
- Garlic
- Cheese
- 1tbsp of olive oil

Method
Heat a tablespoon of olive oil in a large pan until hot. Dice the onion and cook it in the oil for about five minutes until it begins to soften, and then add the garlic. I've used a teaspoon of garlic paste, because it's dead easy to use and a jar lasts ages. Combine with the onion and allow it to cook for another couple of minutes or so before adding the diced chorizo and potatoes.

Stir to ensure that all the ingredients are nicely combined, then turn down the heat and continue to cook it for about ten minutes until the oil from the chorizo begins to impart its excellent flavours.

Spoon the meat and potato mixture onto a couple of tortillas, cover with grated, sliced or crumbled cheese, then fold the tortillas over into semi-circle shapes. Wipe the pan with a kitchen towel or similar to remove the majority of the oil, and return the folded tortillas to the hot pan.

Press them down firmly for a moment or two to encourage the cheese to melt and, after a couple of minutes, when they are beginning to become nicely golden, flip them over and repeat with the other side. Cut them in half and serve immediately.

Clean up: this is the sort of food that you can eat from a piece of kitchen towel (as long as you call it a napkin), so there's just a pan, a cutting board and a sharp knife to wash or simply wipe down.

Camp rules & cartwheels

I spy, with my little eye …

The first thing that you will always see on a campsite, without exception, is children doing cartwheels. I don't understand this at all. For obvious reasons, I've never taken any photographs of this phenomenon, but I think it's something to do with a large expanse of grass. Folk arrive and begin to pitch up, and then, as if they've been tightly coiled up for weeks, their kids suddenly pop out of the car and begin cartwheeling involuntarily all over the place. Oddly their parents don't seem in the least concerned. Perhaps they make the journey to school in a similar fashion each morning as well?

The only thing that I do know, is that there don't seem to be any rules forbidding it, which is odd as there are frequently rules which prevent almost everything else. The rules are something we look forward to reading a campsite – we're grown ups, generally we don't behave like idiots. I think we could camp on almost any site, anywhere, without breaking the rules. Occasionally, we are presented with a veritable tome of things that campers must and mustn't do, and we love to chuckle our way through them.

We once visited a site in the middle of nowhere, which itself was just beyond somewhere hidden away in the centre of the Welsh Marches. An area renowned only for its sheer emptiness.

The cheery site owner asked me if I'd be cooking al fresco, and offered to bring over a concrete slab to protect his grass. I thought that was that until I nipped over to do a spot of washing up after dinner. By the sinks and taps, I discovered the most memorable selection of printed and laminated signs that I'd seen for ages.

The one about chiminea fuel was such a chuckle that I had to photograph it for posterity.

It is of course, sad to think of the repeated damage and the obvious frustration that drives site owners to have to spell out what seems blindingly obvious to anyone, with or without cartwheeling kids!

We do sell chiminea fue

For the Minority

Please do __NOT__ Cut, break, tear, rip, pull or in any other way rem
part of any of our trees.

They are __NOT__ to be viewed as a free source of fuel for the chim

The lack of flame they will produce is only disappointing for a w

The damage caused is PERMANANT.

For the Majority

May I apologise for writing this note..

Squaring up to breakfast

Everyone thinks they know what a full English should be, and the overriding thing is that it's a right palaver to make at home, with a warm oven to keep plates and things in. In a field, it's a nightmare: eggs, bacon, sausage, tomato, black pudding, beans, tomato, fried bread … The list is endless, and it all adds up to an absolutely enormous frying pan.

A couple of years back, I found myself camped up with a bunch of Volvo-driving Scottish blokes. Canny or what? There was no messing with these blokes, they simply rattled up some Lorne* sausage and tattie scones, which they served in a morning roll, and that was your lot. I'd always thought that a Scottish breakfast was a cup of tea and a fag, but there is clearly more to it than that.

I live in the heart of the Midlands and, although Lorne sausage is unobtainable locally, I've found a few places on the interweb that will cheerfully post it to me. Disturbingly, the absolute simplicity of this knocks any attempt at making a half decent, full English breakfast whilst camping into a cocked hat.

Ingredients
- Lorne sausage
- Potato scones/cakes/farls
- Scotch morning rolls
- Butter

Method
Melt just a smidgeon of butter in a hot pan and add a couple of slices of sausage. Cook for about three or four minutes, then turn them over and place tatty scones in the pan.

Butter both sides of a split morning roll and, after a couple of minutes, turn over the scone and cook it on the other side. Remove the sausage and potato cake, and place them into the buttered roll.

In this instance, it's not madness to butter a roll and then fill it with fried food; you'd be surprised how disturbingly dry they make their bread rolls north of the border.

*Lorne sausage is reputed to get its name from Tommy Lorne, a famous Scottish comedian from the 1920s. Sadly, it is more likely to have been named after a geographical region in Argyll and Bute.

LEDs are the future.

Fairy lights

Some things really are all about length, and a string of fairy lights is one of them.

Glamping or not, fairy lights really are great. Lighting is an essential part of a quality camping experience, and fairies provide lots of bright and cheap illumination. There are really only two things you need to know about fairy lights: they last twice as long if you set them to flash on and off rather than stay on all the time, and you simply cannot have too many.

You can easily have too few, and frequently you'll see special fairy lights – shaped like Volkswagen campers, tents, flowers, or even fairies – but these are available only in short lengths. Whilst they may look clever and interesting close up, from the other side of the site they simply don't cut the mustard. They just look like a very short length of dim lights. The very best sort of lights are the huge lengths of two or three hundred solar-powered Xmas lights available from places like The Range or B&Q towards the end of each year.

Solar power means that they'll last as long as you need them to after a day out in the sun, and well into the night. You won't have to worry about conserving batteries or switching them on and off. Take a bit of care setting them out; pick up some spider clips on eBay and you'll be able to attach a huge string of them all around your awning or sunshade.

One final tip is to watch how they are packed, the first time out. With a bit of patience, it's possible to put them away in exactly the same manner. This will help them to last a whole lot longer than if you just roll them up and stuff them in a carrier bag. Solar-powered things aren't known for their longevity, but you should easily see a couple of seasons' use from a set.

And then there are LEDs. These are equally cheap and cheerful, can be wired into your camper in a trice, and look simply amazing.

16

Crispy avocado melt

There really should be more vegetarian recipes in this book. I have repeatedly tried to find out what people who don't eat meat actually do cook when they go camping or sit around a barbecue, but they all become very vague. As a result, there's just a handful of ideas to try, but they are all great.

Ingredients
- 4 soft flour tortillas
- A knob of butter
- 8tsp Parmesan cheese (or vegetarian hard cheese alternative), very finely grated
- Cheddar cheese, grated
- 1 ripe avocado
- 8 moist, sun-dried tomatoes, sliced
- A generous handful of posh crisps

Method
Spread one side of each tortilla with soft butter, then sprinkle it evenly with 2tsp of the grated Parmesan so that the cheese will stick to it. Halve the avocado, remove the stone, and slice and mash the flesh inside the skin. If it's properly ripe you won't need to slice it, and you'll be able to simply scoop it out with a teaspoon. Heat a large non-stick pan over a low heat. Place one tortilla into the pan with the parmesan side down. Working quickly, cover the top with half of the cheddar, the sliced sun-dried tomato, the mashed avocado and the crisps. Now top with the second tortilla, this time with the parmesan side up, and press it all together well. Cook it for about two or three minutes on each side, so that the cheddar on the inside melts and sticks everything together. You will need to turn it over, and the easiest way to do that is by pressing an inverted plate down on top. Holding it firmly in position, flip the pan and the plate over so that the tortillas drop onto the plate.

Then carefully slide them back into the pan!

It's ready when the Parmesan becomes crisp and golden, the cheddar is melted and gooey, and the whole thing is stuck together. Remove it from the pan – it'll lift out on a fish slice – cut it into six portions, and serve immediately!

This is a superb vegetarian meal – you'll have them coming back for more.

Looe Bay Farm

Looe Bay Farm is a superb campsite.

Our first visit was entertaining. I hadn't really been paying attention to the directions, and drove us all the way down into Looe, fully expecting to see a sign. There was no sign, because the site is not at Looe, so I drove back to Millendreath, remembering the pictures I'd seen on Google Maps, and fully expecting a narrow lane leading from there up to the site …

There *was* a narrow lane, and with much enthusiasm, I set off up a 1-in-4 hill – that is, a 25 per cent grade incline – which abruptly turned into a footpath. The fair wife was not impressed with my navigational skills.

This, disturbingly, is something that can happen all too frequently on camping holidays: a chap can be wrong. This is a camping fact. A bonus fact can be slipped in here; it's better to admit your error at the first opportunity. Things can, and do, get much worse.

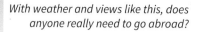

With weather and views like this, does anyone really need to go abroad?

We stopped, we calmed down, we discussed, and we had another go.

We drove far beyond the back of beyond.

The monkey sanctuary is as far as any sane person ever drives – we continued beyond.

We even passed a sign reading 'End of the road.'

Then, suddenly, we had found the campsite at the end of the world.

There was a sign on the wall which said 'If you're unsure where your pitch is, phone Mike.' I phoned Mike.

A voice said, "Look to your left. Can you see that field between the sign and the cliff edge?" I nodded to the phone.

"Park anywhere you like, and I'll be round later to collect some money."

We enjoyed a week there every September, for the best part of ten years.

There were adequate showers and toilets. There was nothing else but the cliff path. Turn left, walk uphill and down dale for miles, and you find yourself on Seaton beach. Turn right, do much the same and you will roll down the steepest hill into The Salutation pub in Looe.

We stopped going only because our dog grew too old to walk the distances involved.

Venison stew

Here's a very simple one-pot stew. Venison is a delicious and very lean alternative to beef or lamb, and for a few months over the winter it is often cheaper than either. If you come across it and the price is right, give it a go.

Ingredients
- 1tbsp oil
- 340g diced venison
- 1 medium onion, diced
- 125g bacon, thickly diced
- A glass of red wine
- 1tbsp cranberry jelly
- 1 beef stock cube
- 1tbsp tomato sauce
- ½tsp dried thyme
- 1tbsp flour
- Boiling water
- Black pepper, to season

Method
Start by boiling the kettle, then put it to one side and heat the oil on the hob in a heavy-bottomed casserole dish.

Add the diced venison and stir it around so that it begins to brown, then add all the other ingredients in something like the order shown above; it's not crucial.

Keep everything moving as you add the various items to ensure that everything is nicely combined. When you add the flour it will suddenly look like it's all gone horribly wrong, but don't worry. Pour over just enough of the boiling water to cover the meat, and then season with lots of freshly-ground black pepper. There's plenty of salt in the bacon – you won't need to add any more. Bring the casserole to the boil, then cover with the lid, turn it right down to a gentle simmer, and leave for two hours.

A one-pot stew always looks a little dull – no matter how great it tastes – so at the insistence of my stylist, and to make the photograph look a little more interesting, I've served this up with a portion of instant mashed potato. I made this with slightly less boiling water than it said on the packet, and a generous teaspoonful of butter.

Smash is a bizarre concept, but it works surprisingly well and a packet will keep in the camper van forever. Alternatively, you could serve it with great big chunks of crusty bread to soak up all that excellent gravy.

The most impractical, yet optimistic, orange camping debacle ever assembled.

FMM 76V

CAUTION WEIRD LOAD

Fun with colour coordination

This is something that everyone with a Volkswagen does at some point, although owners of early bays tend to play it down a bit. I think it's because all of their buses are beige. It also happens less frequently with other, larger motor homes because, like caravans, they are mainly white.

If you've had the good sense to buy a proper late VW, you'll have something in bright red or blue or – the greatest colour of all – orange to play with. For some people it's just a passing phase: buying matching towels, or a set of mugs.

For us, and many others, it became a way of life. We got off to a slightly obsessive start, with a colour-matched motorbike, a little Honda, and even a Trabant that I attempted to A-frame behind the camper van. I can reveal that this was an utter disaster; the steering geometry of the little East German car, for some reason, didn't want to straighten itself, and the Trabbie simply wouldn't follow the camper! Fortunately, I realised this very quickly on a couple of embarrassingly slow test drives around the block.

After the Trabbie fiasco we toned it down a little, but there is nothing that we haven't bought, simply because it's orange and it might look good in the bay: an ancient orange vacuum flask, an orange Mouli grater, multiple picnic and chiller boxes …

We sleep under a quilt cover and pillow cases that we have tie-died in the correct shade, and at the moment we are working our way through a vast stock of orange toilet paper! It's only a bit of fun, but it's great. We seem to have reached the point now where we see something that's available in the correct colour, and wonder not whether it could be fitted in to the camping experience, but how best to change things around to make it work.

For many years, we've used a wine table painted in the exact shade of orange as the bus. It makes an appearance in lots of pictures.

Orange(?) chicken fajitas

This was an attempt at making orange food to go with my orange bus, and, although there were some orange ingredients and an orange grater involved in its creation, I think you can say that I failed!

Ingredients
- 2 chicken breasts, cut into thin slices
- 2 orange peppers, seeded and finely sliced
- 1 onion, finely sliced
- A good splash of oil
- Flour tortillas
- Onion rings and grated cheese, to serve

For the fajita spices
- 2tbsp corn flour
- 2tsp chilli powder
- 1tsp paprika
- 1tsp castor sugar
- 1tsp onion salt
- ¾tsp cumin
- ½tsp garlic powder
- ½tsp cayenne pepper

For the simple guacamole
- 2 Haas avocados
- 1tsp garlic paste

Method
Begin before leaving home by preparing the fajita mix: combine all of the spices in one of those little plastic pots that the pickles from the Indian takeaway come in, or you can cheat and buy a pot or sachet of ready-made fajita spices. This is a meal to make in a big pan; here I've used my trusty old Beauclaire. It's all but identical to a Cadac – an outdoor gas-powered griddle.

Start by heating a drop of oil. Place the frozen – or, in all likelihood, defrosted – battered onion rings around the outside. These will warm through gradually and just need turning once.

Add the sliced onions to the centre of the cooking surface and cook for about five minutes, until beginning to soften. While this is happening, you have time to prepare a very simple guacamole by cutting the avocados in half, scooping out the flesh and mixing together with the garlic paste.

Then add the peppers and chicken to the onions, sprinkle the seasoning mix over everything and stir well to combine. Place a couple of tortillas on the top to warm through.

Keep everything moving around over the heat. It's done when the chicken is cooked through, which will only take about ten minutes. Serve rolled up in the tortillas with lots of grated cheese; the guacamole and onion rings served on the side.

Camping myths & legends debunked!

If you search the inter-google for camping hints and tips that 'you absolutely must know' – the sort of camping essentials that you forget at your peril – you will doubtless come across the hoary old chestnut that says, 'you can afford to forget most things, as there's a workaround: but in the name of sanity, don't forget to take a corkscrew.'

Why? Can anyone really remember the last time they bought a bottle of wine without a screw top?

I can see the chap at the back waving with his fine bottle of 1961 Château Latour, and I totally agree with you, sir, but do you really think that – glamping or not, and possibly with an element of hindsight – you are really cut out for this roughing-it-in-a-field sort of lifestyle?

Similarly, the venerable bottle-opener. The majority of festivals have a total ban on glass, which pretty much dictates that all of your beer, lager and cider will be in cans. The bottle opener can also stay at home.

Then there's, 'my awning/sunshade/windbreak came with all the correct tent-pegs.'

No, it didn't. It came with a bag of the cheapest pegs that just might enable it to stay up at a pinch. You'd be pretty annoyed if it didn't come with any pegs, but the ones in the bag were selected personally by the company's chief cost accountant.

Penny-pinching is too generous a term. Buy yourself a decent set of proper pegs before you try to use whatever came free.

And BBQ tools: why would anyone ever buy extra-long barbie tools, particularly the ones that come in their own super carrying bag holster? Unless you are attempting to smelt iron, there's no need to have a barbecue so hot that you need a pair of three foot tongs to lift something off it. Then there's the luxury leather tool roll that they all come in – where are you going to find the space to store it? Just wait until the BBQ is at the correct temperature and use a knife and fork!

On the next page are a couple of camping cookery myths debunked …

Cheat's chilli taco surprise!

Ingredients
- 1 tin of chilli con carne
- 1 bag of Doritos for each diner
- A couple of ounces of grated cheese

Method

This is the one where you make a chilli in a bag. The theory is that you spoon a tin of chilli that you've heated up into an opened packet of Doritos, then sprinkle some grated cheese over the hot meat. Then, as it melts, eat it directly from the bag with a spoon or a fork. It takes only a moment to make, there's minimal clear up, and it tastes okay, although you'll notice that I haven't included a picture of the finished dish.

'Too hot to handle'

That's because when the bag was full of chilli, it was too hot to hold: the chilli is all at the top with the cheese, and the corn chips are all at the bottom!

It wasn't as good as I'd hoped. It was ludicrously hot and very ordinary. It was something a bit different, and kept me entertained for ten minutes, but I won't bother making it again.

Super easy camping omelettes

Ingredients (per omelette)
- 2 eggs
- Cheese, grated or thinly sliced
- 1tbsp of tinned fried onions!
- 1 slice of ham
- 'Microwave steam cooking bags'

Method

Boil up a saucepanful of water. Then break the eggs into the bag, and add the cheese, ham and fried onions. Scrunch everything up together with your fingers to mix it well, seal the bag, and place it carefully into the pan of boiling water to simmer for about 10 minutes.

But what is the point?

It produced an omelette, it tasted okay, and I have to concede that – once again – it was a bit of fun.

Surely, though, isn't an omelette just about the fastest meal that it's possible to create, using the traditional method involving just a hot pan and some butter? At a pinch, this would work in a boil-safe polythene bag, but unless you have to simultaneously make lots of different flavoured eggy feasts, it's completely pointless.

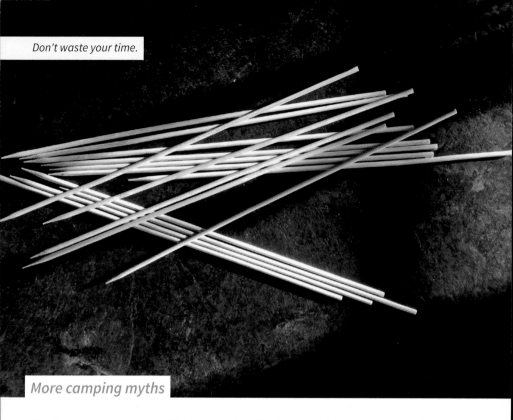

More camping myths

'Gazebos make a good alternative to an awning.' No, they don't. Have you ever wondered why campsites charge a quid for an awning, but a fiver for a gazebo? It's because awnings are designed to be erected in a field and used for camping.

Gazebos are far flimsier, and intended to be used in the relative shelter of a back garden. The reason for the extra cost is that 50 per cent of gazebos pitched on campsites over the season will be wrecked by the wind, and subsequently dumped in a skip for the site owner to dispose of.

This next one is a cracker and you'll find this all over the interweb: 'always soak your wooden skewers in water, so that they don't burn.' Have you tried to do this? Whatever container you use to soak them in, they'll simply bob up and float on the top. Nothing will soak into them, they will not become saturated, and it will make absolutely no difference at all.

The real tip is: 'if your wooden skewers are burning, it's because your barbecue is *too hot!*' Take the food off the rack, put it back onto a plate, and cover it with a tea towel. Relax with a can of cold lager and, after a quarter of an hour or so, it'll be ready for you to have another go!

It's possible that you will be astounded. The saving in the food that you won't have to throw away because of this one simple tip should go some way to paying for this modest volume.

Finally, 'beer can chicken' is another tip that turns up everywhere: 'if you want to cook a super moist chicken on a BBQ, just shove half a can of beer up the egg-laying end of the bird and stand it upright.'

Not only will the bird fall over the moment your back is turned, but the beer will spill all over the bird and will *also* extinguish your barbecue!

On the next page is a far better way to cook a nicely moist bird on a disposable BBQ …

Sunny chicken (GF)

This is a bit of fun. It's an interesting way to get far more out of a disposable barbecue than should really be possible.

Ingredients
- A copy of *The Sun* (other papers are available)
- 4tsp mixed green herbs
- 1 small chicken
- Salt and black pepper, freshly ground
- Olive oil
- 1 onion, thinly sliced
- A disposable BBQ

Method

Remove all packaging and light the barbecue. Leave it for a good 20 minutes or so to reach a usable working temperature. Open the newspaper at the centre pages. It's possible that you could create a slightly more interesting meal if you were to use a copy of *The Guardian* …

Spatchcock the bird by turning it upside down and removing the spine, using scissors to cut along both sides of it. Inside the cavity, you'll see a diamond-shaped piece of cartilage on the sternum. Slice through this with a sharp knife, and the chicken will simply fall open.

Splash some olive oil, and make a bed of onion and herbs on the newspaper for the bird to lie on.

Rub the chicken all over with more olive oil and season well, inside and out. Place the opened bird in the middle of the newspaper and scatter over the remaining onion and herbs. Drizzle with yet more olive oil.

Now wrap the newspaper around the chicken and secure it well with either butcher's twine or a length of wire – lesser string will burn.

Soak the package well; drop it into a bucket of water if you can, then squeeze out the excess water and place the damp parcel onto the barbecue. After about 30 minutes, turn it over and leave for about another hour, or until the barbecue goes out. Take care unwrapping the bird, as much of the paper will have turned to ash. Shake off as much of the ash as you can, or you will have to pick it out of your meal.

This creates a lovely moist chicken: cut it into quarters and serve very simply with crusty bread, posh crisps, and coleslaw or a prepared salad.

Less is sometimes more, so very much more ...

Although I don't advocate going to quite this extreme! This was really the sum total of someone's camping equipment for a couple of days at the Southwold campsite on the Suffolk coast. A young woman and her child were dropped off, presumably by her parents, and this is all that she pulled out of the hat for the pair of them!

Surprisingly, the weather was kind to them both, although various things did blow about the site, and were regularly returned by a selection of kindly people with astonished expressions. At the other end of the scale, we've been pitched up in the bay during quite atrocious wind and rain, and witnessed blokes living and sleeping under little more than a tarpaulin.

As always, moderation is the key. There isn't the need to pare things right down to the bone when you have the carrying capacity of a camper van. There is, however, a huge amount of lightweight and ultra-lightweight camping equipment available. A bonus side effect of the reduction in weight is its corresponding reduction in size. The best example of this that we've taken on board is the humble towel. We used to pack ourselves a couple of bath towels. We'd stuff them into a cupboard, and it would be completely full in an instant. Drying the things would take all afternoon and was a complete pain. It took far too long before we saw a chap produce, with a flourish, a microfibre towel from a string bag the size of my fist.

It was my turn for the astonished expression – I didn't know that teeny tiny towels were even a thing! The saving in weight and capacity is one thing; the ability of the towel to work as a towel and then drip dry in the lightest of light breezes is another.

Lightweight camping items are a game-changer. Things like this simply didn't exist when our camper van was first designed, and I don't even think they were available back in the '90s when we began playing the camping game.

Monte Cristo

This is the ultimate killer sandwich; it looks
and feels like it should have more calories
than the rest of the recipes put together. It is
spectacular, and should probably come with a
government health warning.

Ingredients (per sandwich)
- Three slices of white bread
- Pre-packed sliced turkey
- Pre-packed sliced ham
- Exotic cheese with holes
- American (Kraft) cheese

For the coating
- A couple of eggs
- A splash of milk
- Black pepper, freshly ground
- Oil for frying

Method
The best Monte Cristo sandwich begins life the day before
it is to be eaten. Start by assembling the ingredients in the
following order: on top of the first slice of bread, place a
slice of the cheese with the holes, and a slice of the turkey.
Then, another slice of bread, a slice of ham, a slice of
American cheese, and, finally, the third slice of bread.

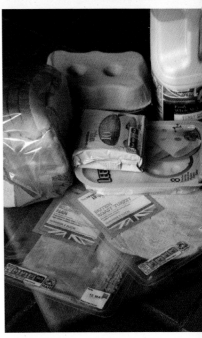

Wrap the whole lot as tightly as you can in cling film,
then place it between two chopping boards and squash
it as flat as you can. Leave the sandwich in the fridge
overnight, placed underneath a chopping board and lots
of heavy cans to keep it as flat as you can.

To serve it up the following day, heat up about three
quarters of an inch of oil in a pan. Meanwhile beat two
eggs in a bowl with a splash of milk and a generous twist
of black pepper. Cut the sandwiches in half diagonally,
and dip them into the beaten egg mixture. Make sure that
they are well covered. Carefully, using a fish slice or similar, lower them into the very hot oil. Cook
for just 3 minutes on each side.

Remove onto kitchen towel and allow them to rest for a couple of moments. Serve on a plate
and eat with a knife and fork. These really are astonishing! They're amazingly light and fluffy,
with lots of melty cheesy inside a crispy shell, and yet they probably contain little more than 700
calories.

Packing

A chap about to go camping simply cannot have too many lists.

One of the best things about a camper van is that it can always be maintained ready to go, filled with all the essentials, in readiness for the apocalyptic four-minute warning, the first murmurings of peak oil crisis, or the inevitable zombie invasion. It should be possible to simply throw in food and water, bedding and clothes, and hit the road – although recent events have revealed that in the event of anything apparently less severe than this, a global pandemic for example, it is simply unacceptable to head for the hills in a camper.

This list makes for a useful starting point that you can further refine, but these are the things that you should aim to leave packed in the bus at all times. Additional items are packed on a trip-by-trip basis. Take your time compiling these things; in the early days you'll take stuff from the house, but, as your camping skills develop, you'll find yourself buying things. Nice, quality things specifically to use in the van.

Packing clothes is a skill. We have friends who pack a suitcase with clothes and bedding, and can be on the road in seconds, but they find themselves spending a fortnight with 'secondary storage dilemma.' Remember those cool cassette holders in 1980s Fords? What did you do with all the original cases?

Rather than fold and pile up all of your garments like you do in drawers at home, roll them tightly and secure with rubber bands or masking tape. Not only can you get much more in, you can also see all the ends of the rolls, so can more easily identify garments from the pile. And the very best bit? The clothes come out and unroll to be far less creased than they would have been if they'd been folded and piled up.

The joy of an empty camper on site – see page 40.

Packing list

The essentials to pack and forget about:

Crockery: plates; dishes; mugs; plastic glasses; tea towels. **Cutlery & kitchen:** knives; forks; spoons; sharp knife; spatula; long necked lighter; basting brush; double skillet; micro stove; kettle; cafetiere; chopping board; washing up bowl, liquid and cloths; scotch cloth; rubber gloves; kitchen spray; kitchen towel. **Dog:** bowl; dried food; lead; snack; toy; ground screw; poo bags; water. **Toilet:** toilet; bog roll; spare bog roll; emergency bog roll; toilet chemicals; toothpaste; toothbrush; soap; antiperspirant; towels; headache tablets; wind tablets; prescription tablets; and your partner's mysterious bag of tricks! **BBQ:** barbecue; emergency disposable BBQ; emergency matches; gas bottle; gas pipe; skewers. **Food:** coffee; tea bags; sugar; salt and pepper; mixed herbs; oil; tinned and dried food (to this you must add food according to your planned menu: water; milk; bread; meat; salad). **Camping equipment** (can be left permanently in situ): awning; gazebo; sunshade; lamps; torch; tables and chairs; umbrella; windbreak; tent pegs and mallet. **Tools:** I am no mechanic and, if things go wrong, I call out a little man with a load of spanners and a flat bed truck. That said, in the bus I always leave: oil and jug; jump leads. **Bedding** (needs to be packed on a trip-by-trip basis or it will go damp. Tick them off as you pack them): sleeping bag or duvet; pillows; blanket; mattress; fitted sheet. **Clothes:** underwear; t-shirts; thick woolly jumper; spare trousers; waterproof coat; sandals; wellies.

Finally, you can pack the glove box with all the things that you'll have to constantly check and re-check that you've not forgotten as you drive along: money; wallet; tickets; sunglasses; phone; car keys; house keys. You don't need to buy all the permanent things in one go. You will gradually duplicate stuff without really trying. A can opener, for example, will only be forgotten once, and you'll just buy a replacement wherever you are. Don't automatically buy a cheap, poorly-made 'camping' version. Have a look around for an interesting lightweight item, or whatever, but buy a quality tool that works well and that you'll enjoy using. The corkscrew in our bus – while not vital (see page 22) – is far nicer to use than the decorative effort we have at home, and we found it on the boundary of a cricket pitch.

The Steve Freer Memorial Toilet in all its battered glory!

Porta Potti

One bog to rule them all,
One bog to find them,
One bog to bring them all,
And in the darkness bind them.
– As JRR Tolkien probably wrote, whilst camping beside the Cherwell.

With a Porta Potti, there is only the One Unspoken Rule.

With the benefit of hindsight, we didn't have a toilet in the camper for a ludicrously long time. This was due to nothing more, really, than the yuck factor. I'm a bit of a blokey bloke, and at the time I worked with a fleet of lorry drivers. I was reasonably content in the knowledge that 'it is legal for a male to urinate in public, as long it is on the rear wheel of his motor vehicle and his right hand is on the vehicle.' Unbelievably, I managed to placate the fair wife with this pearl of wisdom for much longer that I expected. Then, one day at work, one of the chaps was selling off his all-but-unused camping gear. Apparently he had tried it, but camping and caravanning simply hadn't agreed with him or his wife. And so it came to pass that I became the only bloke I have ever met who bought a secondhand, but apparently barely-used, toilet.

Bizarre isn't it? I refused for years to buy a Porta Potti because it would be a bit yucky, and then I bought a secondhand one! Curiously, the old Potti managed to outlast its vendor. The 'Steve Freer Memorial Toilet' – as it then became known – was a game-changer for us. No longer did we have to drag ourselves outside and across the site, or around the back of the bus. We just bobbed out of our warm bed, and when I eventually learned to relax and sit down on it …

Looking back, it was utterly stupid of us not to have had a Porta Potti for so long. I have no idea what the blue chemical is, but it reduces toilet paper to liquid and everything just pours away without fuss and bother.

As I may have mentioned at the beginning, there really is just the One Unspoken Rule …

Pulled pork (GF)

Pulled pork is a bit of a treat.

Cooking a large joint of meat on a barbecue works incredibly well if you have the time and a quiet spot where you can leave the barbecue unattended. Consequently, it's something I've only cooked whilst on holiday – well away from crowds of excitable festival-goers.

This makes enough to feed at least six, and probably a lot more, but we just used it in sandwiches for the next couple of effortless days.

Ingredients
- 1.5kg rolled pork shoulder
- 1tbsp paprika
- 1tbsp brown sugar
- 1tsp salt

Method
Light a generously-fuelled barbecue and leave it for a good 20 minutes or so to reach a usable temperature. Meanwhile, cut through the strings holding the pork together and remove the skin or rind using a sharp knife. Mix together the paprika, brown sugar and salt, and, using your hands, rub the seasoning into the meat. Roll the joint loosely back together, but don't bother re-tying it. Place the pork directly onto the cooking rack and brown it on all sides, turning it regularly with a carving fork. When it all begins to look delicious, remove it from the heat, wrap it in two layers of foil, replace it on the barbie, close the lid and relax. We left it to its own devices and went for a walk to the pub. When we returned almost four hours later, the fire was all out but everything was still warm, so I left it for another hour.

The cooking time is not crucial – it should just be long and uninterrupted. The secret is in the foil's ability to keep in all the steam and moisture; if you peek in early, it simply won't work. When you finally unwrap the pork, you'll discover a joint of meat that really does pull apart using only a couple of forks. Some of the meat towards the bottom may be slightly burnt – just call it caramelised – pull it apart with the rest of the joint and enjoy the extra flavour that it adds.

Fun with tent pegs

If you have anything that needs to be pegged down to the ground, it doubtless arrived with a small selection of flimsy little pegs. You should think about changing these to something far more substantial at the first opportunity, before you bend just one too many at a crucial moment in the back of beyond.

Although we've not tried a huge variety of pegs, the ones that we have kept on using are the type that are little more than a nine-inch nail with a green plastic collar around the top. These are a lot heavier than I would like, but I don't have the patience or the refined motor skills to deal with lightweight aluminium or titanium pegs.

No matter how ham-fisted I am, I seldom manage to bend one. By later upgrading the delicate little rubber mallet that I was advised to buy, I swapped something the size and weight of a toffee hammer for a proper two-pound ball pein hammer. This thing takes no prisoners, and in a trice upgraded my pegs to fully-fledged rock pegs. These go into the roughest ground and they stay there. I also have half a dozen 'delta pegs,' which are curious triangular nylon devices. Again, I haven't managed to break one, and their clever design means that the wind pulls them in a slightly different plane to the one in which they're embedded in the ground. These work particularly well in very wet, muddy fields, and although they can occasionally be seen to have moved, I have never had one come out in well over ten years.

I've recently become tempted to invest in, or at least temporarily borrow, some screw-in pegs that you embed in the earth in an instant using a drill. I'm fundamentally a bit low-tech at heart, and don't actually own a rechargeable drill. Bearing in mind that I had to replace my smartphone with something much simpler because I couldn't remember to keep it charged, I don't think I'll bother!

Chicken fusion tagine (GF)

I've made many attempts at creating a decent Moroccan stew – this is by far the simplest and best, and occurred as the result of a very fortunate freak accident. The chickpea dhal had been in the bus for ages, unloved and unwanted, until one hungry evening when we used it as a filler to go with chicken fillets. Originally that was to be that, but the only rice we had in the camper was Mediterranean. Its addition suddenly moved a nominally Indian dish closer to the borders of the African continent. A note was duly made, and the next time we cooked it, apricots were added and a killer dish was born.

Ingredients

- A knob of butter
- 1 medium onion, finely diced
- 1tsp garlic paste
- 2 chicken fillets, cut into 1cm cubes
- 1 can of chickpea dhal
- 50g dried apricots, chopped
- 1 pack of Mediterranean rice

Method

This is the sort of dish that can be cooked inside the camper without fear of spitting oil or fat, and minimal chances of lingering smells.

Begin by gently heating up a knob of butter in a pan until it starts to foam. Add the finely diced onion and sweat it over a medium heat before adding a teaspoon of garlic paste. Turn down the heat still further, until the onion turns translucent. Increase the heat slightly, add the chicken and stir everything together. Cook for ten minutes, stirring occasionally until the chicken begins to colour. Scrape in the can of chickpea dhal – this drops out in chunks, so stir it all together – and cook for two or three minutes until the dhal is softened and everything becomes as one. Add the packet of rice, loosened as per the instructions, and the dried, chopped apricots.

Give everything a final stir and serve up.

Sadly, one-pot dishes always look a little dull. My food stylist wanted to add a riot of green herbs, which in reality would have added nothing. The dish is spectacularly filling, and given its apparently mismatched ingredients, is a veritable taste sensation!

A fridge is a total game-changer: pack it well.

The fridge

If your bus doesn't already have a fridge, you should invest in one as soon as you possibly can.

Our bus originally came equipped with what was described as a 'cool box' – a clever little cupboard in the corner with a plastic dish thing on the top. The idea was that you filled the dish with water, which in turn, presumably filled passageways running around the cupboard until you were left with a pool of water on top. This water evaporated over the course of the day, and then the scientific bit involved the evaporation drawing heat from its environment causing the little cupboard to stay cool. Which it did, to a point … It was only ever relatively cool, and never properly cold, so the number of mornings we awoke to stinky milk became a little depressing. There is only so much food that a chap can throw into campsite hedgerows before anyone else gets up without beginning to get upset. I reached that point whilst enjoying cottage cheese on my cornflakes just once too often.

Enough was enough – we bought ourselves a teeny tiny little gas-powered fridge that fitted snugly into the gap vacated by the cooler. The difference that this apparently simple device made to our lives was incalculable, it really was a total game-changer. Originally, going to a three-day festival meant eating a mountain of fresh food on day one, a load of defrosted food on day two, and then chucking out everything else and buying food from burger bars on the final day. Now we could relax, safe in the knowledge that we could take anything we didn't eat back home with us, and could pick and choose what to eat and when to eat it. Recipes have become more adventurous, and we enjoy icy cold lager and the occasional exotic cocktail. We even managed to be completely self-sufficient for food over the full five days of the Glastonbury festival. When parked up in a field, miles from anywhere, fridges are worth their weight in gold – this is a camping fact.

Lamb koftas

Here's a tasty alternative to burgers that's just as easy to cook, and has only four ingredients. Because I'm lazy, instead of serving koftas as a sausage shape, cooked on a wooden skewer, I made them into oval discs and cooked them like burgers. Far less mess.

Use a disposable barbie and there's practically nothing to clear up: everything can just be thrown away apart from your knife and teaspoon.

Ingredients
- 400g minced lamb
- 2tsp garlic powder
- 2tsp dried coriander
- 1tsp dried cumin

To serve
- Pitta bread
- Rocket or other posh lettuce
- Mint sauce

Method
Light the BBQ and leave it to warm through for a good 20 or 30 minutes. While you are waiting, mix the herbs and spices into the minced lamb using your fingers. Traditionally, this is done in a bowl, but it's just as easy to do in the polythene bag or tray that the mince comes in.

Divide the mixture into four balls and, using your fingers again, make them into flat, pitta bread-sized patties, and make a depression in the centre with your thumb. Cook on the barbecue rack for about ten minutes, turning once. Splash the pittas with water and place them onto the BBQ for a few moments until they swell ready to split, then fill with the meat, a handful of rocket and lots of mint sauce. I sometimes make this by stirring a teaspoonful of traditional British mint sauce into a small carton of natural yoghourt, but I found something very similar, ready-made in the corner-shop, so I've used that instead.

Stick your thumb in it?
There aren't many rules for making successful homemade burgers, but you should remember to make them slightly thinner in the middle than at the edges. This is because they like to plump up when you cook them. You can spend some time doing it evenly and aesthetically or, like me, you can just dob your thumb in it!

Kelly Kettle meets COBB

Here's a clever trick for all those who enjoy playing with fire!

As barbecues go, the COBB heats up relatively fast, is ready to use in around 20 minutes, and is incredibly easy to light. This is in contrast to the Kelly Kettle that I treated myself to a few years ago and really struggled to do much with. A new KK apparently leaks from all of the soldered seams until a bit of soot and tar has built up to seal them: I lit the fire, the seams leaked, the water ran into the fire pit, and the fire went out: brilliant! I was well and truly stuck in the proverbial 'cleft stick.'

Then, whilst enjoying a quiet pint one day, I was taught an incredible technique – the unlikely fusion of two disparate camping tools – by an elderly, canal-dwelling couple sat at an adjacent table. In what can best be described as a flash of inspiration, they told me how they'd used the warming stage of their COBB to boil a Kelly Kettle.

It's so obvious!

They put the two things together. I have owned and used both of those things for a decade – why in the name of all things air-cooled had I not thought of such a thing?

In a brilliant bit of lateral thinking, they simply placed the kettle on top of the charcoal basket in place of the cooking surface, and have made it a BBQ-lighting chimney. The conical shape of the KK chimney draws a blast of air through the coals, has the flames roaring in a matter of moments, and, as a by-product, produces a litre-and-a-half of boiling water!

Unbelievably clever, and, like all the best ideas, amazingly simple. The kettle is probably more stable on the charcoal basket than on its own base.

Barbecued Buffalo wings   (GF)

In much the same way as buffalo do not actually have wings, Buffalo Sauce originates from Buffalo, a city in New York State, and has nothing to do with cattle. With that in mind, it adds a great flavour. This appears to be a huge quantity for just two people, but there's barely any meat on them! 60 per cent of this will be thrown away, but cooking chicken on the bone helps to infuse the meat with a strength and intensity of flavour that you simply don't get when it has been filleted.

Ingredients
- 750g chicken wings
- 50g butter
- 1tsp garlic paste
- 1tsp sugar
- 1tbsp Tabasco sauce
- 2tsp Worcestershire sauce

Method
As always, light the barbecue to enable it to reach a usable temperature before you add any food. Make up the sauce by combining the garlic, sugar, Tabasco and Worcestershire sauces into an almost empty carton of soft butter. Stir everything to combine it thoroughly.

Using a sharp knife, separate the wings into two at the joint. Place them onto the BBQ rack, well away from the source of direct heat – I placed them all around the outside of my COBB. Using a brush, paint the sauce onto the wings, cover them with the lid, and relax with a glass of fine ale.

These are simplicity itself to cook on a barbie, they just need to be turned over and basted with the remaining sauce every fifteen minutes or so. You're adding moisture and butter every time, and after about an hour they will be done to succulent perfection – crisp and slightly charred on the outside, yet tender and moist on the inside.

Buffalo wings are traditionally served with a blue cheese dip – I also served up a selection of ready-made dipping sauces intended to accompany Mexican food. What had initially looked like far too many wings were soon gone in just a few, deliciously silent, minutes.

Multiple guy lines provide an easy solution to an age-old problem.

How to fasten down a sunshade – properly!

Sunshades can make a very lightweight and far more practical alternative to a fully-fledged awning. The secret is knowing how to make them work. All manner of camping companies make and sell them. Similarly, all sorts of people buy them and use them just a couple of times before leaving them at home, because they always blow down.

They are essentially all much of a muchness: there's the fabric sunshade itself, which is a sheet of cotton or nylon with some reinforced holes for a couple of poles. Then there are a couple of guy lines to support the outside end, and a method of attaching it to your camper at the other.

I have always used a figure-of-eight rubber to attach mine to the gutter, but a pole and clamps would work equally well.

The problem with the thing blowing down always occurs at the end supported by the poles and guy lines. The instructions suggest that you should put it up so that the pole is vertical and the guy line runs to ground at an angle. If you erect it like this, it will blow down.

However, try setting up the pole so that it's almost as long as it will go, and angle it at about 30 degrees to the vertical, then use two guy lines on each of the poles, with both arranged at roughly 30 degrees. Then, if you arrange it so that the bottom of the pole and the tent pegs that secure the guy lines form the shape of an equilateral triangle on the ground, your sunshade will never blow down again.

You will doubtless have to buy a couple of additional guy lines, which you should use in combination with a handful of decent-quality tent pegs, but coming back to find your sunshade in a heap on the ground will be a thing of the past.

Barefoot biryani

A good curry makes a superb meal, but it can sometimes be a swine to make a decent one given the constraints of a camper van in a field. Just boiling enough water to drain the rice properly is the first of your problems. I stumbled across this recipe, which claims to be a simple biryani but which I feel is much closer to a decadent keema rice. Whatever it really is, it makes a very simple, great-looking meal (which is unusual for a single-pan dish), in about half an hour.

Ingredients

- 1 onion, finely diced
- 125g lamb mince
- 1tsp garlic paste
- 3tsp rogan josh paste
- 125g basmati rice
- 125ml stock, made up with a vegetable stock cube
- 80g frozen peas
- Black pepper, freshly ground
- Mint raita and fresh coriander, coarsely chopped, to serve

Method

Into a pre-heated and heavy-bottomed pan add a teaspoon of butter and the diced onion. After a few moments, add a teaspoonful of garlic paste. Stir everything together well, and then add the lamb. This will yield enough extra fat to cook everything else, and will also impart its spectacular flavour. After about ten minutes or so, mix in the rogan josh paste, stir everything together well and cook for another couple of minutes. Then stir in the rice, pour over the stock and quickly bring everything to a boil. Cover with the lid, turn down the heat, and continue to cook over a medium heat for ten minutes. Then, finally, add the frozen (or more likely by now defrosted) peas, stir into the mixture and replace the lid. Remove the pan from the heat and leave it to rest for five minutes.

Give everything a really good stir, season with lots of freshly ground black pepper, and serve up the meat and rice mixture onto a couple of plates. As a decorative touch, you can scatter it with the freshly-chopped coriander, and lashings of mint raita in artistically-daubed stripes!

Possibly the largest awning in the world?

The best awning is no awning at all

Way back in the last century, when we first bought the camper, we soon spent more money on an awning that we could fasten to the side to create more space …

We've subsequently experienced the 'joy' brought about by no fewer than four awnings. We started with a traditional frame tent style, which was made of something akin to canvas and weighed a metric tonne. This was followed by a huge 'space-saver tunnel,' which turned itself into scrap after just ten erections when a small component – apparently made from unobtainium – failed, rendering the entire construct incapable of remaining upright. We then invested in yet another which was okay, but, after pitching camp and nipping to a nearby pub for a pleasant hour or so, we returned to find that it had blown down and all our possessions were scattered far and wide. We currently own a small, single-hoop inflatable.

They've all been okay, but we tended to sit outside our awning, rather than outside our camper, as the awning inevitably filled up with the extra stuff that we felt obliged to take with us. We even had a pop-up bookcase at one point! It's what's known in plumbing circles as a vicious circlip.

Finally, we rejected awnings completely in favour of just a lightweight sunshade and a pop-up tent. Originally one of those dreadful round, self-erecting things that leapt out of its bag and pitched itself about five feet away from where I intended, we've since upgraded to a different design that folds away much smaller, has a proper inner tent, and unfurls like a huge umbrella.

Now we can pack the bus really tightly for travel, knowing that when we arrive at the campsite, not only will it only take five minutes or so to pitch, but when we've flung everything out of the van and into the pop-up tent, we'll be left with a pleasingly empty camper, furnished with just a dog bowl, a couple of glasses of wine, and a bowl of elegant canapés.

Spicy chicken picnic burritos

Everyone has seen these: they sell them in KFC, the bloke on Man vs Food loves them … but I couldn't make mine stay together. No matter what I did, there was chicken and rice all over the place whenever I tried to lift one to my mouth – and then, a Eureka moment. It's the foil that holds them together! A superb picnic treat that, sadly, is only suitable for preparing at home, within comfortable reach of hot running water.

Ingredients
- 1 large chicken fillet
- 25g rolled oats
- 1tsp paprika
- 1 egg, beaten
- 1tbsp flour
- 1 packet microwave 'Mexican' rice
- Flour tortillas
- Greaseproof paper and tinfoil.
- Yoghourt and mint sauce, to taste

Method
Wrap the chicken fillet in cling film and beat it viciously with a rolling pin until it's about half an inch thick. Remove the film and dip the flattened fillet – the escalope – into three shallow dishes containing, in turn: the flour, the beaten egg, and finally the mixed oats and paprika. Shallow fry for about five minutes on each side, whilst simultaneously microwaving (or otherwise preparing) the rice according to the instructions on the packet.

Place a couple of tortillas onto two slightly larger pieces of waxed paper and tinfoil, and cover each with half the rice and the chicken escalope sliced into half-inch-wide strips. Add mint sauce to taste and roll up the tortilla. Immediately wrap up the whole lot in the paper and then the tinfoil, making certain that you tuck in both ends tightly. It will stay held together and remain warm for a surprisingly long time. I packed ours into a trusty old Lakeland 'cool bag' with a bottle of hot water.

If you take these to a picnic, there is just the tinfoil to dispose of. The multiple dishes used for preparation, with the sticky egg and oats, can just be left out for your partner to clear up when you get home!

Equipment

My cooking equipment is not particularly comprehensive or exotic. In addition to the Fellows stove that was built into our camper back in the 1970s, there's normally only a very small camping stove and kettle, my double skillet and heat diffuser, and an emergency disposable barbecue on board. The two items that I use for the majority of the food I cook can be seen throughout these pages, and consist of a COBB barbecue and a Beauclaire gas-powered griddle. Anything else that I occasionally use, such as the wok or the ridged, square pan, are brought from home as and when they are specifically required.

I've had the COBB for almost 20 years; it's a fine piece of kit, but can be a pig to clean. I never really got on with the standard cooking surface that came with it, so I bought some expensive accessories in the form of a wire rack and a non-stick 'frying pan,' which both suit me much better.

The Beauclaire appears to be very similar to a Cadac, although I've never actually used one. In a similar fashion to the VHS/Betamax dichotomy, it looks like I backed the wrong horse, as I've not seen another one for sale in years. My choice was made in part by the manufacturer selling off a load with faulty legs very cheap – not that it really matters, I have never used the legs, as I always put it on a table. There's not much to it besides a cast-iron griddle pan, which is incredibly heavy. There's also a cast-iron gas container to lug about with it. It heats up in about three minutes, is seldom blown out by the wind, and doesn't seem to mind being stuffed in a thick polythene bag to be cleaned when I get home!

Anything else that I need, such as a microwave, I pack and take with me as required by my menu plans.

A proper winter warmer, and something to look forward to as the camping season draws to a close – just as the shooting season begins! This is a proper sit-down meal that you can cook inside your bus on the built-in hob as the summer evenings begin to draw in.

Ingredients

- 1 pheasant
- A splash of sunflower oil
- 1 glass of white wine
- 1 apple, roughly chopped
- 1 onion, roughly chopped
- 1tbsp strawberry jam
- 2 wine glasses of vegetable stock
- Mixed herbs
- 1 wine glass of double cream
- Salt and pepper, to season

Method

Begin by jointing the bird. This is actually much easier than you'd think: simply cut down each side of the spine with a large pair of scissors, remove the spine, and the pheasant will practically fall apart in your hands. Snip through the flesh that still holds on the legs, and finally through the centre of the breast bone. Heat the oil in a large

That's home-made strawberry jam in the pickle jar.

heavy-bottomed pan, and add the four pheasant joints, turning regularly until they are browned on all sides. Then add the roughly chopped onion and apple, a good dollop of strawberry jam, two glasses of vegetable stock and a glass of white wine. Season well with salt and pepper and mixed herbs, stir the whole lot thoroughly and bring to the boil. Turn the heat right down until the stew is bubbling very, very gently. Cover the pan and relax with another couple of glasses of wine whilst the pan simmers for a good hour.

Finally, remove the joints of pheasant from the pan and stir the double cream into the sauce to thicken it. I forgot to take any potatoes, so accompanied mine with two varieties of tinned beans, which I simply warmed through in a second pan.

Clear up

You can't get away with serving this in a bit of kitchen towel: it needs to be done properly on real plates with knives and forks. So there's all that, but there's only really two pans and a chopping board involved in the actual preparation.

Words fail me now, as they failed me then!

Smashed roof

More recently than I care to remember, I picked a glorious sunny morning to drive my camper van out into the street. Here, I popped up the elevating roof and leisurely fitted a new sparkly door curtain to the underside. It looked gorgeous and shimmered in the bright August sunlight. Thrilled with it, I went back in to phone the fair wife with the exciting news, and then drove the camper back on to the drive and under the car port.

Has anyone spotted my schoolboy error yet?

A Dormobile pop-up roof is incredibly strong in all the ways it's required to be strong; I imagine the triangle structure which keeps it up is probably strong enough to withstand gale-force winds. It is, however, incredibly flimsy in all the planes in which strength is not required, and smashing it against a gutter was akin to being showered with broken eggshells.

I don't think furious quite covers my mood that afternoon. There was far too much damage for a proper repair, and a complete new cap had to be installed via the insurance company.

How we all laughed as I related my story …

But to make the exciting tale even more nail-biting, we need a bit of increased jeopardy – the 'will he make it in time?' thing. And, sure enough, I was booked in at a campsite in Cornwall some 300 miles away the following weekend!

Obviously, there was not the remotest chance of being able to get the bus booked in, taken down to Dormobile for a new roof and bellows, and then recovered back to the Midlands for a replacement headlining in six days … so we compromised.

The insurance company quite cheerfully let me pay to have it hurriedly put back together with a couple of steel plates, a whole load of big bolts, and a tub of mastic. This little lot was skilfully attached by my man with the spanners and the bemused grin, and managed to provide just enough strength to hold the thing together until it could be repaired properly.

Shish kebabs

Ingredients
- 1lb lamb, diced
- 1 red onion, cut into wedges
- 1 green pepper, sliced

To make the marinade
- 1 onion, finely grated
- 2tbsp olive oil
- 1 lemon, grated rind and juice of
- 2tsp garlic paste
- ½tsp oregano
- ½tsp thyme

To serve
- Pitta breads
- Crisp lettuce, shredded
- Cherry tomatoes
- Chilli sauce
- Lots of kitchen towel

Method
Begin by making the marinade. You can, of course, do this pitched up somewhere exotic, but it's fiddly and messy, and far easier to do at home and bring it ready to use. Grate the onion very finely to produce lots of juice, and combine this with the other ingredients in a Tupperware-type container. Then add the meat, stirring to ensure that everything is well covered, and refrigerate until you're ready to cook. I always reuse the cartons that the local Indian takeaway bring me – that way I've doubled their useful working life, and this gives me the option when camping of chucking them away, guilt-free, instead of washing them!

On-site, begin as always by lighting the barbecue and leaving it for a good 20 to 30 minutes to reach an even temperature that's suitable for cooking. Anything much less and it will still be far too hot, and guaranteed to produce blackened, charred food that is still pink and raw in the middle. Meanwhile, slice the pepper and cut the onion into wedges, then remove the lamb from the marinade and, with sticky fingers, thread it onto the skewers, alternating with the two vegetables. If you use two skewers instead of just one, it makes the kebabs a thousand times easier to turn over.

Cook over the barbie for about eight to ten minutes, turning and basting frequently with the remaining marinade. Remove the skewers from the grill and use the tines of a fork to slide off the meat and vegetables. Split the pittas, fill them with the lettuce, the hot lamb, peppers and onion, and top off with sliced tomatoes and lashings of chilli sauce.

Miscellaneous tips

This is a selection of miscellaneous tips and oddments that don't really need any further explanation, but which will all make small – but invaluable – improvements to your camping experience:

- ALWAYS take a fire extinguisher.
- I urge you never to take proper glass glasses camping. Despite the fact they appear to be capable of surviving years of rough treatment at home, they always manage to get themselves broken, and the multiple tiny shards are impossible to extract properly from grass. Plastic or stainless steel is the way forward here.
- Mugs and plates are different: I heartily recommend the use of proper crockery. Melamine really is dreadful, and there's no excuse for it – pretty pictures of camper vans all around or not, you wouldn't use it at home. Do take an extra setting: three mugs, three plates, etc.
- An emergency spare key can be attached to the underside of the camper using a large magnet.
- We have learned to give names to the various drawers and cupboards. There's the cutlery drawer and the other drawer; the china cupboard and the other cupboard. We even have a wardrobe and a larder, which saves having to think about left and right when things need to be found.
- 'A place for everything, and everything in its place' is never more relevant than when camping in a tiny van. Always put everything away unless you are actually using it.
- Take a small clock for the living area, as the one in the dash is no use when you're chilling in the evening.
- When friends suggest a drunken game of twister – this happens more frequently than you'd imagine – always try to be the bloke with the dice, and cheat. Don't let things happen at random; take the time to tie them in knots.
- A Moroccan Rug is a curious name for a form of clever plastic matting woven from polypropylene; it is completely waterproof, and great for placing outside the camper. No matter how much it rains, it will prevent walking mud inside with you. Any mud left on the rug folds up on the inside when packing up, but the rug doesn't pack away particularly small.

Barefoot chicken & chorizo (GF)

Chicken and chorizo is a match made in culinary heaven, and I'd been after a suitable recipe for ages. Eventually, the absence of something as simple as I was looking for forced me to come up with my very own. Apologies for the lack of an exotic name.

Ingredients
- 2tbsp butter
- 1 medium onion, diced
- 5cm chorizo, finely diced
- 1tsp garlic paste
- 2 chicken fillets, cut into 1cm cubes
- Mexican rice mix

Method

Melt the butter in a pan over a medium heat and add the diced onion. After about five minutes or so, as it begins to soften, add a teaspoon of garlic paste and the finely diced chorizo. Mix together and leave for another five minutes, until the oil begins to run from the sausage. Cut the chicken into 1cm cubes and add to the pan, stirring so that everything is well combined and the flavours begin to mix. After about another ten minutes, as the chicken begins to change colour, it's time for the rice.

Normally, I would make this as a one-pot dish in a single pan. However, my food stylist – who has done nothing but moan for as long as I've known him – in an endless drone complained that the photographs might look dull, and so I was coerced into using a second saucepan for the rice.

Option one is to add a pack of microwave Mexican rice to the pan. Stir to combine, continue heating for about three minutes, and then serve up.

Option two, which is the version illustrated here, involves finding a second pan from the cupboard, which was blocked by a folding table. Warming it, and then heating the rice for three minutes, stirring occasionally until it's warmed through.

Serve the spicy Mexican rice onto the plate first, forming a lush bed, and then lay the chicken and chorizo mix over the rice in an elegant, decadent and luxurious fashion.

As alluded to at the top of the page, this is a taste sensation.

And so it needs to be because, when you've finished, you'll have double the washing up to do!

The carburettor is the thing at the back, with the big spring, just to the left of the top pulley.

'These old Volkswagens go on for ever, you know'

I've heard this story so many times that, if I didn't own one, I might actually begin to believe it. Of course they don't. They were a commercial vehicle built down to a cost/price, with a design life of no more than about 100,000 miles. And, like every other kind of motor car anywhere in the world, they'll keep going for just as long as you're prepared to keep spending money on them. The only reason VW owners seem prepared to pour vast amounts into them is because most of them are past the point of no return.

A huge bill for a replacement gearbox? What's the alternative? Sell it as a project as opposed to the glorious, reliable camper is was just a fortnight ago?

One of the problems owners encounter is the poor quality of replacement parts – presumably the result of our throw away society, with its endless cost cutting. A good example of this was my old carburettor. It had managed to mix a bit of fuel and air in roughly the right proportions for 30 years, and then things like seals and bearings eventually wore out and the camper began to run a bit rough. I popped onto the old interweb and countless online suppliers were more than happy to post me a 'direct replacement' for the old Solex.

A carb arrived which certainly looked the part, and it bolted into the same place using the same bolts. Once again, the engine ran as smooth as a sewing machine … For about eighteen months, and then it, again, started coughing and spluttering.

Back then, there was an old chap who used to recondition the old carburettors. I like to think of him working in a dusty shed, wearing thick, bottle-bottom glasses and with multiple ink stains around his top pocket. In any case, he did it – my old Solex arrived back in the post looking brand new and fitted with a whole bunch of extra smoothness.

A decade later, and it's still there, still doing its stoichiometric trickery!

Fat sausages, braised in cider & mustard (GF)

This makes a lot – it will serve four.

Ingredients
* 8 fat, gluten-free pork sausages
* 400ml dry cider
* 2 large leeks, sliced
* 2tsp garlic paste
* 450g new potatoes, halved
* 2 apples, cored and sliced – keep the skin on
* 2tbsp wholegrain mustard
* Salt and coarse black pepper
* 2tbsp butter
* 50ml of double cream
* Splash of olive oil
* A large handful of fresh parsley, chopped

Method
Pour the oil into a heavy-bottomed saucepan and heat. Then, cook the sausages until they are nicely browned on the outside, remove them from the pan, and put to one side on a plate. Melt the butter in the pan, add the leeks and let them 'sweat' gently for about ten minutes until really soft.

Now return the sausages to the pan, together with half of the sliced apple, the potatoes, and the cider. Bring to the boil, then turn down immediately. Put the lid on and cook on a gentle simmer for about ten minutes. Remove the lid and season well with salt and pepper, then let the dish cook for another 15 minutes until the potatoes are tender.

Melt the remainder of the butter in a second small pan and add the rest of the apple slices, along with a sprinkle of sugar. Cook gently for a few minutes until the apple begins to soften and the edges start to caramelise. Add the cream and the mustard to the sausage pan, mix everything together, and heat it a little. Then remove from the heat, lay the caramelised apples over the top, and garnish with the fresh parsley. Give everyone a bowl and a hunk of good bread and let them dig in.

The weather was shocking the day I cooked this, so it was all done inside the bus. I didn't really have the space to make the caramelised apples, so I just added the extra butter and apple slices to the first pan and left out the sugar!

'Fun weekends with wild friends'

For anyone wondering whether VW shows and festivals are worth visiting, I have to say that it depends entirely on the attitude that you take with you. If you go along prepared to join in with the idiotic fun, you will have a whale of a time. Go to look at displays of old and interesting camper vans, buses old and new, to see how different people have solved the same old problems, and you will learn. As soon as things get back to proper BC* normality, it is more than likely that the fair wife and I will be back out there in the thick of it with the best of them.

For the sheer variety of bands we've seen that we wouldn't normally have even thought of seeing, Volkswagen shows are unbeatable. We've enjoyed versions of Amen Corner and Showaddywaddy, have been introduced to the legendary Gwen Dickie of Rose Royce, and became good friends with the bassist from popular '80s rock legends Spider. I am one of a very select number of people who know Jenson D Groover's real name, I even have his home number … somewhere. The sheer variety of people we've met and had a laugh with beggars belief. I couldn't honestly tell you which shows were the best, or are the best, or even which will continue to be great.

After a quarter of a century, the shows have become blurred and have begun to merge into one another. Some shows have disappeared along the way, but new ones spring up to take their place. It's been an odd experience. Some of the people that I met years ago, and who I have nothing to do with in any other aspect of my life, greet me like a brother from a different mother. It can't be simply the bond that is Volkswagen, there has to be something else …

Some of these people I can put names to, others I have to call 'mate,' but at the top of the page, there's a picture which speaks volumes: he is now a political analyst, and she works for the United Nations.

*Before Covid

A suggestion for a full weekend of easy food.

In addition to the usual, you'll need a couple of disposable BBQs, some wooden skewers and a wok. It's just as easy to cook a pork chop on a BBQ that's spent two days marinading in a delicious Chinese sauce with garlic, ginger, five spice, hoisin sauce and honey as one that hasn't.

The hard work – all ten minutes of it – was done at home.

Menu
Thursday tea time: Char Siu pork with egg fried rice, *recipe on page 113.*
Friday breakfast: Oatcakes with bacon and cheese, *see recipe below.*
Friday lunch: Coronation chicken and Waldorf salad, *recipe on page 64.*
Friday tea time: Lamb shish kebabs, *recipe on page 45.*
Saturday breakfast: Oatcakes with bacon and cheese.
Saturday lunch: Coronation chicken and Waldorf salad.
Saturday tea time: Tournedos Rossini, *recipe on page 99.*
Sunday breakfast: Oatcake with bacon and cheese

Oatcakes with bacon & cheese

Ingredients
- Pack of 6 oatcakes
- 6 rashers of bacon, rindless
- 2 packs of exotic cheese slices

Method
In a dry pan, fry the bacon on both sides. Meanwhile, open the packet of ready-sliced cheese and place a slice on one half of the oatcake. Remove the bacon from the pan and place it on top of the cheese. Fold the oatcake in half and drop it back into the hot bacon fat and cook for a couple of minutes until the cheese is nicely melted, turning once.

Serve immediately with HP sauce, knives and forks and a mug of hot tea.

Brighton

We've been to a lot of Volkswagen shows over the years, and have concluded that they are all very similar: there's a selection of camping areas, rated from 'silent' to 'drunken hooligan'; there're bands to see, which rate from 'utterly hopeless' to 'far better than expected'; and there are VW concours events, where the chaps in the anoraks hang out and debate exactly which month in 1963 it was that VW changed the stud pattern on the cab door hinges. Then there are endless traders, club games, food and drink … unless you're at Santa Pod, with its drag strip, or at Weston Park, by the stately home, it can occasionally be difficult to tell one from another.

Then there's Brighton Breeze: an endurance event masquerading as a gentle day out in the camper van. This begins on a Friday evening, at Hook Road Arena in the outskirts of London. A few hundred VWs gather around a burger van and a portable toilet, where they pitch camp for the night, ready to wake up in the gloom of an October morning. Then they'll all head off in a glorious convoy down to Brighton, some 60 miles south. The convoy always breaks up, participants always get lost around Brighton, and there's always a queue to get down and parked up on the seafront. After a day by the seaside, it's time to move on again – this time to the racetrack, where there's a warm indoor bar, a band, and more very basic camping facilities.

We love it. The Hook Road experience is unbelievably basic, but a day spent in Brighton more than makes up for it. We don't often get involved with the VW things, we just go for a potter around the touristy areas of the vibrant and cosmopolitan city. The place is heaving with young, glamorous university types, and the sheer variety of trendy shops, pubs and cafés is incredible. Then, at about tea time, as the contenders head off towards the racetrack and a second night of excess, we begin our long drive back home towards the Midlands.

ABC: Avocado & blue cheese burger

As everyone secretly knows, you can't camp, and you can't barbecue, without the appearance – at least once – of a burger. The problem is, shop-bought burgers taste of cardboard.

This is a camping fact.

I haven't bought a burger, even from a butcher, in a decade. There's no need. They are so simple to make, and once you've taken it onboard, you'll quickly become very slick at making them. You can use a burger maker, but there's really no need. This is my attempt at a sophisticated, grown-up burger for adults, which I made when we all went to watch popular '80s beat combo ABC at the very first Camper Calling show.

Ingredients
- 250g minced beef
- 1 ripe avocado
- 1tsp garlic paste
- Blue cheese, sliced
- Cob rolls, buttered

Method
Scoop the flesh from the avocado and mix it in a bowl with a teaspoonful of garlic paste. Heat up a non-stick pan: I used my Beauclaire because I was cooking outside – it's a huge cooking surface, and it seldom blows out in the wind.

Slice the cobs in half, drizzle the insides with olive oil, and drop them onto the hot pan until they start to crisp up and brown on their cut sides. As you remove the cobs from the heat and onto a wire rack, divide the minced beef into two 125g balls, place the mincemeat balls into the pan, and squash them with your fingers to make burger patties. Experimentation reveals that around 125g/5oz is the optimum size: a quarter pounder is a bit lightweight, while 6oz and heavier can be a bit hefty! After a couple of minutes, flip over the burgers and top the cooked side with the blue cheese. Spread the inside of the toasted cobs with the avocado mix and then, when the cheese begins to melt, place the burgers onto the bread. Leave them for a minute or two to rest, and then consume with sticky fingers.

All the gear, no idea …

You've all heard the expression, 'I know the very man.' Well, I've camped with him and his lovely partner on numerous occasions. There are so many tales I could tell, but I'm just going to recount the one where he upgraded the ICE in his bus. He had the usual dash-mounted radio device that used to play CDs, and it was loud. It wasn't loud enough for Kieren, though, so he visited a car hi-fi professional, who offered him louder. It was considered, but ultimately rejected because he didn't want loud or louder: Kieren wanted loudest. Numbers were discussed, and eventually 1000watts was mentioned. There were potential drawbacks with such a system, but 1000 was the magic number, and that was the one that was to be installed.

At the very next VW show we all met up, and the new ICE was revealed in all its glory. The music began to play, and it was turned up, and up …

Then the drop-outs began, a sudden brief pause here, and another there. Just a couple of seconds, but enough to spoil the ambience. "Installer said this might happen," was the response. The engine was fired up, the drop-outs ceased … and then they began again.

It seemed to work okay if the engine was held on the throttle at a fast idle. You couldn't actually hear the engine above the throb of the bass, although the treble response may have been a little muffled …

We went for a walk around the stalls instead. Just because you have the loudest stereo in the entire world doesn't mean you have to turn it up to 11 all of the time. Surely the point is that, at normal volumes, it's barely working with lots in reserve – but apparently not. Our campsite for that particular weekend was filled with the second-loudest music system in the showground (after the band). It was also marked out by the clouds of exhaust fumes.

The next time we met up with them for a weekend of Volkswagen fun, the original radio was back.

Cheat's tandoori chicken kebabs

Real tandoori chicken is cooked in a clay oven: this is a bit of a barbecued cheat. The red food colouring is optional, but it does help it to look the part.

Ingredients
- 2 chicken breasts, cut into chunks
- Natural yoghourt
- 1tsp chilli powder
- 2tsp tikka curry powder
- 1tbsp garlic paste
- 1tbsp ginger paste
- A couple of drops of red food colouring
- Naan bread
- Mint raita

Method
It's far easier to do all of your marinading at home, and simply take the meat bagged up and ready to cook. Pour the yoghourt into a food bag and mix in all of the spices. Place the chicken chunks into the frightening-looking bright pink gloop, and move everything about with your fingers on the outside to ensure that all of the meat is well-coated. Tie up the open end and pack it into the fridge in your van.

At the campsite, light the barbecue and wait for at least 20 or 30 minutes for it to reach the correct temperature upon which to cook. Curiously, this is exactly the same time as it takes to drink a pint of fine ale or a glass of wine.

Thread chicken pieces onto skewers, leaving enough wood exposed to use as a handle away from the flames. Cook the chicken for a good 20 minutes, turning it frequently, until cooked through and the edges are beginning to darken; another drink may be called for. After about 15 minutes, place a naan bread on top of the skewers to warm through.

Remove the chicken from the skewers by pushing them off with a fork, and serve on the warm naan with a dainty-looking lettuce and tomato salad and a good squirt of mint raita.

According to my stylist, "if you're going to the trouble of an overnight marinade that smells great all across the campsite, you might as well make sure that it gives folk something to look at when they pop over for a nosey."

The majority of people assume that my old Volkswagen is way past its sell-by-date, and obsolete in every conceivable way.

Usually, I am happy just to let this go. Its flat-four air-cooled engine, for example, is incredibly compact in comparison to the more usual inline-four, but when Ford can extract 138bhp from a turbocharged 1-litre 3-pot for the latest Fiesta – essentially a shopping trolley – 50-odd-bhp from 1584cc is a little bit on the pathetic side of dismal. Similarly, the Type 2's steering box lacks the precision of a rack and pinion, and its gearbox … although it enjoys the long-forgotten convenience and simplicity of just four forward ratios, selecting them isn't exactly as light and unambiguous as it might be, given the linkage is the best part of 14ft long.

Then there's the dashboard, which was fitted from the factory with just two knobs: one for headlights, and another for the hazards. Instruments consist of just a speedometer and a typically non-functioning fuel gauge. There's no indication of temperature, because the low-revving standard engine will probably never overheat. Heater controls are present and correct, although they don't do very much, and there is no option to recirculate or condition the air.

There are stalks for indicators and wipers, but, sadly, the steering wheel has only one button which operates just the horn.

There is, however, just the one area where an old bay – and, unbelievably, even the much-older split screen vans – must have been at the absolute zenith of cutting-edge technology at the time of their release. From new, they were fitted with something that remains today exactly the same as it has for the last 70-odd years.

It still shares with Volkswagen's very newest model range, on both sides of the cab a bit of foam on a stick that Volkswagen persists in calling a sun visor. I appreciate there's a cost/benefit ratio that needs to be balanced, but is that really the best that the finest minds of Wolfsburg can achieve in the 21st century?

Welsh rarebit or VW rabbit?

This is ideal comfort food to enjoy for those evenings when you're forced into your bus early because of a spot of adverse weather. You know the sort of thing: it's blowing a gale outside and one retires inside with an elegant glass of red …

But then one fancies something to eat. For many years we've been rattling up a bit of cheese on toast. Bread, a sliced cob – anything would do, and it did. There's always cheese and there's always something to put it on. Welsh rarebit is a nice idea, but it's really only a posh variation of cheese on toast, and it's a whole lot of effort for what it is.

VW rabbit, on the other hand, is the work of a moment.

Ingredients
- Bread – absolutely any kind will do
- Cheese – again, whatever is about
- Red onion marmalade
- Walnut pieces

Method
Working the grill on the old Fellows stove is an acquired skill. Use it like any grill you've ever used before in your life, and you'll be thrilled at the impressive-looking stripes that it burns into anything you put under it. But by lighting it and running it on maximum for about three or four minutes, you can then turn it right down onto the simmer setting. You should also turn over the grill rack to its lowest (upside down) position. You have created a tool that actually works.

This is dead easy. Toast the bread on one side, turn over and spread the uncooked side with the onion marmalade and sprinkle over some broken walnuts. Cover with a couple of generous slices of cheese and stick it back under the grill until it's nicely melted, bubbling, and beginning to brown.

Walnuts and onion marmalade are the sort of things that last forever if left unopened, and the marmalade will probably see the season out even after.

Pack both ingredients into your bus today while you think about it. They'll be waiting for you on that chilly summer evening when you fancy a bit of a snack.

BABY CRYING IN
CHALET

Camp	Row	Number
Red	F	27

Weekend hippies: a good thing, or bad?

Some years ago, we found ourselves spending time at Volkswagen shows with people who enjoyed doing the 'weekend hippy' thing, and dressing up to match their camper van. This went on for some time and then, strangely, it became the norm. Peer pressure meant that for a moment (it was actually at a show called VWoodstock), we were obliged to join in with the whole Jimi Hendrix/'60s-hippy vibe.

It should have been okay, but my time as a fancy-dresser came to a rather abrupt end following a bit of a breakdown on the southbound M1, on the way to the show. In true comedy fashion, the nearside wheel parted company with my trailer, and bounced up alongside us on the hard shoulder to our left. At the same moment, there was a bit of a jolt as the trailer amusingly assumed a rather jaunty angle. The problem and the solution was obvious, but we tend not to bring along a trolley jack just on the off-chance it's needed.

As I wandered back down the shoulder rolling the wheel ahead of me, I noticed that the traffic had slowed to a bemused crawl, as folk pressed their noses to the window to see a shoeless bloke, dressed in far greater quantities of cheesecloth than would normally be considered acceptable in the 21st century.

I called out the fifth emergency service, and the man – a very nice, very kindly man – had the decency not to mention my bizarre hipster-cut, flared strides. I think I even got away with the silver flowers embroidered into them.

I had honestly thought that this was just a Volkswagen thing. I don't, for example, suddenly snap on a pair of red braces each time I nip out in my old 944, and there was no one doing the old cravat/blazer/panama thing at a meeting of Rover 75s that I once attended.

It turns out, though, that I was wrong. When we visited a 'vintage nostalgia' weekend, we discovered ten years of rose-tinted British postwar history packed into a single weekend …

Sweet & sour chicken

This is definitely not one to cook inside your camper!

In contrast to some of the more relaxed recipes, this one is totally frantic. It's essential to have everything weighed, measured and chopped, ready to fling straight into the hot pan. It cooks from start to finish in just a few short minutes. A chap at the local Chinese supermarket told me that the secret to sweet and sour is this 5:4 sugar/vinegar ratio. It certainly works, but, as always, the interweb offers a thousand alternative ratios.

You'll need to take a proper, very cheap Chinese carbon steel wok, and a very hot source of flames. I used the base of my Beauclaire.

Ingredients
- Sunflower oil, or similar, with a very hot smoke point
- 1 green pepper, diced
- 1 small tin of pineapple chunks
- 25g white sugar
- 20ml cider vinegar
- 2tbsp of tomato ketchup; a big splash
- 2tsp light soy sauce; a small splash
- Cooked chicken, diced
- 1 bag of bean sprouts
- 1 small head of broccoli

Method
Add the oil to the wok and heat until it just begins to smoke. Add the diced pepper (it will spit and be very noisy), and stir-fry for about three minutes. Add the pineapple and keep it moving for another two minutes. Working quickly, use your spatula to move everything away from the centre of the pan and sprinkle in the sugar. Do not stir it at this point, but watch it closely and, as it begins to caramelise, add the vinegar. It won't be happy, and will once again spit viciously. Begin stirring again and quickly add the ketchup and soy sauces. Mix everything together well, and stir the sauce around the pepper and pineapple to coat them, then add the cooked chicken and finally the bean sprouts and broccoli. Two or three minutes of brisk stir-frying action should see everything nicely covered in the sauce and properly heated through.

Serve it up immediately, and you'll wonder why you ever bought that orange gloopy stuff they sell at the local takeaway.

This really is the occasion when we were told that the site was 'rammed.'

Green Hill Farm

Green Hill Farm was a campsite that we tripped over entirely by accident.

We were on our way back from somewhere in the south of England when the fair wife decided she didn't want to go straight home. We discovered this campsite, in the pre-internet days of old, tucked away in the Caravan Club's brochure, *The Book of Lies*. Arriving unannounced, it was superb – although we picked a particularly poor spot, which was afflicted by early evening shade (see page 104) and a valuable lesson was learned. The following year, I phoned to book a pitch for a lengthier stay, only to be told that they were completely full that particular week: "We are absolutely rammed."

With nowhere else planned, we turned up anyway. The slightly strange woman on the gate was as nice as pie, and directed us to the very pitch on the top of the hill we'd talked about. The field was empty! For a memorable couple of days we had it entirely to ourselves.

New Forest campsites are extreme: they are either massively regimented, or they are little more than a gap in the trees with no facilities. This odd little site curiously ticked all of the boxes. The facilities were best described as adequate, but a gate on the far side opened up directly onto a vast area of common land.

It was gorgeous, and populated by cattle, sheep, pigs, donkeys, and, of course, the ubiquitous ponies. Although they took some finding, there were pubs on all sides, in the days when such places were still open. We could spend the majority of the day simply walking a couple of very beautiful miles for lunch, and then gently back again.

Then, after about a decade or so, the campsite changed hands, and it was no longer the ramshackle organisation with a couple of daft old folk in the little hut. Suddenly, there was a one-way system around the field, pitch numbers, and a kid's play area. I'm sure that it made a lot more money, but for us it was the end of a golden era.

Lamb shawarma (GF)

Lamb shawarma is a very simple BBQ treat for garlic lovers everywhere.

As with almost all of these recipes, it's more than possible to make this from start to finish in the middle of nowhere, in a camper van, using only the most basic of facilities.

If, however, I was going to a festival or for a quick weekend away, I would make the marinade at home and bag it up with the lamb, so that I could take it ready to unwrap and cook. I don't like to waste valuable socialising and drinking time.

Ingredients
- ¼tsp cinnamon
- ½tsp turmeric
- 1tsp of paprika
- 1tsp of cumin
- 2tsp garlic paste
- 2tsp lime juice
- 2tsp olive oil
- 500g of diced lamb
- Serve with corn chips, shredded lettuce, diced cucumber, tomato, pickled dills, and lashings of garlic aioli

Method
Mix together the first seven ingredients in a polythene bag, and add the diced lamb. Shuffle everything around with your fingertips to ensure that the meat is evenly covered in the spice mixture. Leave it to marinate for at least an hour, and preferably much, much longer.

Light a barbecue – I used my COBB, although this is very simple and a disposable BBQ would be more than adequate. While you're waiting for the barbie to heat up, thread the cubes of meat onto half a dozen skewers. Ensure that you wait at least 20 to 30 minutes for the coals to reach an even, and usable, temperature. This part is crucial; if you have any doubts, crack open a can of ice-cold lager. By the time you've drunk it, the BBQ will be ready.

Lay the loaded skewers onto the grill and cook for 20 minutes, turning once. Remove the skewers from the coals and slide the meat from the skewers using a fork. Wrap the cubes of lamb in tinfoil and leave to rest for ten minutes.

Serve the lamb on a bed of corn chips, and cover with the diced salad and lashings of garlic aioli.

The definitive picnic

I recently watched the 1955 film, *To Catch a Thief* with Cary Grant and Grace Kelly. It wasn't very good. The heroine did, however, lure our Archie up into the hills for a picnic with the promise of "chicken and beer." How times have changed, when you consider how utterly decadent that must have been intended to sound half a century ago. I love a picnic, and spent the next few minutes glued to the telly to see how it was done. I watched as the blue Talbot Alpine roared up through the hills, thinking to myself 'I'll bet that's a bit awkward to have a picnic in.' And it was!

If you look closely at the movie still, you can see that the passenger seat has been removed to make room for the picnic basket. I'm guessing that, sat perched on the sill like that, Cary's film-star buttocks must have been all but purple.

Picnics are great. Sometimes you just don't have the time, or the inclination, to pitch up for the weekend: that's the time to pack up a picnic. You should get yourself a proper picnic basket: these are brilliant, and, despite having a camper van at your disposal, you should still indulge yourself with one – but be careful. There are dozens to choose from, but most picnic baskets – either the old-fashioned woven wicker efforts, or the modern lightweight, insulating fabric versions – are so full of plates, cutlery, salt/pepper shakers, and the ubiquitous corkscrew, that there's barely room to shove in a bag of Wotsits!

After some research, we found a cheap and cheerful wicker basket, and have sourced the contents ourselves. We normally take just a couple of paper plates, titanium sporks, a bag for rubbish, and a very sharp Opinel knife. That's it, that's all we need, and there's plenty of room left for food and drink. Sometimes we take a bottle of wine together with elegant plastic glasses. Sometimes we take beer in tins and a flask, or just pop in cans, with or without paper cups.

Picnicking for absolute beginners

Faff about all you like with your fancy picnics: when it boils down to it, the simplest picnic, a proper bloke's picnic, and the ultimate outdoor food combination, are all the very same. It's a pork pie, an apple, a bag of crisps and a bottle of beer. Each item travels well, can be bought in a variety of qualities, and each is instantly ready to unwrap and consume. It can be ingested properly from plates using a knife, with mustard and even napkins, or you can simply bite into it. This is a picnic fact. And when you're finished, the whole lot – the plates, cans, packaging, whatever – goes into a polythene carrier bag

and from there into the nearest bin. Picnicking is a skill. Once mastered, it will serve you well. That said, the following pages have a few posh picnic alternatives to serve as inspiration.

Chicken & beer picnic

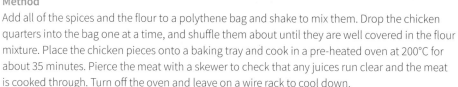

Here's a quick and dirty chicken and beer picnic recipe, so you too can play at being Cary and Grace, but without the brightly-coloured bottom!

Ingredients
- 2 chicken quarters
- 2tsp celery salt
- 1tsp garlic salt
- 1tsp paprika pepper
- 1tsp cayenne pepper
- 1tbsp corn flour

Method
Add all of the spices and the flour to a polythene bag and shake to mix them. Drop the chicken quarters into the bag one at a time, and shuffle them about until they are well covered in the flour mixture. Place the chicken pieces onto a baking tray and cook in a pre-heated oven at 200°C for about 35 minutes. Pierce the meat with a skewer to check that any juices run clear and the meat is cooked through. Turn off the oven and leave on a wire rack to cool down.

Wrap the quarters first in greaseproof paper, then in crisply starched white cotton napkins, and place carefully into your picnic basket along with a salt shaker, a glass for the lady, and a couple of bottles of ice-cold Italian lager. And then it's time to head for the hills!

Coronation chicken & Waldorf salad

Ingredients
For the chicken
- 150g chicken, cooked
- 200g crème fraîche
- 1tsp curry paste
- 4tsp mango chutney
- 80g sultanas
- 40g flaked almonds

For the salad
- 120g crème fraîche
- 120g walnuts
- 2 sticks celery
- Lettuce and posh cobs to serve

Method
In a bowl, combine the curry paste and mango chutney with the crème fraîche. Cut the cooked chicken into 1cm cubes and add to the mixture. Stir to ensure that the meat is evenly coated, then add the sultanas and almonds.

Use this to make sandwiches with quality bread rolls, and garnish with rocket. Wrap them in waxed paper, kitchen towel and foil.

To make the salad, place the chopped celery into a Tupperware box, add the broken walnuts, and stir through just enough of the crème fraîche to bind everything together. Waldorf is traditionally served on a bed of fresh lettuce, and this simple, but elegant, touch adds a soupçon of sophistication, out of all proportion to the effort involved.

Shooter's picnic

A shooter's sandwich travels particularly well, but you need to make it the night before.

Ingredients
- 1 ciabatta loaf
- 1 chicken fillet
- 6 rashers smoked bacon
- 1 can of Batchelors Cream of Mushroom Condensed Soup, or similar
- ½tsp thyme
- Greaseproof paper and string/baking bands

Method
Cut the bacon and the chicken into 1cm chunks and cook them in a hot dry pan for about ten minutes, stirring frequently. Meanwhile, cut the ciabatta in half horizontally and hollow out the

loaf using your fingers. Spread the top and bottom of the loaf with the condensed soup, then add the cooked meats to the bottom of the loaf. Sprinkle with the thyme and assemble the sandwich. Do this while the meat is still warm to keep the sandwich moist.

Wrap tightly in greaseproof paper. Traditionally, this is tied with string, but it's far easier to hold it all together using baking bands, which you can scrounge from any good butcher. Place it in the fridge, under a chopping board weighed down with tins, and leave overnight.

The following day, the sandwich will have maintained its shape; the flavours will be well merged. Slice between the strings into individual sandwich-sized portions and enjoy.

Vegshooter's picnic (V)

The best vegetarian picnic sandwich; here's a vegetarian alternative to the shooter's sandwich. A lot of traditional sandwich favourites – like tomato, lettuce, cucumber and mushrooms – won't work in a sandwich like this, because they'd go mushy overnight and make the bread soft.

Ingredients
- 1 crusty demi-baguette
- Mozzarella cheese, sliced
- Provolone cheese (or vegetarian alternative), finely sliced
- A handful of walnuts, chopped
- 3 figs, sliced
- 3 onions, thinly sliced
- Butter
- 4tsp Demerara sugar
- Greaseproof paper and string/baking bands

Method
Begin by making an onion marmalade:
melt two generous tablespoons of butter in a pan, add the thinly sliced onions, and sprinkle over four teaspoons of Demerara sugar. Cover the pan and leave for about ten minutes, then, give everything a good stir, put the lid back on, and turn the heat right down. After another ten minutes or so, The onion will be reduced and the marmalade will be ready to use.

Cut the loaf in half horizontally and scoop out most of the soft bread to leave slightly more than a shell. Line the bottom of the loaf with finely-sliced provolone cheese, and cover it with warm onion marmalade. On top of this add the sliced figs, the chopped walnuts, and the sliced mozzarella. Put the loaf back together and wrap tightly in greaseproof paper. Secure the package at regular intervals using baking bands that you probably had a carnivorous friend scrounge from their butcher! Leave the sandwich in the fridge overnight, pressed down beneath a chopping board and as many cans of food as you can manage.

On the following day – the day of the picnic – the flavours will have melded together nicely. Again, this is served by slicing vertically into individual portions. Although I am the first to admit that this can be a bit of a faff to make and assemble, it travels well, the flavours improve overnight, and it makes a spectacularly good picnic sandwich.

Dealing with children

I am utterly useless when dealing with children.

Here, then, are a couple of suggestions for fun games for kids from a particularly inept bloke: experiments that proved to be an unqualified success. It was just as much fun for the organising adults as for the kids taking part.

The first is a yoghourt-eating competition. I recommend the use of plastic spoons and, obviously, the pots of yoghourt can be tailored to the size and age of the competitors. Contestants form themselves into teams of two: a 'feeder' and an 'eater.' The feeders hold the spoons and stand behind the seated eaters. The yoghourts are opened and lined up, the spectators gather … and, at the last minute, blindfolds are produced for the feeders!

This is a right chuckle. It can go on as long as you like, depending on the mess, because the feeders won't know whether or not their pots are empty. You can call a winner as soon as you've had enough!

The second game is designed to be played on a long walk. It's called 'Squirrel Hunting,' and you need nothing more than a pen knife and a length of ⅜in rubber. The first part is where the competitors build a catapult. They just need to find a lovely bit of Y-shaped ash from which to construct their catapult. The problem is, they'll never find one which will meet your stringent criteria for making a top quality, super powerful, super accurate example. Whatever they bring back can be rejected for any number of daft reasons: too long, too short, too flimsy, whatever.

In the unlikely event that they do find something suitable and you have to trim up the rubber and construct a weapon: one, they'll probably not see a single squirrel for the rest of the walk; and two, they don't stand a chance of actually getting a projectile anywhere near it. Obviously, it's not the intention that any animal is hurt.

Hopefully though, it's been a pleasant enough walk with the kids, who've been distracted enough not to pester you with how soon they'll be able to go back and fire up the PlayStation.

Hungry man's goulash   (GF*)

I appreciate what you're all thinking: that looks like a huge number of ingredients to make anything with in the middle of a field. The only time you'll think that is at home, when you're sorting stuff to pack in your camper. This really is such an easy and forgiving dish to make, you can almost chuck everything into the casserole single-handed, with a glass of wine in the other.

Ingredients

- A splash of olive oil
- 1 onion, diced
- 1 carrot, diced
- 1 pepper, diced
- 1tsp garlic paste
- ¾lb/350g stewing steak
- 1tsp paprika
- 1tbsp cornflour
- A glass of red wine
- A tin of chopped tomatoes
- 1tbsp of cider vinegar
- 1tbsp tomato sauce
- 1tbsp Worcester sauce
- 150ml beef stock

Method

Begin by boiling the kettle and making the stock. Then, using a heavy-based casserole dish and starting at the top of the list, just bung in everything. You can do it in the order it's written, or you can do it in the order that ingredients come to hand.

Stir the mix if it makes sizzling noises, but don't worry too much about it. When you reach the end of the list, add just enough stock to ensure that everything is covered. If there's not quite enough, an extra drop of hot water from the kettle will be fine. Bring it to a boil, stir everything through again, cover with a lid, and turn the heat right down. Leave it gently bubbling away for about an hour and a half. You can give it a stir every so often, but this is not crucial.

If you cut the stewing steak into bite-sized pieces, the goulash can be served very simply in a bowl, with just a spoon and a big chunk of crusty bread.

This is another one-pot recipe that looks a bit dull in all of the photographs. My food stylist wanted to brighten it up with scattered green herbs, and was discussing placing a poached egg in the centre to create a 'splash of vivid colour' when I pushed him under the camper van.

My overriding memory of France is just mile after mile of endless motorway!

France

Back in the last century – when we first bought our camper – we were filled with enthusiasm. Once upon a time, we bought a book of road maps of Europe, and off we went. Our first proper stop was to be the south coast of France: the Mediterranean. Somehow, I had calculated that it was 900 miles from our home, in the centre of the UK. So, intermediate stops – determined by squinting a bit and dividing the map into three – at Paris and Clermont-Ferrand would make for an easy, relaxing trip.

300 miles a day, at 50mph, is just six hours' driving. I'm writing this, and I cannot believe our naivety. 300 miles in a VW T2 takes all day. And it took all day, for three of the longest days of my life. This was back in pre-interweb days, so I was totally unaware that the whole of France takes the month of August off work and heads south: the journey over the Massif Central was nothing but a desperately slow-moving procession. What's more, unknown to me, I'd also taken 70kg of water over the mountain range and back, in the on-board water tank that we never, ever used.

We finally arrived on the Mediterranean coast, at a harmless looking little place called Cap d'Agde. This, you remember, in the days before the world wide web: in the days before we'd had the opportunity to look up our destination before leaving home. Three days, we'd travelled, to spend a week in the largest naturist resort town in the whole of France.

It came as something of a surprise to us both.

Looking back now, some 20 years later, the biggest surprise is that during the French national holiday fortnight, we actually managed to find ourselves a pitch on the only campsite in town that didn't insist I left my under-clackers in the van.

The town, the bars, the beach, and the whole resort were very pleasant. The holiday was tempered only by the knowledge that we'd got another three days of solid driving ahead of us at the end of it!

Mushroom burgers   (V)

This burger recipe was given to me by my
vegetarian editor at a magazine I once
contributed to. He says that if you don't get it
quite dry enough, and the burger becomes a
bit gloopy, don't worry, as the washing up will
be done in seconds! Makes four burgers.

Ingredients
- 450g mixed mushrooms, finely diced
- 3-4tsp dried and reconstituted shiitake
  mushrooms
- 1tbsp olive oil
- 1tsp of truffle oil
- 1 onion, diced
- 1tbsp breadcrumbs (and extra to coat)
- 1 egg
- 1tbsp flour
- Parmesan cheese (or vegetarian
  alternative), grated
- ½tsp cayenne pepper
- A healthy splash of soy sauce
- A sprinkle of parsley

Method
Although it is possible to make these out in a
field somewhere, it's a bit messy for a camper. I
heartily recommend that you make and freeze
the burgers at home, ready to take with you.

In a large pan, over medium heat, add a
tablespoon of olive oil and cook the finely diced mushrooms until they release their liquid and
begin to dry up a bit. Add the diced onion and cook for a few more minutes.

Allow the mixture to cool slightly, and then add it to all the other ingredients in a large bowl
and mix to combine everything well. Depending on the amount of liquid in your mushrooms, you
may need to add more flour or breadcrumbs. The mixture should hold its shape, without being
dry or crumbly. It should be pretty wet and even a bit sticky.

Pour the remaining breadcrumbs into a baking dish, and, as you form the burgers, dip them
into the breadcrumbs to form a crust. This helps them to retain their shape and gives them some
structure, but it won't dry them out on the inside.

Finally, and crucially, leave the burgers in the breadcrumbs for half an hour in the fridge, so
that a good crust forms, and then freeze them in readiness for a camping expedition.

These are best cooked in a pan with a drop of hot oil for about five to six minutes per side,
until the outsides become golden and crispy. Serve them in buns with all the usual trimmings.

The Barefoot Bishop's knob!

The three generations of rear-engined Volkswagen campers all have one characteristic in common: a ludicrously long gearshift mechanism. The linkage is the best part of 14ft long, and it needs to be adjusted with great precision for it to work at all, never mind properly. There are multiple rods, all linked together with rubber grommets …

Assuming that the linkage is in good order and set up correctly, a lot of owners upgrade their gear selector to a shiny American Hurst-style shifter or similar. Whilst I'm the first to appreciate that these do improve the feel of the gear change, their much-touted quick shifting capabilities appear to be completely wasted when the gearbox they're operating is still attached to a stock VW engine, with its low compression ratio and huge heavyweight flywheel. Although it's possible to change the ratios much quicker, the engine will still take the same amount of time to slow down to the correct speed to make a smooth transition. This is very much a personal thing, but in my opinion, the whole thing feels wrong for what remains a leisurely old van.

Many years ago, when I was messing around with a dreadful two-stroke Trabant, I met a fascinating chap called Tim Bishop. Best known for importing all manner of East German oddities – including the spectacular Tatra 613 – we talked about many things. I learned from him that the perceived quality of the gear change is determined by the weight of the knob. Think about it for just a moment: the VW has an odd-feeling gearshift, topped by little more than a 15g button. Chances are that everything else that you drive has a proper heavy knob.

I went home and filled the hollow underside of my gear change knob with small chunks of lead, all held in place with lashings of epoxy resin. I am very pleased with it: from the top it looks entirely standard, but the improvement in the actual gear change was noticeable immediately.

This recipe isn't a recipe at all, it's just an idea; an idea for you to develop, personalise and hopefully tailor to your needs. I first tried this out during the 2014 season, and over the last few years it has developed slightly. I appreciate that it is far from perfect, but it does make getting up in the morning, as a couple, much easier and stress-free. We call it simply 'the breakfast basket,' and it contains everything a chap needs to be able to leap straight out of bed and make that crucial first mug of coffee. We go to great lengths to ensure that it's all stocked up in the evening, and then the first one up – inevitably, it is me – can dress and nip outside, with the little basket tucked under their arm, and rattle up a brew. There is no messing, and no hunting about for something hidden deep in an inaccessible cupboard.

This, then, is the breakfast basket.

Ingredients

- 1 small self-lighting stove
- 1 very small, 500ml kettle
- 1 equally small windbreak
- 1 small gas bottle
- 500ml water
- Two mugs
- A pile of easy coffee sachets
- 1 teaspoon

Method

It enables a totally stress-free start to the day, and embodies the spirit of compromise that pervades many aspects of camper van ownership. I normally drink my coffee black, but the fair wife takes hers white: in an ideal world we would involve milk in this, but we have a dog who sleeps in front of the fridge, and he suggested that we should drink dodgy three-in-one coffee rather than ask him to move. There's just enough water for two mugs to ensure a rapid boil. I simply don't function as a human being before that first caffeine hit, but as soon as it's drunk, I am ready to face the world with either a proper, percolated cup of strong java or a steaming hot mug of tea.

An apposite solution to the great early morning cuppa dilemma.

Three-in-one coffee sachets

These are a total oddity. Dismissed, I'd imagine, by the majority of coffee lovers as cheap, tacky and over-sweetened – and I totally agree. I like my coffee to be strong, with just enough sugar to take the edge off it, and black. Once you go black, you can never go back!

There's an old and very battered classic stove-top espresso maker in the bus, together with a hand-cranked coffee grinder and fresh beans. That's all well and good, but when the dog and I stagger out of the camper van first thing in the morning, ready for our overdue comfort breaks, the last thing we want to be messing about with – and I include the dog in this – is coffee beans.

Then there's milk: the fair wife can't drink hers without it; I can't drink mine with it. Over to the coffee sachets, then. I can be out of the van with a brew in my hand before anyone even knows that I'm out of the pit. The sachets aren't shockingly bad. They're just adequate to put a hot sweet drink into me before I start to worry about not having had one. The curious thing is that I bought a load of them from the corner shop on a buy-one-get-one-free deal, and the freebie was a frighteningly-flavoured coffee. I think it was 'toffee coffee' or something similar – they certainly had far too much sugar in them.

Toffee? In coffee? What is the world coming to?

We were laughing about the sheer horror of these things with some camping friends of ours – an elegant and sophisticated couple, you might even describe them as the coffee cognoscenti – and the odd thing is, I made up a couple of toffee coffee drinks for a chuckle … and they loved them!

They had the rest of the packet off me, and the last I saw of them they were heading home to tell their friends. They phoned me a few days later to let me know that they'd found something very similar in Waitrose.

The mind boggles.

Lemony Chicken! (GF*)

Ingredients
- 2 chicken fillets
- 2 lemons, cut into wedges
- 2tsp garlic granules
- 2tbsp olive oil
- Fresh sage leaves

Method
This is another recipe involving a marinade. These are so much easier to do in the kitchen at home, where you have the relative luxury of hot running water! Spoon the garlic granules and the olive oil into a polythene bag – I generally use one intended for frozen food. Cut the chicken fillets into 1in cubes, add them to the bag, and mush everything around with your fingers to ensure that the meat is evenly coated. Put this into the camper van fridge, and by the time you're ready to cook it, the garlic will be well infused into the chicken.

Light a barbecue and, as always, leave it for at least 20 to 30 minutes for the flames to die down, and for the coals to stop smoking and become covered in a fine white ash. Putting the meat onto the grill before this is a recipe for disaster.

Whilst you're waiting, make up the skewers. Start by threading on a piece of chicken, followed by a sage leaf and a lemon segment. Repeat until you have threaded everything. If you arrange the meat and lemon at the pointed end, and leave yourself a longish length of skewer at the other to make a bit of a handle, you will make your life so much easier!

Lay the skewers over the coals and cook for about 20 minutes, or until the chicken is thoroughly cooked, turning every 3 to 4 minutes. You should check to confirm that the meat is properly done by piercing it with another skewer to confirm that any juices run clear.

The very simple flavours combine to make something that tastes greater than the sum of its parts; the lemon and sage compliment each other beautifully. Remove the contents using the tines of a fork to steady the meat whilst you pull out the skewer. Serve the chicken with a finely-diced salad and posh lettuce.

It seemed like a good idea at the time …

You know how it is: you go for the big awning, you keep buying the additional stuff to put in it, and, eventually, you find yourself needing to take so many extra toys to fill out your new expansive camper/awning combo that, ultimately, a trailer is needed to carry all of the extra clobber!

If the camper van that one drives is modern, white, and propelled by front wheels and the magic that is a forced-induction diesel, one can nip down to Halfords and pick up a little ERDE trailer for a couple hundred pounds. Everyone is happy.

If, like me, you drive a 'classic' orange Volkswagen, that simply won't do at all. What I had to find was either a single-wheel rigid trailer – made by some utterly obscure German manufacturer who probably went bankrupt in about 1950, having made about ten examples – or a half Beetle trailer. These look superb, they are so cool, they are so heavy, so impractical, they have such a hopelessly limited capacity …

They are clearly the ones to have, and, as luck would have it, a friend of a friend was selling one locally. I could hardly contain myself. I rushed round, money was exchanged, and I was the owner of slightly less than half a Beetle welded to an A-frame. There were no windows, wings, bumpers, rear valance or paint. I was thrilled. I rebuilt the shell of the car, fitted some glass, installed a camping oven, and lashed on some paint: the Barefoot Bistro was born. It was hopeless to tow, and reversing was a nightmare. I can reverse an articulated lorry, and I can reverse a tug and dolly laden with air containers, but the steering in the bay simply wasn't fast enough to catch this little trailer as it stepped out of line.

The final straw came when the nearside wheel chose to part company with the rest of the trailer on the M1, just south of junction 16, on the way to VW Action …

Beef stroganoff à la rock track   (GF)

I'm using this very simple stroganoff as an introduction to cooking along to music. Having decided that you'll be making this and have bought all your ingredients, you'll then need to put together a suitably-timed playlist for your mp3 player/smartphone.

It's a fun way to get consistent results, whilst at the same time look as if you're barely trying.

Ingredients
- 1tbsp butter
- 1 large onion, finely sliced
- 1 nice slice of rump steak, about 450g/1lb, sliced into thin strips
- 2tsp paprika
- 225g/½lb mushrooms
- 1 carton of soured cream or crème fraîche

Method
Heat the butter in a large frying pan for the duration of the Prodigy's 'Firestarter' (3:46). Finely slice the onion, add it to the pan and cook along to 'Disasterpiece' by Slipknot (5:00) until softened. Meanwhile, slice the steak into thin strips. Add the steak to the pan, stir in with the onions, and cook for the duration of Dan Hartman's 'Relight my Fire' (3:30) until just beginning to brown.

Slice the mushrooms in half, add to the pan and stir-fry until the very end of the guitar solo in Queen's 'We Will Rock You' (2:00).

The stroganoff should be served on a bed of rice, which, in a camper van without access to endless quantities of boiling water, is much easier said than done. I advise you to cheat with a packet of Tilda or similar microwave rice, which reheats easily in a pan, in about the same time as it takes to rattle through The Spencer Davis Group's 'Gimme Some Lovin'' (3:00, a track that really deserves to be much longer)!

Add the rice to a second pre-heated pan at the same time as you lower the heat in the main pan and stir in the paprika. Simmer gently whilst enjoying Spencer Davis.

Finally, stir the soured cream into the mixture and cook very gently to (appropriately enough), 'The Meal' by Ashton, Gardner and Dyke (1:00). Be careful – if it boils, it will curdle.

Season to taste, and press 'stop.'

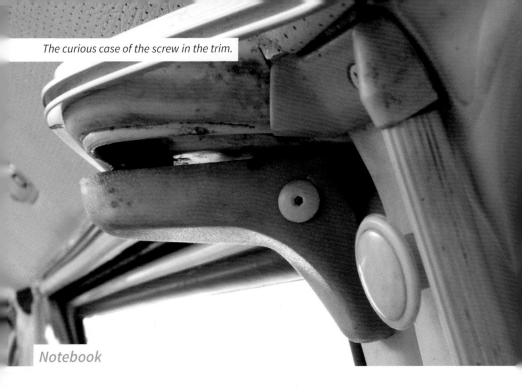
The curious case of the screw in the trim.

Notebook

This is an oddity, but get yourself a notebook and pen.

You will read this, think 'hmm,' and then promptly forget about it. You will only remember it when you are sat in your camper one night, relaxing with a beverage …

There'll come a time when you'll find yourself chilling on a site, spending a longer than usual amount of time in your little home-from-home, and you will spot something that will irritate you.

It will catch your eye the following night, and the night after that. It won't be anything major, it won't be crucial, but it will brass you right off. You'll tell yourself that you will resolve the issue when you get home, when you have access to the correct tools, or can order a new one, or whatever.

In reality, you'll go home and forget about it. It may creep into the periphery of your thoughts, but by the time you are able to nip out to the bus to sort it, the memory will be gone. You won't actually remember what it was you'd promised yourself you'd do, until the next time that you're sitting, once again on-site, in your camper, chilling with a mild alcoholic beverage … and again, it will catch your eye.

My personal elephant in the room was a missing screw. It served no purpose. It was supposed to hold on a bit of plastic trim that didn't even have the decency to fall off because of the missing screw. It haunted me for what felt like an eternity.

Finally, I packed myself a little notebook and a pen. I placed it in the 'other drawer' – the one without the cutlery. The very next time we were camping, I spotted the missing screw and made a note of it straight away in my little notebook.

When we returned home, I took the bus to the garage and pointed at the little hole. I have many screws, but I instructed the garage to source and fit the correct screw.

My turmoil was finally at an end.

Loaded tortilla chips

I appreciate that many people are concerned about cooking inside their buses. Since I've recently had a new pop-top roof installed – with a luxurious fluffy lining and a replacement perforated headlining – I am one of them. This, however, is an incredibly simple meal that doesn't spit or smell, and can cheerfully be made inside the camper without worrying about any kind of undue mess.

Ingredients
- Corn tortilla chips
- A selection of cheeses
- About 7cm of chorizo, finely diced
- Ready-made tubs of guacamole and sour cream dip

Method

This is something to cook under the built-in grill. There's a reason why people don't use these more: it's a nice idea, but if you've used it, you'll know that the only thing it does well is burn stripes down the centre of your toast. To make it work a little better, light it and turn it to maximum. Leave for a good three to five minutes, and use this time to pour the chips into a baking tray. Sprinkle them with the finely-diced chorizo, and cover everything with thinly-sliced cheese. In the photographs,

I've used Red Leicester and Gouda. Mixing a variety of cheeses makes far more difference than you'd expect: it brings out the best aspects of the cheeses to create a taste sensation.

When you're ready, turn down the grill to as low a setting as you can manage without it going out, and slide the baking tray underneath.

Close the front flap and pour a couple of glasses of Mexican lager to get yourselves into a chilled out state of mind. Your nose will let you know when the food is ready, as the oils from the chorizo begin to seep into the corn chips and the hot cheese melts.

Using a tea-towel or similar, remove the baking tray, divide the corn chips between a couple of plates, and add some exciting sauces and dips. We only had the two shown here, but you can add refried beans, sliced jalapeños, whatever … the world is your onion!

Campsite etiquette

Or, how to camp well without irritating any of your fellow inmates.

The side of the camper van without the sliding door is known in restoration circles as the 'long side,' due to the length of the side panel. When camping, this same side becomes the 'dead side,' as nothing ever happens there. The first rule of camping (unless you are pitching with friends as a group) is to park up with this dead side facing the open side of your neighbour's bus. This works both ways: by the time you have your curtains drawn you'll have forgotten that they're even there, and they won't be looking back to see if you are looking back at them.

Meanwhile, you can get on with having lots of fun around the other side, by the opening door, and away from prying eyes.

Theoretically, campers should follow the 30ft rule … unless you're at a festival, when this often becomes the 30cm rule!

Whoever they are, however near or far they may be, it's always worthwhile saying a quick hello to your camping neighbours. You might be surprised at the difference it can make. Things become much, much easier …

On one occasion we found ourselves camped next to a bunch of drunken young lads. Very, very drunk – but very happily drunk! We didn't have a lot to do with them, but they were totally smashed and we laughed because they were funny. As the sun began to go down, we set off to watch a half-baked Oompah band (it was that sort of a show). They all stayed behind, hanging about near their vans so they could snort some vodka. When we came back a couple of hours later, we found their buses all unlocked and open, and every last one of the lads totally passed out. We checked that they still had pulses, rolled a few of them over into the recovery position, and went to bed. It was the least we could do!

Portobello blue!

For the last few years we've generally tried to plan the meals for our trips and holidays in advance. That way, we don't have to take enough cooking gear and assorted ingredients to be able to cook anything we come across. We've not always done that, though: here's a meal we made whilst in Southwold.

We were wandering back from the pub towards the campsite when we saw these absolutely huge mushrooms displayed outside a greengrocer …

Ingredients
- 4 Portobello mushrooms
- 4 chestnut/brown mushrooms, diced
- Butter
- Cooked rice
- Cheese, thinly sliced
- Dried basil
- Black pepper, to season

Method
Light the barbecue and leave for a good 20 or 30 minutes to reach a useful working temperature. Lay the large mushrooms on their backs, remove the stems, spread butter liberally around the rims, and dice the stems together with the smaller mushrooms.

Place the mushrooms – butter-side down – onto the barbecue, and melt more butter in a small pan. Add the diced mushrooms, and cook until beginning to soften nicely. Add a packet of microwave rice, stir to mix everything together, and leave to warm through while you slice some cheese.

Remove the large mushrooms from the barbecue. Spread the gills liberally with more butter, and then top with as much of the rice and mushroom mix as you can. Season with a twist of black pepper, cover with the thinly-sliced cheese, and replace them on the barbecue. Sprinkle with the basil and relax whilst you wait for the cheese to melt.

Serve at once; you really won't need anything to accompany this.

I encourage you to try this recipe, the texture of the mushroom was almost like steak, and the huge quantity of butter ensured that it was completely lush!

The next time I made this I planned for it before leaving home, and took along some mozzarella, which melts far better and gives an exotic Italian feel. As you can see from the photographs, on this occasion – although I had cooked rice and basil – I only had a bit of cheddar for the cheese.

The barefoot foldaway harem; what fun, what decadence, what an absurdity …

Glamping

Glamping is about more than fairy lights, but not very much more …

It's a recent phenomenon, and an unimaginative fusion of two words that manages to come a close third to 'staycation.' The clear winner, by a couple of laps, remains 'Brexit.'

I don't much care for glamping – it can often get a bit silly – and we've been camping in our own sophisticated and glamorous fashion for many years.

Glamping was already quite bizarre to start with, and has since mutated to the point where it signifies little more than sleeping in a shepherd's hut, a chicken coop, a pigsty, or simply a knackered old shed. As a child of the '70s, the thought of being dragged to spend a week's holiday in such a place would have driven me to hysteria, and necessitated a solo bus ride to the nearest orphanage. Now such places are described as 'vintage,' and decorated with a load of old tat that you'll find has been rebranded as 'shabby chic.' The whole lot is gentrified only by that ubiquitous string of fairy lights!

I've even seen a caravan decorated with an old shower curtain, masquerading as a sunshade. It looked okay, and clearly a lot of work had gone into it, but it was still a shower curtain. Amongst other things, the little fishes gave it away! Tiny, dated old caravans have suddenly become the thing to be seen in, and if you can find a 'Dandy' folding cardboard version (essentially a pile of hardboard sheets that you assemble on-site until they look like a bit like a caravan) for less than a king's ransom, you are a better man than me. What began as a clever way to add a bit of appeal and glamour to camping has become skewed, in a media-led attempt to make places you'd have never even considered for a holiday a decade ago appear desirable.

Back here in camper van circles, the venerable old Volkswagen – for years the poor relation, on account of its performance and cramped accommodation – has recently found itself the epitome of all that is perceived as cool.

Mexican steak with queso fresco (GF)

Queso fresco is Spanish for 'fresh cheese,' and is a crumbly cheese like feta – but it sounds far more exotic!

The food stylist was let loose on this, but left the project immediately afterwards …

Ingredients
- A nice slice of rump steak
- 2tbsp olive oil
- 3tsp garlic paste
- 1tsp chilli powder
- 1tsp cumin
- Salt and pepper
- ¼ bottle of lager

For the dressing
- 1 avocado
- 1 tub of Greek yoghourt
- Fresh coriander, chopped
- 2 limes, zest and juice of

For the salad
- 1 romaine lettuce
- ¼ pack black beans
- Cherry tomatoes, halved
- 1 avocado, cut into chunks
- ⅓ pack of queso fresco or feta cheese
- Fresh coriander, to garnish

Method
Mix together the olive oil, garlic, chilli powder, cumin, salt and pepper in a polythene bag. Then add the steak and pour the lager into the bag, and seal it. Leave it to marinate for at least as long as it takes to consume the rest of the beer, and preferably for much, much longer.

You can then make a great dressing by mixing the ripe avocado, yoghourt, coriander, lime zest and lime juice, but on this occasion the weather forecast wasn't brilliant so I took the marinating steak in its bag and bought a tub of guacamole!

I cooked this outside on my gas-powered Beauclaire, which I lit and left for about five minutes to come to temperature. Remove the steak from the bag of marinade, place it onto the hot griddle pan and cook, turning once. About two minutes per side is spot-on for medium-rare, three minutes a side for medium, and so on. Remove the steak from the pan and wrap it in a couple of sheets of tinfoil, then leave to rest under a tea towel for about five minutes. Slice the lettuce and place it, together with the drained beans and the halved tomatoes, onto a couple of plates. Slice the steak across the grain into thin, ¼in strips, and lay this over the salad together with the avocado, then sprinkle over the crumbled feta.

Finally, pour over the guacamole, garnish with the freshly chopped coriander, and serve. It's a taste sensation!

Takeaway

Many, many years ago – I think we were camping on the Caravan Club site in Minehead – we saw the couple opposite us have an Indian takeaway delivered.

It had never occurred to me that such a thing was even possible. It was our last camp of the season, and so the idea was put on a back burner. I filed it away somewhere in the back of my mind, ready to drag out at some indeterminate point in the future.

Early the next year, we were arranging to visit a VW show about 20-odd miles from home. The takeaway thing popped into my head for a moment, only to be replaced with an even better idea. What if I could get a Sunday paper delivered, direct to my camper, as the people around me were just waking and setting up for the day?

The map was consulted, the nearest village identified, and the newsagent pinpointed. The idea was to let the folk on the gate know, and point the paperboy in my direction. 'Paperboy' is where it all began to go badly wrong.

Fortunately, I rang the papershop, rather than turning up at the counter, but the conversation went something like this:

'Good morning miss, do you deliver papers?'

'And do you deliver on a Sunday?'

'Do you think you could deliver one to me in my little orange van, which will be parked in the show field, at the end of the road?'

'I appreciate that it's a bit out of your way, but I'd be prepared to pay handsomely.'

'And would I be correct in thinking that it would be delivered by a paperboy?'

'Like a school-age child on a little bike …'

It was only at this very late stage that I realised: although I was asking for something very innocent, which might have been mildly amusing for a half a dozen friends, I had gone about it all wrong. There was a fair chance that if I continued, I'd be leaving the festival in a police car.

I still think it was a clever idea!

Orange chicken casserole (GF)

Rather than make a British casserole, which is traditionally a bit heavy for camping and often a bit brown, I've found a Mediterranean chicken dish with a delicious combination of rice, olives, peppers and orange! All of this can be done on-site, but if you measure and slice before you leave home, you'll make your life even easier.

Ingredients

- 3tbsp olive oil
- 2 chicken fillets
- 1 medium onion, sliced
- 1 large red pepper, sliced
- 1tsp garlic paste
- 4 sun-dried tomatoes, sliced
- 7cm chorizo sausage, sliced
- ¼tsp paprika
- 100g rice
- 12 olives
- 1 glass of fine white wine
- Boiling water
- Tomato ketchup
- 1 orange
- ½tsp mixed herbs
- Salt and pepper, to season

Directions

Begin by boiling the kettle; use the waiting time to slice the onion, pepper and tomatoes. Heat a generous splash of olive oil in the casserole dish, add the chicken portions, and brown them for a few minutes, then remove and place on kitchen towel. Add a spot more oil and turn up the heat. When the oil is hot, add the sliced onion and peppers, stirring occasionally for about five minutes. This is a good time to taste the wine before it's too late …

Add the garlic, sun-dried tomatoes and sliced chorizo, and stir for a couple of minutes. Then stir in the rice, and add the tomato ketchup, the paprika, glass of wine, and just enough hot water (from the kettle) to cover. This is probably another good opportunity to grab a bit more wine for another tasting – just to check that everything is okay – whilst you bring everything back to the boil, before turning the heat down to a gentle simmer.

Season to taste, then add the chicken to the pan, ensuring that the rice remains submerged in the liquid. Add the herbs, the orange and the olives. Cover with the lid, sit back, and take the time to enjoy some quality time with another glass of wine (because you've earned it) while the casserole continues to cook for about an hour.

Disposable barbies are great!

When it comes to cooking equipment, there's normally only a kettle, a double skillet, and a disposable barbecue tucked away in the bowels of the van. If I'm going to use anything more specialised, I'll load it when I pack the bedding, the clothes, and the food required for the trip. There's no point humping around an extra gas bottle and a bag of charcoal if you're not going to be using them.

In the good old days, throwaway barbies used to be three for a fiver at the supermarket, and I used to buy loads of them. More recently, environmental concerns have meant that not only are they frowned upon, they also cost a whole lot more!

I still like them; for something relatively simple, they can be ideal, and when they work, they work well. On occasion, though, you get a bad one and they become a pain in the parts. Some years ago, I met a Spanish bloke on a campsite – an interesting chap, who said that he'd show me how to cook mushrooms successfully on a barbecue. Off to a promising start, he ran a skewer through half a dozen plump white mushrooms, laid them – nicely oiled – onto the barbecue rack, and then out of the blue ...

... his disposable barbie went out, as on occasion they are wont to do. It's happened to me, and it can be a right palaver trying to persuade a tin tray full of dead coals to show some interest in burning once the lighting paper has gone. It didn't cause this chap the merest moment of annoyance, however.

Taking a couple of moments to dismantle his barbecue, he lifted the top wire rack and put it onto his gas stove. He then picked up the majority of the good-sized charcoal, placed it on the rack, and fired up the gas.

Within about ten minutes he had a healthy selection of nicely glowing charcoal nuggets. He then simply tipped them back into the tray and replaced the rack – an amazingly simple idea that I won't forget in a hurry.

Pan haggerty (GF*)

A traditional one-pot wonder, perfect for cooking inside the camper to warm you through on a chilly evening.

Ingredients
- 1tbsp vegetable oil
- 125g streaky bacon
- 3 potatoes, thinly sliced into rounds
- 1 onion, peeled and sliced
- 1 vegetable stock cube
- 75g cheddar cheese, grated
- Salt and black pepper, to season

Method
Boil the kettle and make up about 125ml of vegetable stock. Meanwhile, heat the vegetable oil in a deep-ish oven-proof pan and fry the bacon for three to four minutes - or until it begins to turn golden-brown and slightly crisp. Remove it from the pan, and set to one side to drain on kitchen towel.

In the same pan, arrange a layer of the thinly-sliced potatoes over the bottom of the pan. Cover the potatoes with a layer of sliced onions. Layer over some of the crispy bacon, then season with salt and pepper. Repeat the process with the remaining potatoes, onions and bacon, finishing with a layer of potatoes. Season with more salt and freshly ground black pepper.

Pour over the stock, so that all of the ingredients are just covered, then bring to the boil. Cover the pan with a lid, and reduce the heat to a simmer. Continue cooking for around 15 to 25 minutes, or until the potatoes are tender.

Preheat the grill to high! This, of course, is the notorious Fellows comedy 'black line special' grill.

Uncover the pan, and sprinkle over the grated cheese. You must turn the grill right down to its gentlest simmer setting before putting anything you ever plan to eat anywhere near it. Once you've done so, put the pan underneath the grill until the cheese is bubbling and golden brown – if this were a conventional grill, I'd write, 'for about five to six minutes,' but I can't do that. Even though it's turned right down, you must watch it like a hawk, and keep moving the pan about and from side to side, or it will be black-striped!

Transfer the pan haggerty into bowls and serve with fresh, crusty bread to mop up the juices.

Another weekend festival, and lots more fun with a sunshade

This was the very local 'Off The Tracks' festival. It's held within the boundaries of Donington Park, just outside the racetrack fence, and, quite literally, off the tracks. It's a great idea: there are multiple stages, both inside and out; there's a beer and cider festival; even a meditation village. There's entertainment for kids, and without doubt the most laid-back, chilled out vibe I have ever experienced. This is a proper hippy-fest.

We saw well known bands like Big Country; the original rude boy, Neville Staple (from the Specials), and lots of up-and-coming young artists. I even met a bloke that I'd been to school with, and not seen in 30 years. The only problem, for me, was that I hadn't been before and I chose my pitch particularly badly. It looked okay – it was close enough to the action without being right next to the toilets, or on the wet grass by the forest. It should have been exactly right.

But I'd camped far too close to the race track, which I hadn't realised would be in action that weekend. Just beyond an entirely innocuous-looking five-bar gate was an entrance lane that led to the pits. Not only was there the incessant howl and crackle of racing engines slowing down rapidly, there was also a siren to alert people in the pits to the swiftly approaching cars. Sitting around the camper between acts was, sadly, not an option. A bit of a disaster – and then there was the rain …

The picture shows my sunshade, which I'd pitched as described earlier in this book, using multiple guy lines, and the poles at a jaunty angle rather than vertical. You'll see that on this occasion I also set up the sunshade with one end much higher than the other, in an attempt to encourage the copious rain to run straight off. This normally works well. On this occasion, the rain was practically biblical, and, despite the extreme angle, still pooled in the middle.

We abandoned and went home early!

Spam & baked beans (GF)

When it comes to survival in the wilds, everyone knows that it is possible to survive for weeks and weeks armed with just a hat, a Swiss army knife, and a decent pub.

I like to buy the odd tinned, or long-life, food item when I'm perusing the supermarket – so that I'm prepared for the inevitable zombie invasion – but a recent stocktake revealed Pot Noodles, ancient tinned steak and kidney puddings, frightening-looking meatballs, corned beef, spam, baked beans and Poultry Pâté! I have no idea where this came from, but it apparently contains seven per cent preservative, and needs no refrigeration! All of this stuff is tinned, dried, or otherwise long-life, and will probably last another 20 years without me worrying about it. Here's a bit of a cheat: the quintessential British camping meal. It's not quite the Famous Five, but it's close.

Ingredients
- 1 tin of Spam
- 1 tin of baked beans
- A splash of oil
- Black pepper, freshly ground

Method
Empty the tin of beans into a pan and heat gently on a stove. Remove the Spam from the tin. If you have a can opener without handles (I'm not kidding, these things are brilliant and last for years), you'll find that you can remove the top and bottom of the tin, and simply push the meat out!

Cut the Spam into half-inch cubes and fry in another pan using a drop of oil. Aficionados of Spam cookery suggest that the curved ends should be removed and given to the dog or otherwise discarded, as these detract from the true symmetry of the meal.

When the meat begins to turn a slightly darker colour and the edges look like they are becoming crispy, discard the fat, add the Spam to the beans, and mix gently.

Season only with a twist of freshly-ground black pepper, and serve with a crisp white wine.

When the zombies do come to town, you'll be pleased that you tore out this page and tucked it away in the back of your van with some tins!

I'm not entirely sure about having the heaviest part of the camper hanging out way beyond the back axle of the recovery vehicle – its steering must have been incredibly light!

Breakdown ...

It's a 40-year-old van, and, with the best will and all the maintenance in the world, on occasion, the thing is bound to pack up. I think our most frustrating tale – which involves not one, but multiple instances of a 'failure to proceed' – dates back to the Brighton Breeze event of 2002. The plan was to drive down to London, pitch up overnight, and then drive down to Brighton in convoy with a couple of hundred other air-cooled buses the following morning. Our camper had been running faultlessly in the weeks leading up to its biggest endurance test of the year. We left home, together with friends in another bus, and, 20 miles down the M1, our camper died. It simply cut out.

We diagnosed a faulty coil, and somehow managed to restart it. We left the motorway at the next junction, and it cut out again. We left it on a farm track and drove in the second bus to a local scrapyard, where we found a replacement coil.

With the coil swapped over, our bus fired up as good as gold, and off to London we went. The next morning, all was well until we joined the M25, and it cut out again. Now, we had two faulty coils instead of the single unit we had the previous day. By swapping the overheating coil with the other, which we put into the fridge to cool down in the meantime, we covered the 58 miles to the seaside in far-too-many eight-mile sections. We were exhausted, but knew we'd be able to buy a brand new one when we arrived. Oddly, we weren't in the mood for taking any photographs of this debacle, and the photograph shows a far more organised disaster when the old van was spluttering, but continuing, along the M1.

Before entering a new, hi-tech section of carriageway, with all lanes running and no hard shoulder, we bottled out. We pulled into a service area and called out the very nice recovery people to come and give us a ride home.

Barbecued rib of beef

This is less of a proper recipe and more of an exercise in how far it's possible to push a disposable barbie.

Ingredients
- A single rib of beef – I had the butcher cut mine just slightly wider than the bone, at about 2in thick. It weighed just over a kilo.
- Salt
- Butter
- Crusty cobs
- Horseradish or mustard
- Lots of foil
- A cheap and cheerful ten-bob barbecue

Method
Light the barbecue and leave it alone for at least 20 – probably 30 – minutes.

When it's up to temperature, place the rib on a sheet of foil and then onto the cooking surface. If you place it straight onto the grill it will stick. You could oil it, but that would involve all sorts of smoke and flames.

Leave it to cook for between ten to 15 minutes, then turn it over and onto a fresh sheet of foil (the first one will be flimsy, brittle and worn out). Leave for another ten to 15 minutes, then remove from the heat and

wrap in a third sheet of foil, then in a tea towel, and leave for the essential 'rest' – at least another 20 to 30 minutes. This will help the joint to retain its heat, re-arrange its fibres, and continue cooking to ensure that it is cooked throughout.

When you unwrap the meat, you'll find that it is not cold, red or bloody, but properly pink in the middle and spectacularly crunchy, blackened and caramelised on the outside.

While it's still hot, cut into thick, chunky slices and add horseradish (or mustard), lashings of butter, salt, and then serve in crusty cobs. There'll be lots left for tomorrow, when you'll be able to slice it much thinner and be more sophisticated with salad, mayonnaise, and even dainty brown sandwiches with the crusts removed.

To say that it practically filled the little disposable barbecue isn't an exaggeration, as you can see, but it worked out very nicely and made sandwiches for the two of us, *and* provided scraps for the dog for three days.

I've not backed onto my levelling blocks because I'm not really using them – I've just put them out of the way, under the camper.

Windbreaks

The fair wife and I often find ourselves at loggerheads when it comes to the issue of windbreaks. She's a big fan of them, not only for their innate ability to fend off the wind, but also for the privacy they afford. The problem is that I totally disagree: on a warm sunny day, they can often shut out the wind completely, creating a small area that's not only too hot and too stuffy, but no longer has a view.

We also disagree on where we should put them up. I'd prefer a straight-ish run down the windward side, with just a kink at the end to keep it upright, whereas she'd have one on all four sides.

The only thing we manage to agree on is that the traditional British seaside windbreak – with lots of scratchy, stripy nylon fabric, and half a dozen wooden poles – is completely useless. If you remain unconvinced, take a look around the campsite the next time you hear someone spending an extended period of time hitting something with a big hammer.

You can beat the poles into the ground as hard as you like, and for as long as you like, but it won't be very long before they blow over, and you'll find yourself hammering them back in before you know it. These things don't even really work in soft sand, and they take up a relatively huge amount of space when they're rolled up.

Alternative versions designed specifically for camping are available, which fold away into small bags, and use lightweight folding alloy poles and lots of guy lines to keep them upright in the strongest winds.

For our next trip away, we're planning to take a camouflage net, which I appear to have acquired, in place of any kind of windbreak. The thinking is that, because of its multiple holes, it will provide some protection from the wind, whilst not even threatening to blow down. By simply throwing it over the sunshade and securing the corners to the ground, it should be an absolute breeze to put up!

Smoked salmon, barbecued on a wooden plank!

Barbecuing on a piece of wood is surprisingly similar to cooking in a pan: it provides a stable surface to work on, although may smoke and catch fire. The smoke is a welcome addition, because it adds another dimension of flavour to the food. The fire is not so great, and you'll need a squirty bottle filled with water to put out any untoward flare-ups. The plank also insulates the food from the direct heat of the barbecue coals, and lengthens the cooking time by about 50 per cent, which is particularly useful when barbecuing delicate foods like fish and vegetables. Look out for a clean, untreated piece of hardwood, about an inch thick and just larger than the food you plan to cook. If you leave it outside and under your bus the night before, it may just soak up enough early morning dew to help prevent too many flames.

Ingredients

- 1 salmon fillet, about 700g
- A bunch of trimmed spring onions
- Lemon juice
- A generous splash of maple syrup, about 2tbsp
- Another splash of dark soy sauce
- 1tsp garlic paste
- 1tsp ginger paste
- 1 avocado to accompany, peeled and sliced

Method

Begin by lighting the barbecue. Leave it for a good 20 to 30 minutes, until it settles down to a usable temperature, and make a garlic and maple glaze by combining the maple syrup, lemon juice, dark soy sauce, chopped ginger and chopped garlic in a small pan or empty tin. Place this on the BBQ to warm through, and stir well.

Wipe the top of the plank with a little oil. Arrange the salmon on a bed of spring onions and place the plank onto the barbecue. Baste the salmon regularly with the glaze. There is no need to turn the food over when you cook it like this.

Cooking times are a little arbitrary, as it will depend on the thickness of the wood that you're using! Remove the plank to the table, and serve the individual portions onto plates directly from it.

Bikes

I have a bicycle. I knew it was flat around the campsite here, so I brought my old bike specifically to bring back fish and chips from the harbour while they were still hot. Look at the state of it! I'm not a keen cyclist – I'm barely a reluctant cyclist – but I bought a 1966 Raleigh Small Wheel Mk1. The RSW was a very low-cost alternative to the Moulton cycle, but instead of clever suspension it has fat, low pressure tyres, making it an absolute drudge to ride. It cost a derisory sum from eBay many years ago: I'd bid whilst watching an episode of *The Prisoner*, and it seemed like a good idea at the time, but I'd failed to take into account that it had been snowing for a week, and the bike was in Manchester. At that time, I had a camper van with badly-holed heat exchangers and no bike rack …

I originally planned to paint it to match my camper van, but it has a strange sort of charm with its own co-ordination going on. I'd never seen brake cables that match the metallic red frame before, so instead of re-building and re-painting it, I just replaced the brake blocks and the tyres, cleaned it up, and made it usable again.

I keep getting it out of the garage and looking at it. I've sourced new decals, and found people who will powder coat it and re-upholster the saddle for me. But, as the years have passed, I have grown to be intrigued by its unique, low-drag cycle basket, and realised that it's a ready-made 'rat look' bike. And then I looked again, and I saw the number plate that I bought for it. It's a laminate vinyl in the wrong, post-2001 font.

I would love to buy a period-correct pressed-alloy plate in the earlier typeface, and 'distress' it by driving back and forth over it until it matches the patina of the bike, but I couldn't bring myself to wilfully damage something that's not only shiny and new, but cost more than the bike.

Posh Pot Noodle

This is the platter that I designed, cooked and constructed immediately after the food stylist and I had been obliged to part company, because of what we agreed to tell people were 'artistic differences.' He was all right, but he made such a meal out of everything we made together.

He wanted everything to look 'just so.' The point of this book is that you can make all of this relatively simple grub in a field, or in the back of a camper van with the standard two-burner hob. Chances are that you're fighting the weather, as well as the cramped conditions. There is no time for sprinkling masses of freshly cut herbs, or adding a soft poached egg, just for a splash of colour, to something that tastes great, but looks – for want of a better expression – too brown!

Here, then, is how you can appear to be not only a very elegant glamper, but more than that: a camping guru.

This recipe is just a bit of fun. The best bit is probably the posh paper plate which contrives to transform a very simple and humdrum snack into a decadent-looking meal.

Ingredients
- 1 Beef & Tomato Pot Noodle
- 1 can of cheap and cheerful meatballs
- Fresh coriander

Method

Boil the kettle. Make the Pot Noodle as per the instructions, and gently heat the meatballs in a saucepan. Using a fork, lift the noodles from the pot and arrange them on the plate to create an even layer. Top with the meatballs, and, finally, sprinkle a generous handful of freshly trimmed coriander leaves over the top.

Not the most sophisticated meal to appear in this slim volume, I grant you, but certainly one of the better-looking ones! At the right event, in the right company, this can be made to look like the best thing since sliced bread.

Don't forget to call your kitchen towel 'napkins,' and add the chopsticks. These couple of things really do add sophistication and a pleasing aesthetic touch, lifting this cheap and cheerful snack into far more debonair and gentrified territory.

Be scene, be safe

Back in the days when I still had reasonable eyesight, and a printer to go with my computer, I used to spend hours making amusing slogans for my spare tyre. I'd print out the words at the correct size onto a couple of sheets of A4 paper, and then, using masking tape, I'd secure them to a sheet of what the lovely Valerie Singleton used to call 'sticky-backed plastic.' I'd spend a pleasant hour relaxing to some mellow tunes, whilst painstakingly cutting out all of the letters with a pair of nail scissors.

Aligning them on the vinyl tyre cover is relatively simple. I simply used more masking tape to create a straight baseline, and stuck them on – by eye. I made no end of them – there's a few scattered about in the various pictures – but, sadly, it never occurred to me that I should make a record of them all.

It was whilst reviewing this particular photograph that it suddenly dawned on me that my number plate was completely wrong. That's a 1979 plate in a post-2001 font. I was mortified, and utterly embarrassed. How could I have been so stupid?

It's one of those curious things that, until the difference is pointed out to you, you remain blissfully unaware of, but then once seen, it is completely impossible to unsee. The later font, sometimes called 'Charles Wright New,' was designed to make space for a Euro logo on the left hand side, is marginally narrower, and has serifs on the Bs Ds and Ps. Everything suddenly looked completely wrong.

An internet search was commenced, and it was soon revealed that I had no fewer than three period-correct options. First, either pressed aluminium plates in either the original 'Charles Wright' font, or the now-unobtainable 'Serck' font. Or, I could enjoy the luxury of plastic digits on an alloy background. I plumped for the latter, and spent an additional 70p on a handful of decadent yellow and white nylon nuts to fasten them on with.

Diffuser frittata   (GF)

One of the many problems you encounter when cooking in a camper is that the pans are much lighter and thinner than the ones at home. This has led to me unexpectedly burning food in the centre of my pan, and having to spend the best part of an aeon scraping it clean.

A heat diffuser solves this problem in a moment. You can probably tell that mine is ancient – I bought it from a stall on the market – but you can get them from the ubiquitous Amazon and elsewhere. They're nice and shiny when new, but they go rusty and begin to look dreadful almost immediately. It's simply a double-skinned disc of steel that sits on the hob, under the pan.

You can then turn down your stove, secure in the knowledge that there won't be a great mass of black matter bonded to your nice new pan as soon as you turn your back on it for a moment or two.

It helps to make this frittata recipe work much better. I realise that 'real men (probably still) don't eat quiche,' but frittatas don't have the pastry and claim to be the new superfood.

Ingredients
- 5 eggs, beaten
- Ham or bacon, cut into 1cm cubes
- 1 small potato, cut into 1cm cubes
- 1 onion, diced
- 50g of cheese, cut into thin slices
- A sprinkle of thyme
- 2tbsp olive oil

Method
Heat the oil until hot, and add the potato, onion and bacon. Turn down the heat, place the diffuser under the pan and fry everything gently for a few minutes. Then add the cheese and beaten eggs and continue to let it cook very, very gently. It's not like an omelette: this cooks relatively slowly, and can sit there for a quarter of an hour.

Finish off by placing the pan under the hot grill. The eggs will fluff up nicely, but be careful that you don't allow a plastic pan handle to burn. Slide the frittata onto a plate, and cut into wedges. Serve hot or cold.

Fuel gauge

My fuel gauge has packed up. It stopped working more than a decade ago. I remember it well; it was almost as if the Volkswagen was designed and built with a 100,000-mile life expectancy. At that point, things began to fail with an alarming, but short-lived, frequency.

For a moment being without a fuel gauge was disconcerting, but I realised that all I'd have to do would be to pay close attention to the distance I covered. Like an idiot, I still managed to run out of fuel on a couple of occasions. Since then, though, my lesson has been well and truly learned. I now automatically check my mileage each and every time I fill up, and the failed gauge has been replaced by a Post-it note with a five-digit number on it.

It's odd – I've stopped paying any attention to the fuel gauges in the other vehicles that I drive. They all swing about wildly once they get down below about a quarter, anyway. I simply fill up the bus every 200 miles. Occasionally, over the winter lay-up, I lose track and rush down to the petrol station before it runs out. Once I put in £2.70's worth; the woman on the till was not impressed.

I have subsequently discovered an online fuel consumption calculator tool. I rush home after a week's driving holiday, with a wallet full of petrol receipts, and excitedly enter them all to discover just how good – or bad – my fuel economy has been. The best I have ever recorded was barely a tad above 30 miles per gallon, despite it being a straight motorway run between two service stations, at about 55mph.

The real point is that any sudden drop in fuel economy should alert me to the first sign of a potential fault. It gives me the chance to drive the van to my man with the spanners, to let him take a closer look, before it leaves me stranded somewhere remote, cold, and with a fair – but distinctly grumpy – wife.

Chips

Everyone loves chips! It's a curious thing, cooking when you're camping – at home, surrounded by the comprehensive facilities of my kitchen, I automatically make 'a meal.' In its most obvious form, it's meat and two veg. When I'm out in the back of beyond, I love to barbecue an exciting piece of meat that's been marinading for hours. The problem is, what can I be bothered to make as an accompaniment? I could make a simple salad … but the easiest solution is simply to stick it in a cob, a bread roll, or whatever.

Over the years, I've found a variety of solutions, and you'll discover a few of them scattered about this book. Packets of 'microwave rice' heat up well in a hot pan in just a couple of minutes, or posh crisps, coleslaw and ready-made salads work well and are dead simple.

I spent a lot of time experimenting with oven chips, onion rings, and the like. They will cook surprisingly well in either a double skillet, a COBB with the lid on, or on a Beauclaire/Cadac.

In all cases, you need to keep shaking or turning them regularly. Cheesy chilli chips, in foil parcels, were a dismal failure!

Then, for a laugh, I bought myself one of those bargain 'BBQ frying pans' – strange devices with holes in. Advertised as 'ideal for cooking healthy vegetables over a barbecue,' it spent time in the back of the camper, taunting me with my failure to come up with a decent use for it. Then, whilst messing about with oven chips, it struck me …

It worked, and it worked surprisingly well. I placed this odd little pan on a barbie that was up to a steady working temperature. I oiled the pan, wiped it round with some kitchen towel, added a portion of oven chips and a handful of onion rings, and cooked them over the barbie, stirring and shaking regularly to ensure that nothing stuck.

Everything cooked properly and looked fine. It was all hot throughout and beginning to colour nicely within about 30 minutes.

Heater

We survived for a ludicrously long time in a very, very basic camper van. The changes that we've made have, to some degree, been forced upon us. First, the radio in the dashboard packed up, so I went to buy a new one. Foolishly, I was talked into an all-singing, all-dancing CD/DVD model, which did nothing but constantly flatten the battery. Before I thought it through properly, I'd had a leisure battery fitted. The new radio managed to repeatedly flatten that, too, and before I knew it, I'd been persuaded to have a mains hook-up installed, to top up the second battery. With the ECU came the luxury of three-pin sockets, which coincided with a trip to Dunelm, which had teeny tiny oil-filled radiators on special offer …

Oil-filled radiators in camper vans are not a good idea.

This is a camping fact.

I'm unsure how to describe the heat that they give off – there is presumably a scientific word that will – but it's not the right kind of heat. It warmed the air, a bit, but it also caused massive amounts of condensation to form on the vinyl of the pop-top bellows. It was actually raining inside the camper van! Even after we wiped things down, switched everything off, and went to bed, the condensation was still there – enough for a single drop every now and again, just as a chap was dropping off to sleep.

The final straw came with a bitterly cold trip to the Inner Hebrides. We went in the spring to avoid the midges, and spent the evenings wearing every stitch of clothing that we'd taken, before retiring to bed long before dark.

We eventually returned home and researched heaters and the people who fit them. The thought of a petrol-burning Eberspächer frankly terrified me, and a local boat builder convinced me, instead, of the sheer joy of a Propex heater. It was promptly installed somewhere underneath the bus, and all I have to do is to turn the knob. Lovely warm – and, importantly, dry – air is blown in within moments. Here, I hope, begins our lasting joy.

Tournedos Rossini

Exotic steak dishes, done dirt cheap.

Tournedos Rossini is a French steak dish that was practically de rigueur 30 years ago. Here is a very simplified version, re-imagined for campers of the new millennium, using that long-forgotten and cheap sandwich ingredient, the minute steak. You'll need to ask your butcher for this, as it doesn't seem to be readily available any more. It can be made from slices of topside or inexpensive braising steak. Whatever you use, you must tenderise it to within an inch of its life, either with a special textured steak hammer, or you can do it by placing it between two chopping boards and pressing down on it very hard ... with a Volkswagen.

Ingredients

- Minute steaks
- Soft cobs
- Pâté
- Mushrooms, thinly sliced
- Butter

Method

Tournedos is traditionally served on a crispy sautéed croûton, topped with foie gras and truffle shavings. On the campsite, some compromise and creativity is called for.

Heat the butter in a hot pan and add the halved and buttered cobs, together with some thinly-sliced mushrooms. When the bread begins to colour, remove the cobs from the pan, re-assemble, and place to one side whilst you stir the mushrooms and fry the flattened steak for a minute on each side. Remove the steak and place it in the cob, whilst you add a 1cm-thick slice of pâté to the meat juices in the pan and heat for another minute.

Assemble the Rossini sandwich with the steak, the mushrooms and the pate. Press it down and leave for a moment or two, so that the flavours can combine and begin to intensify.

Pedants may point out that there should really be a trickle of demi-glace sauce made from a Madeira reduction, but I remind you: you're in a field, and the preparation of this pseudo-elegant sandwich involved backing an old camper van over a lump of cheap meat. If, however, you remain determined to impress your fellow campers with your attention to detail, you should start five minutes earlier and boil a drop of cheap red wine in a small pan until it thickens.

The double skillet

The stuff of legends. This is the renowned double skillet, and I make no apologies for the shabby appearance of my example. It's had some hammering over the last 20-odd years and the non-stick interior is still as good as it was when I bought it. The skillet was recommended as the answer to all my camper van cooking problems by an old girl I met at a Volkswagen show towards the end of the last century.

It's very clever, and works in a variety of different ways: simply as a couple of pans, with a Pyrex lid for one of them, or you could stack them, if you're the sort of person who likes to cook meat and vegetables separately. Where it really scores, though, is in its ability to attach the two pans together so that they form a very small, hob-top oven. Although comparatively expensive for what it was, it works as well now as it ever did. I was probably more sceptical when it arrived than you are now, reading this, but – and I remember this vividly – we were parked down by the seaside in Cornwall when we tried it out for the first time. To give it a proper test, we bought a box of frozen, oven-ready SFC chicken and chips from a supermarket. I kid you not, people were drifting past on the gorgeous smells emanating from our little van. We even heard a little girl ask her father where the nearest KFC was!

As a couple of top quality pans, and a way to cook oven chips, battered onion rings, and other frozen supermarket frippery, it is unbeatable.

You will find this on the inter-google after the briefest of searches. It only seems possible to buy them from one place, which I assume to be their ultimate source in Lancashire. Given that the address is 'the workshop, behind the car wash,' I fondly imagine a tiny company, run by a chap in a brown warehouse coat, with a fine collection of coloured biros and, quite possibly, a lathe beside his television set.

Pork shoulder

I've spent quite a while experimenting with barbecuing large cuts of meat. Here's one that works particularly well, which is known in America as the pork butt. The butchers on this side of the Atlantic joint their pork slightly differently, and, in English, this is a shoulder of pork. I've made it a handful of times using rolled and unrolled meat, and this makes surprisingly little difference.

Ingredients
- 1.5-2kg pork shoulder
- 3tsp brown sugar
- 3tsp paprika
- 2tbsp barbecue sauce
- 1tsp liquid smoke

Method
Mix together the dry ingredients to make a rub, and stir the liquid ingredients together to make a marinade. Fire up the COBB and, as is traditional, leave it for a good 20 or 30 minutes for the flames and smoke to die down, and for the coals to acquire a coating of white ash. Rub the joint all over with the dry spice mix and place it on the rack. Save the marinade to brush on later, when you turn the meat over at the halfway stage.

There's a lot of fat in a pork shoulder, and it will flare up and smoke in a most disconcerting fashion. I had to refuel the barbie with extra charcoal after about 90 minutes, but I kept the meat on the covered barbie for two-and-a-half hours.

On my first attempt I thought I'd ruined it: the joint was black and charred all over, but I wrapped it up in foil and left it to rest whilst I used the tail-end of the still hot barbecue to cook some sweetcorn. I'd managed to get hold of a couple of cobs still wrapped in their silks, and I simply ran them under the cold tap for a minute or two before placing them on the grill for 30 minutes.

The corn was perfectly steamed throughout, and the pork was utterly superb. Despite the superficial char – that on something smaller would have been ruinous – when cut into slices, it was excellent. It was incredibly moist on the inside, and with those lovely rings of redness that only smoking can create.

There is obviously an extinguisher very close at hand.

Tiny awning

As I've already mentioned, I'm not really keen on awnings: too big, too heavy, too much trouble, and then you have to take loads of extra stuff to fill them up!

I was recently given the opportunity to test out this very small, single-hoop inflatable version.

It answers one of my biggest criticisms of such devices, by being incredibly quick and simple to put up. You really do just attach it to the gutter rail, spread it out across the area you'd like it to be, and then simply pump it up whilst pulling on a couple of guy lines.

Secure the guy lines with pegs, and hammer in another half-dozen tent pegs, and that appears to be it: erection is complete. The awning is in place, and, on the occasions that we've used it, appears to completely shrug off the wind. It feels very secure.

Obviously there are no poles, which makes for one bag instead of two, and it is reasonably compact, tucking away behind the seat without drama – although it was surprisingly heavy for its size. I'm pretty sure that's because the air-beam weighs far more than a single pole would have done. There's also a big old pump and a length of hose to stash away.

Grudgingly, I was obliged to accept that it provides a far greater degree of shelter from the wind and rain than my old sunshade, and I can zip up my chairs and table inside it rather than using my pop-up tent when I leave my pitch.

I think that the real problem is that the fair wife and I just don't seem suited to awnings any more, having had three previous models blow down on us. We don't really sit inside them unless it's raining. We tend to sit just beyond them, so that we still have a view. Even if, like here at the Camper Jam Volkswagen bash, the view is just a spot of furtive people-watching, with lots of merry strangers walking back and forth amid the general hubbub of the show.

Pizza on the COBB

The COBB barbecue doubles as a small oven, which makes it ideal for a pizza.

If you wanted to do this properly, you could mix up a pizza base from scratch, and, in theory, you could roll it out on a chopping board with a wine bottle …

It's all well and good making a proper pizza at home, in the surroundings of a proper kitchen, but while you're out and about in the great wide-open, taking a break from the hurly burly of everyday life, you should just cheat and use a ready-made pizza base from the supermarket. I, for one, can't be bothered to scrape all that dough from under my fingernails when I'm camping.

This was actually cooked outside, and was only put into the van for this picture.

Ingredients
- 1 long-life pizza base – these are not chilled, and keep fresh for about 3 months
- 1 small tin of tomato puree
- A selection of meats from the Italian delicatessen; here I've used salami, mortadella, and – because he didn't have Parma ham – Tyrolean Speck!
- Mozzarella, thinly sliced – this is a really nice smoked version
- 1tsp dried oregano
- A little olive oil
- Or, of course, any other combination of pizza toppings that you fancy!

Method
Fire up the COBB, using lots of charcoal briquettes and the non-stick frying pan base. Put on the lid, and leave for about 15 minutes to become very hot.

Make up the pizza using the cheating base. You could create an authentic tomato base with onions, garlic and oregano, or you could cheat again and just use a small tin of tomato puree like in the pictures. Cover this with layers of the sliced meats, top with the thinly-sliced cheese, sprinkle with the oregano, and then drizzle a little olive oil over the top for that continental touch.

Place the assembled pizza into the very hot COBB, cover with the lid, and cook for about 15 minutes.

Using the COBB tool, you can simply lift the pan and slide the pizza onto a chopping board. Cut into slices and serve with a tub of coleslaw.

The good camping pitch paradox

A good pitch is so many different things to different people. I love the sort of sites that are little more than a field, either with or without numbers. I'm not keen on 'fully serviced' pitches where, although I can connect up to electricity, I also have to park in a line surrounded by other campers, and my only view is of endless white caravans. I appreciate that there are times when you could do with a shower, and your batteries actually do need recharging. I do insist on a toilet, but I much prefer a site and a pitch with a view.

Assuming that you are in the sort of touring site where it's a bit of a free-for-all, take some time to have a good look around and check the position of the sun. You don't have to have the navigational skills of Sherpa Tenzing or Scott of the Antarctic to appreciate that in the northern hemisphere – and when facing south – the sun appears to move from left to right, through about 180 degrees in spring and autumn, and closer to 270 degrees during the summer months, passing through the midpoint of its travel at around lunchtime.

It doesn't really matter where the sun will be at midday, as there's a good chance that you'll be away taking a leisurely lunch in a public house, or doing something even more interesting. What you don't want, though, is to be plunged into shadow before you have to. Look out for those trees, that barn, or even that mountain, as deep shade can be surprisingly cold relatively early on, whilst you watch other folk still bathed in gloriously bright warm sunshine. Ideally, it'd be nice to catch a few rays over breakfast, too, but it's not the end of the world if that's not on the cards.

With the sunshine sorted, the only other thing you should try to look out for is an angle from which you can take a photograph, for all your social media friends. Ideally, you'll want to show just your camper van and nothing but a gorgeous view behind it, with not another tent or caravan in shot.

Houmous & pea fritters

A quick vegetarian recipe that'll line up your Chakras!

Ingredients
- 160g frozen peas
- 200g tub of houmous
- 125g boiled rice
- ½tsp parsley
- ½tsp mint sauce,
- 1 chilli, deseeded
- ½tsp coriander
- ½tsp cumin
- 1 lemon, the zest of
- Olive oil
- Flour – gluten-free, if necessary

Method
Despite the frighteningly long list of ingredients, these are the easiest things to make, ever.

Flying in the face of my usual advice to mix and make things at home, then take them to a show or on holiday ready to cook, these really are simple enough to make anywhere, armed with just a spoon.

Mix together all of the ingredients and some flour at the end – enough to firm up the mixture, so that it becomes manageable. I used gluten-free plain flour so that the fair wife could have a couple, but It really doesn't matter what sort you use. Divide it into four equally-sized balls, and heat a small quantity of oil in a frying pan.

Carefully place the balls, a couple at a time, into the hot oil, and then, using your fingers, flatten them into burger shapes. For an easy life, try to make them the same sort of size as your bread rolls.

Fry them for about five minutes on each side: you'll be able to see the edges beginning to colour, indicating that they're ready to be turned over. They're still a little fragile at this point, so turn them over very carefully.

I photographed these and ate mine in a bread bun, while the fair wife had hers with a quick and dirty salad; they really are a taste sensation. The strength of the garlic in the houmous is countered well by the sweetness of the peas and the sharpness of the mint and lemon.

Beaten by the weather ...

From time to time it happens. The pictures show an occasion in the New Forest when the supermarket had run out of disposable barbecues and, in their place, for just a few quid sold me a small BBQ described as 'ideal for camping.' It soon became apparent that it was not actually ideal for anything. As the rain became progressively heavier, and the flames on my sparkling new grill failed to catch with the urgency required, I decided that discretion was the better part of sitting outside under a brolly any longer, and retired to the shelter of my awning. Once inside I was quickly distracted by a few cans of beer from the fridge, a big bag of crisps, and a secondhand paperback thriller that we'd brought from home. For me, the smell of the ink and the grubby pages of an old, well-thumbed book beats technology every time.

We have never even entertained the thought of installing a television screen in the camper, but did flirt briefly with the idea of keeping the bus online with an interweb dongle. On a couple of occasions we even took an iPad with us, loaded with a handful of things to watch ...

It simply didn't work out for us. We disagreed constantly about what to watch, finally agreeing that we'd each loaded stuff that was disliked by the other. As if that wasn't irritating enough, it then transpired that whenever we did watch anything, we were constantly distracted by things going on outside the camper van: the westering sun, and a chap walking past with a dog. In our little camping world, people-watching trumped technology every time, and whereas the action in a paperback pauses the very instant you glance up, the iPad demands more involvement, and so its days were short-lived.

The only concession we've really made to camping in the digital age is our constant use of an MP3 player. This links wirelessly to what, I understand, is known as the head unit (the thing on the dashboard where the radio used to go).

Cheatin' chicken Kievs

Everyone loves a garlic Kiev, but what a performance they are to make. All that triple-dipping in egg and breadcrumbs is almost enough to make a bloke weep and buy a packet of oven-ready frozen ones. Here's a relatively easy alternative that you might like to try: they really are worth the effort, as they taste significantly better than frozen.

Although it's quite possible to make these on-site, to be completely honest, the last couple of times I made them at home and took them, ready to bung on the BBQ. You'll also need a barbecue with a lid to cook these.

Ingredients
- 2 chicken fillets
- 4 rashers of streaky bacon
- ½ tub of cream cheese with garlic

Method
Using a sharp knife, cut a pocket in the underside of the chicken fillet – as deep as you can, but just short of cutting all the way through. Pack this with as much cream cheese as you can persuade to go in. Then, lay the bacon on a chopping board and, using the blunt edge of a knife, stretch out the bacon. It will become much thinner and about 35 per cent longer. Push the chicken back together to enclose the cheese and wrap it in the bacon. Hold everything together with baking bands, and wrap the parcels in tinfoil to keep them intact for transportation.

Fire up the BBQ, and leave it for about 20 or 30 minutes to come to a sensible temperature. I used my old COBB and the non-stick surface that's called a frying pan. Unwrap the chicken parcels and place them around the outside of the pan, cover the barbecue with its lid, and leave for about half an hour. As always with chicken, check that it is cooked through by either using a meat thermometer, or piercing with a sharp knife to check that the juices run clear. Remove the Kievs onto a plate, cover them with fresh foil to rest, and then, if desired, use the still-hot barbecue to heat up a packet of spicy microwave rice.

More miscellaneous tips

Here's another selection of miscellaneous tips and oddments:

- Compression bags will reduce a double quilt to a size small enough to pack, but don't leave it compressed for longer than you have to. It won't recover!
- Don't hang decorative lamps from your sunshade or awning, or, if you do, wear a cycling helmet.
- I haven't seen a proper 'Tupperware' box since I was a child; the plastic food boxes that I use throughout come from the local Indian takeaway. Washed and reused, I have effectively doubled their design life, so I can wash and take them home again, or I can simply bin them whilst shouting, "Chase me, Greta!"
- Items that don't really need names, are named. There's 'the cover of discretion,' which is daft, but it beats shouting across the site, "Where's the rug for the top of the bog?"
- Always pack a CO alarm for your safety. When it inevitably goes off for no reason at all, don't panic – it can be silenced simply by blowing into its vents, which floods it with carbon dioxide.
- When wrapping food to eat later, use greaseproof paper against the food, a piece of kitchen towel to use as a napkin, and wrap the whole lot in foil to avoid spills.
- To save on washing up, serve food wrapped just in kitchen towel.
- A digital food thermometer is well worth buying, and costs only a few quid from eBay.
- Magnets keep draughts from the bottoms of the curtains, and a spare key under the van.
- When camping at a festival, teamwork and speed are of the essence. Pull up and immediately define your camping area by setting up tables and chairs. Reserving an area for friends who will arrive later is difficult, and involves subterfuge. Immediately define the area with garden canes and red and white tape. Tell anyone who asks that it was done before you arrived, and never, ever quote me or the book on this point.
- When you pack the area behind the seat, you should ensure that the pop up tent and levelling blocks go in last so that they can come out first without drama.

Chorizo & tomato pasta

For fans of one-pot cookery, here's an easy chorizo and tomato pasta. The best bit is, for a dish cooked in a single pan, it doesn't look too shabby (even without my food stylist, who by this point had moved on to pastures more glamorous!).

The instructions specify a relatively deep pan, and this is important: too shallow, and the pasta won't be sufficiently covered by the stock and will be excessively 'al dente.'

Ingredients
- 1tbsp olive oil
- 1 medium red onion, finely diced
- 50g chorizo, sliced
- 1tsp garlic paste
- ¼tsp chilli flakes
- 250g small tomatoes
- 500ml vegetable stock
- 150g dried penne pasta
- 2tbsp cream cheese
- 30g Parmesan, grated
- 100g of spinach
- Salt and pepper, to season

Method

This superb-looking pasta dish is ideal for cooking on a late summer's evening, as the

sun finally begins to go down. It can be made on the stove inside the camper van, without fear of spitting fat or lingering smells, although obviously you can make it outdoors as well.

Begin by heating a generous splash of olive oil in a deep-ish pan, then add the finely-diced red onion and the sliced chorizo, and cook for about three minutes, until the chorizo starts to release its gorgeous-coloured oil and flavours. Add the garlic and the chilli, followed almost immediately by the cherry tomatoes, the vegetable stock, and the pasta.

Turn up the heat and bring this little lot momentarily to a boil, and then turn the gas back down and allow it to simmer gently for 15 minutes.

Stir though the soft cheese and the grated Parmesan, then turn up the heat for about five minutes or so to encourage the liquid to reduce slightly. Remove the pan from the heat and stir through the spinach, season everything generously with freshly-ground black pepper and a sprinkle of salt, and leave it to rest for a final five minutes until the spinach has wilted.

I don't know how that happened. The healthiest-looking meal in the entire book was created and cooked long after the departure of both the nutritionist and the stylist!

Goyt Camping

This is the tale of a weekend spent at Goyt Camping, one of the most curious campsites we have ever visited. It was on the very northern edge of White Peak, in Derbyshire, and right next door to a pub that served great food. It was run by an interesting old guy who had apparently started it to give himself something to do in his retirement. Hidden right down in the depths of the valley, there were no views to speak of, but it was out of the wind, very sheltered, and, curiously, a total sun-trap. We'd phoned ahead to book and to confirm that it was okay to take Stephen the collie, but we arrived to find 'No Dogs' signs everywhere. These were seemingly because of the chickens running all around the site, but Steve would be fine just so long as I kept him "tied up, so I don't have to shout at you."

Inside the toilet and shower block there were lots of those lovely handwritten signs that old folk do so well. It was also very apparent that, at some point, the site had come under the auspices of the Camping and Caravanning Club. To become a certified location, or whatever they're calling them now, there had obviously been some hoops the owner had been required to jump through: facilities he'd been obliged to provide, and some boxes that someone somewhere had seen fit to require ticking. The one that reduced us to fits of stifled laughter whenever we visited the loo was the 'baby changing area.' It appears that whatever the specific requirements are, they can be satisfied quite simply by an imaginatively placed and clearly signed ironing board!

I know very little about babies and toddlers. I imagine that it is quite possible to deal with them on an ironing board if push comes to shove, but the ironing board in question had clearly seen much better days – a very, very long time ago. Despite my Mickey-taking, this really was an excellent little site with lovely, friendly owners and lots of good walks nearby.

The most incredible 'baby changing area' you will ever find anywhere!

Toad in the hole

Let's not beat about the bush: this is never going to be the best toad in the hole. It's not even a proper one, but I made it in a field, using only a barbecue with a lid and a kettle full of boiling water.

Ingredients
- 0.5kg of your favourite sausages
- 2 frozen monster Yorkshire puddings
- A packet of instant mashed potato
- 4tsp instant gravy

Method

Here's another recipe that uses the old COBB barbecue and its lid to create a small oven. As is customary, fire it up and leave well alone with the lid off for a good 20 to 30 minutes, or until the flames and smoke really are finished and the coal is beginning to acquire a coating of fine white ash. At this point, and not a moment before, it is ready to cook on.

Place the sausages on the cooler outer part of the grill, and cook them for a generous 20 minutes, turning them regularly until they're all but done.

Then, just as they're about ready for their final sizzle, it's time to add the (by now) defrosted Yorkshire puddings. Spread out the sausages and place the Yorkshire puds on top of them, again trying to keep everything away from the direct heat. Put the lid on the barbecue and leave it alone for ten minutes.

While you are waiting, boil the kettle and make the mashed potatoes and the gravy according to the instructions on the relevant packets. There's no need to take a measuring jug specifically for this, I marked a couple of quantities onto a pint glass at home using masking tape: 425ml of water to make the potatoes, followed by 280ml for the gravy. A pint glass half-filled with gravy is a sight that you will long struggle to forget, but it's soon poured out and the glass rinsed.

Serve up the pudding on a plate, with the sausages and mash inside, and gravy poured over the whole lot.

A spill-proof water bowl makes a huge difference.

Dogs in vans

Dogs love camping. This is a camping fact.

We've always brought up ours to believe that going away in the camper van is the best walk ever. They're effectively outdoors and on an adventure from the moment they jump into the van, until they get home a week or so later. Our dogs (the sharp-eyed may have already spotted two different Merle collies in the photographs) have been quick to learn that a camping pitch has mysteriously defined boundaries, and they both manage to stay within them. It can sometimes take a while, but teaching them involves the initial use of a long lead, a ground anchor, and repeatedly walking them around until they mark out the limits for themselves. Once these are established in their clever little doggy minds, tying them down is no longer needed.

On a fine day, it's amusing to watch them as they lay down at the very edge, with smug grins on their faces, and watch other dogs on the site getting themselves into trouble for barking and straying.

We have found that, as long as they are given a quick constitutional first thing (normally as soon as a chap's had his first mug of coffee), they are happy to hang about watching the world go by until we're ready to go for a proper walk. This is normally about an hour before lunch, and often involves stopping at a public house.

It appears that the vast majority of UK pubs are dog-friendly, although common courtesy and the fair wife always dictates that we check it's okay before getting too comfortable.

Technically, I think that I should really attach the dogs to a seat belt when travelling, but both of them were reluctant, and would spend their entire journey wrapping the restraint tightly around things. In the end, the dogs and I agreed that, as long as they were happy to lay down on the floor behind the seat riser so that they can't be thrown forward under braking, there was no need for me to force the issue.

112

Char siu pork (GF)

Pork chops are practically crying out to be barbecued. Marinate them in Char Siu sauce, and you'll have campers' noses twitching for hundreds of yards all around you. It's that gorgeous red-edged pork that you get from the Chinese takeaway.

Ingredients

- 4tbsp hoisin sauce
- 2tsp garlic paste
- 1tsp ginger paste
- 1 star anise
- 4tsp caster sugar
- ¼tsp five-spice powder
- 2tbsp honey
- 2 pork chops

Put all of the ingredients, minus the chops, into a polythene bag and scrunch with your fingers to mix. Add the chops and scrunch a bit more to ensure they are well coated. Seal the bag and leave to marinate. This is a step that I normally do at home, taking the bagged chops ready to cook.

As always, you should light the barbecue and let it warm through for at least 20 minutes. Give it a good shake to even up the coals, and then place the chops on the rack for about 20 minutes, turning frequently. They will blacken, but this is not a disaster. Remove them from the heat, wrap in tinfoil, and leave covered with a tea towel whilst you make the rice.

Egg fried rice (GF)

Ingredients

- 2tbsp sunflower oil
- 1 egg, beaten
- 1 packet of microwave long grain rice
- 40g peas
- 4 water chestnuts, sliced
- 4 spring onions, sliced
- Chinese sausage or chorizo, finely diced
- 1tbsp light soy sauce

Method

Before you leave home, slice the water chestnuts, the spring onions, and the sausage/chorizo and pack them together with the peas in a Tupperware container, or similar.

With a wok over a gas stove, heat the oil until it is blisteringly hot. Carefully add the beaten egg, and scramble with a spatula. Working quickly, break it into pieces and add the cooked rice, stirring and mixing all the time. Add the pre-packed mix, and continue stirring to ensure everything is well mixed, finally adding a generous splash of light soy sauce. Serve the rice immediately onto plates, lay the chops on top, and garnish with a couple of sliced spring onions.

This is something I will never forget.

Glastonbury

Glastonbury festival is a once-in-a-lifetime experience.

I've been to a lot of VW shows, and many, many music festivals, but I've only been to the Worthy Farm bash once. As such, I make no claim to be any kind of authority on it, but it was far, far bigger than I ever expected. We arrived in the camper van on the Tuesday night, and pitched up as early as we possibly could. Despite that, it still took us 40 minutes each day to walk from our camper to the entrance. I have since read that the festival site is eight miles from one side to the other.

I knew that there were to be roughly 1000 acts on something like 100 stages, and I realised that I had no chance of seeing even a fraction of them. This really is an event like no other.

Although there was no music, the showground was open on the Wednesday and Thursday, which gave us plenty of time to walk around the different areas and begin to form an idea of how the various stages related to each other, and get to grips with where things were. Had the event been on for three weeks rather than three days, I would still have only managed to scratch the surface of what was there – it really was astonishing. There was so much to do besides just watching the bands, and entertainment was apparently running round the clock …

I couldn't swear to that, though, as I was in bed about an hour after the headliners left the pyramid stage each night, and wasn't back in the arena until after lunch.

My only problem with the whole event was the traditional long-drop toilets, about which much has been written over the years. Not only can I still see them in my mind's eye, I can still hear the gulls wheeling overhead when they were cleaned in my mind's ear, if such a thing was to exist. And in my mind's nose …

I can still smell the things!

Lamb tzatziki

This is great because it's absolutely delicious, and looks like it takes an age to produce. In reality, it's one of the easiest and quickest things in this book. If I can make this in the rough at Glastonbury, you can make it anywhere!

Ingredients

- 1 pot of natural yoghourt
- ¼ cucumber, peeled, seeded, and finely chopped
- 1tsp garlic paste
- 1 lime, juice and grated zest of
- Pitta breads
- 1tbsp olive oil
- 1 red onion, thinly sliced
- 225g minced lamb
- 1tsp cumin
- ½tsp coriander
- ½tsp cayenne pepper
- 50g frozen peas
- ½ bunch asparagus, trimmed and cut into 2in chunks

Method

Begin by making the tzatziki sauce. Mix together the yoghourt, cucumber, garlic, and lime in a small bowl and reserve. Toast the pittas in a very hot, dry pan until lightly browned, then put them on plates, wrapped with tinfoil and covered with a tea towel to keep them warm.

Using the same pan, heat a splash of olive oil until hot. Add the onions and a pinch of salt, cooking until softened – a good five minutes or so – and then add the powdered cumin, coriander and cayenne. Stir together and cook for just 30 seconds, and then add the lamb. At this point, if anyone is camping close by, you may see their noses begin to twitch …

After adding the lamb, stir it into the onion and spices until it's just beginning to cook through, but is still pink in places – just three minutes should be adequate – then add the peas and asparagus. Once again, stir everything together to mix well, place the lid on the pan and cook for a final two minutes.

Serve immediately on top of the warmed pitta, and slather with the tzatziki. The chap in the next tent, the one with the nose, will be amazed that you've gone from "that smells good" to served up and sat down eating in little more than five minutes!

If you can find a way to sprinkle freshly-chopped mint over the top, then do it!

Volkswagen clubs: to join or not to join?

There used to be clubs for specific marques: the Split Screen Van Club, the Type 2 Owner's Club, and so on. There were also local clubs: Nottingham Air-Cooled, Rugbydubs, etc.

Then, like a flash, with the dawning of the interweb came the age of the forum. This spawned a whole host of new and exciting clubs with cool and exotic names, such as: VolksZone Interactive, the Natural Born Dubbers, and Spooky VW. For all their promised exoticism, many of these turned out to be much the same local clubs as they were before. The difference was in their endless ability to self-destruct and fragment. No sooner had a chap pledged allegiance to one bunch of air-cooled nutters, than a handful of mates would fall out with another bunch and a rival club would be formed, that, in turn, would splinter and fragment further – and so it continued, seemingly endlessly. We once visited Santa Pod to find that the club we had ostensibly gone with was now divided into four different factions, all scattered far and wide across the fields.

As this endless disintegration and dilution reached a kind of fever pitch, there briefly dawned the age of the Volkswagen 'micro club': a gloriously short-lived entity that faded away almost as soon as it was born. I've recently found my member's shirts from 'MandyMicra's Gang' and 'Fingy's Aircooled Outlaws.'

Great memories of some great times, but ultimately just a bit of fun, and I never camped with either mob. Now clubs have become facebook-based and membership has a totally different kind of fluidity.

It worked well for us for a time, as we camped with a group of people who shared a common bond, over and above the whole VW thing. We used to have large pitches either marked out for us by the organisers or blagged by early-arriving members. Clubs provided a degree of security and camaraderie whilst camping at festivals. Some of the people we met back then remain friends some two decades later, and that can't be a bad thing, can it?

Onkar's lamb

This recipe really belongs to the mother of a bloke called Onkar, who I used to work with many years ago.

Ingredients
- 450g lamb, cubed
- 2tbsp Patak's Tikka Masala Spice Paste
- 1 small pot of plain yoghurt
- 2tsp traditional English mint sauce
- 2 apples, finely sliced
- Flour tortillas or Warburtons wraps

Method
It's marinade time again, and while, as always, this is entirely possible to do on location in a field just about anywhere, it's far easier to do it whilst you're sorting out the food to pack for the weekend. As a bonus, you get a much longer marinading time, too.

Place the lamb in a polythene bag and add the Patak's curry paste. Rub it around with your fingers to ensure that the meat is well covered. Squeeze the excess air from the bag and tie up the top.

Light the barbecue and leave to warm through for at least 20 minutes. If you're using a disposable, it's well worth giving it a bit of a shake to even up the coals at the ten-minute mark!

Thread the cubed lamb onto BBQ skewers, but don't push them on too far. It's always better to use more skewers with slightly less meat on each, to leave yourself a bit of a handle.

Place the loaded kebabs on the grill; these will cook through in about 20 minutes. Keep turning them regularly. They may stick a little at first, but when they're all lifting up cleanly from the mesh, they're done.

In the meantime, make up the mint raita: eat two teaspoons of yoghourt to create space to add the same amount of mint sauce, and stir well.

To serve, make a bed of apple slices on the tortillas, then slide the meat off the skewers using the tines of a fork and pile it up onto the apple. Add a generous lashing of the mint raita, and either roll it all up and eat with your fingers, or you could feign sophistication and eat from a plate with knives and forks!

Flags

Flags and flag poles are a big thing at festivals and other outdoor events, and although they are less prevalent on campsites, they still make an occasional appearance. The only advice I would offer is to make sure that you buy the tallest flag pole you can, since they all fold down to about the same size and weight. Also ensure that you don't forget some method of making the pole stand upright. There are all sorts of solutions: some are very lightweight, but not much use, whereas others work brilliantly, but are huge and weigh the best part of a metric tonne!

After much frustration with poles toppling over in strong winds, taking a variety of lightweight supports with them, I eventually hit on the idea of utilising a handful of bolts on one of my bumper brackets. These were left over from a long-unused motorbike rack, and I had a supporting pole welded and attached to them.

My man with the electric sparkly stick was a little bemused that anyone should want to create such an unwieldy thing, but it satisfies my long-established Bauhaus sensibilities of 'form follows function.' It's not overly heavy, can be removed if required, and it comes in useful when camping properly or even when just out on day trips. There's no longer any need for me to be messing about screwing poles into the ground, and it was also designed so that its position could be adjusted for it to support a garden parasol – which, at the time, seemed like a moment of genius.

It will never blow down, even in a hurricane. The flag or other device that you fly from the top of the pole is entirely up to

you. Curiously, in the photograph it would appear that I'm flying a large, fluorescent pink bra, for which I'm sure that somewhere, there's a perfectly rational explanation. Have a good look around at the next festival and see what normal folk have, but be warned: they all become surprisingly noisy in a stiff breeze!

Rolled beef

For a while I've been serving up a variety of snacks and smallish food items wrapped up in kitchen towel – which I have pretentiously been calling a napkin – just to save me some washing up.

I've just been introduced to the art of eating from a brown paper bag, which knocks your average napkin into the proverbial cocked hat. It's brilliant, there's no washing up, the food doesn't fall apart, and it even keeps your hands clean.

This is an effortless variation on an old favourite, made using my Beauclaire with the ribbed side up, to create some charred stripes of interest on the steak and peppers. Light it and let it burn on full power for about five minutes before turning the gas right down to the mark marked 'mark.'

Ingredients
- A couple of Romano peppers
- Goat's cheese
- A sprinkle of basil
- 10oz of thick-cut steak
- 'Squarish' wraps, or flour tortillas

Method
Begin by halving the peppers lengthwise and de-seeding them. Place into the hot griddle pan and cook, skin side down, for five minutes or so. Flip over for another five minutes on the other side. Turn back, and fill the hollow side with lots of goat's cheese, then sprinkle over the basil and continue cooking until the cheese begins to melt.

Now place the steak on the griddle, cooking for two minutes on the first side before turning and cooking for between two and four minutes on the second side, according to how well done you like it. Place the wraps or flour tortillas onto the grill to warm through, as you remove everything else to a chopping board. Slice the peppers/cheese and steak into thin slices and tightly roll up everything in a wrap. Then drop the filled wrap into the bottom of a brown paper bag.

Roll up the bag tightly and cut it in half with a sharp knife: you may need to stab it to start the cut. Then relax and enjoy a snack of quality and distinction with a fine drink of your choice.

My man with the spanners

There are many air-cooled owners who do all their own mechanical work. I am not one of them. I would love to be able to nip out of a Saturday morning and spend a couple of pleasant hours re-aligning my grungle pins.

I understand how the engine/transmission/suspension works, and I can perceive how the whole shebang is designed to work together. More importantly, I can tell when there's a problem, I can appreciate what is causing it, and I know which component needs adjustment or replacement. My problem, for want of a better way of explaining it, is that I am utterly cack-handed.

If I need to remove a crosshead screw, I can guarantee that I'll mash the head before it moves, and if I have to nip up a bolt, I will inevitably tighten it until the head snaps off.

As a direct consequence of this exceptional skill set, I have become very good friends with a lot of mechanics over the course of my motoring life, and many of them are more than mere mechanics – they are true craftsmen.

It has also come to my attention that, back in 1979, when my particular van was built, there was no FIAT Strada: the phrase 'built by robots' did not exist. My old bus was built by a handful of German blokes on a production line, probably holding a fag in their free hand, and maybe thinking about going home to their wives, where they'd consume vast quantities of beer and bratwurst over the weekend.

Despite their possible lack of interest, though, the majority of the components that they fitted, and the assembly work they did, have lasted 30 or more years. I like to make a point of reminding the chaps who work on my bus, these 21st-century artisans, that – considering the money they're charging, and the time they're planning to take doing a proper job – the work should last a sight longer than 30 years; it shouldn't need doing again in my lifetime.

How they laugh …

120

Gammon, with broad beans & new potatoes (GF)

This is a recipe that was given to me many, many moons ago by an old Yorkshire farmer. He claimed that it was the only way to eat gammon. The story goes that it was his favourite meal, and that he would always order gammon if he went to a restaurant. He would also ask how it was to be cooked, and would insist that it was done this way. You'd wonder why he bothered eating out, but once you have tasted it, you will understand.

I've used his method at home, obviously with fresh vegetables, for a long time, but have been a little wary of doing it in the camper van because of the potential lingering smell and mess. There's also a lot of stuff to clear up. In practice, though, with a fine day, the sliding door wide open, and tinned veg, it didn't turn out too badly!

Ingredients
- 2 gammon steaks
- 1 tin of new potatoes
- 1 tin of broad beans
- 2tbsp of demerara sugar

Method
Adjust the grill rack to its lowest position: ie, turn it upside down and pre-heat the grill for about five minutes. Tip the contents of both tins into a single, lidded saucepan, and place onto the hob, ready to light later. Using scissors or a sharp knife, cut through the rind of the gammon at 2cm intervals. Sprinkle the fat liberally with the sugar, turn the grill right down, and place the gammon under it for about ten minutes. Turn over the gammon, sprinkle more sugar onto the fat on the other side, and replace it under the grill for another ten minutes.

When it's done, remove the gammon, wrap in two layers of tinfoil and a tea towel to keep it warm. Then take the grill pan outside. Place it on a brick or rock to protect the grass, and fill it with water and washing up liquid.

Warm through the vegetables while the meat rests, and serve on warmed plates if you can, with lots of black pepper. You won't need to add any salt.

The campsite at the end of the world!

Mull

After our trans-European holiday and other long distance nightmares, we've tended to limit our longest journey to Cornwall, at about 300 miles. We were, however, sorely tempted by the Scottish Inner Hebridean Islands, and departed on a meticulously-planned journey to cover the 400-or-so miles to Mull. This time, the journey was broken into far more manageable sections of just 150 to 200 miles. Our idea was to drive in a similar way to lorry drivers' tachograph breaks: for no more than about four-and-a-half hours at a time.

We spent what felt like months poring over endless maps on the interweb, and, with the aid of our magic random pin, booked sites in advance at Keswick and Loch Lomond on the way up.

For once, everything went like clockwork: we'd spend a suitable period of time driving, and our campsite would appear on the horizon. A quick pitch was followed by an evening's lightweight camping, and we still had the enthusiasm to walk the dog to a local hostelry.

Mull was incredible as a final destination. Our directions told us to follow the A849 the 30 miles to Fionnphort. We were aware that it was a single track road with passing places, and would take us a couple of hours. What we weren't expecting was the utter isolation of the landscape, the fact that the campsite was at what appeared to be the end of the world, or the sheer beauty of the place.

After a bitterly cold night and a brisk thunderstorm at breakfast time, the skies cleared, the sun emerged, and the last vestiges of cloud disappeared to leave a clear blue sky. The sea turned from dull grey to a spectacular turquoise, the sand turned a gorgeous shade of pink, and the rocks became a bright iridescent white. The weather also became pleasantly warm, and stayed that way – it's apparently something to do with the Gulf Stream. With temperatures and scenery like those we were treated to on this curious little island, we don't need to head abroad.

Even when we can!

Deconstructed scrumper's crumble (V & GF)

It's not often that I make multi-course camping meals, apart from the obvious G&T as an aperitif, or a snifter of brandy to signal the end of a meal. Generally, it's because I can't be bothered and they're more trouble than they're worth, but I thought I'd better show willing and include a dessert to round off this slender volume.

This really is simplicity itself, and if you take the time now to pack the dry ingredients into the back of a cupboard, then, at the tailend of the summer, when you inevitably come across luscious fruit growing in the hedgerow, you'll be a hero. It certainly puts a whole new spin on being camped up next to an unruly bramble hedge – and it seemed like an interesting idea for a final recipe!

Ingredients
- Blackberries, apples, etc
- Dark muscovado sugar
- Gluten-free oats
- Flaked almonds
- Desiccated coconut
- Butter
- 1 tin of custard

Method

Surreptitiously gather a bowl of apples, blackberries or other summer fruit …

Apples will need to be diced, but smaller fruits can just go straight into a small pan. Mix together with a couple of generous teaspoons of dark muscovado sugar (you can use any sort of sugar, or even maple syrup at a pinch) over a medium heat. Stir together, and set it bubbling. After about ten minutes the fruit will become tender and sweet, but still maintain some of its shape, without degenerating into total mush.

For the crumble topping, mix together a handful of oats with some flaked almonds and desiccated coconut. Stir together with another couple of teaspoons of sugar. Then, melt a generous knob of butter in a frying pan and cook the topping mix, stirring occasionally until it's beginning to become gently browned and fragrant – you may need to add even more butter!

Serve by placing the fruit into a couple of bowls and then spooning over the deconstructed crumble topping.

Finish off with a couple of spoonfuls of thick canned long-life custard to make this the ultimate summer fruit indulgence.

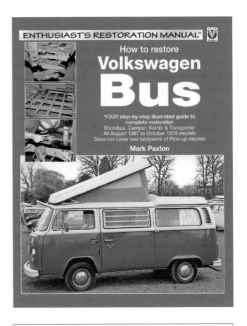
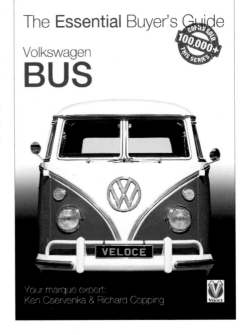

Convert your own VW panel van to a Camper, and you've got the best of all worlds, as the author of this manual shows. A detailed step-by-step guide with 1500 illustrations, covering every aspect of the conversion: you'll save a fortune, learn a lot, and get a great recreational vehicle! Covers T5 models 2003 on.

ISBN: 978-1-904788-67-6
Paperback • 27x20.7cm • 272 pages
• 1786 colour and b&w pictures

Have a great time converting your VW van to a Camper – and save a fortune! With 800 colour illustrations, this manual guides you every step of the way.

ISBN: 978-1-903706-45-9
Paperback • 27x20.7cm • 224 pages
• 861 colour and b&w pictures

Wonderful walks from **dog-friendly campsites** throughout the UK

Anna Chelmicka

Hubble & Hattie

Stride out with your dog from a campsite. Follow nearby footpaths and byways to explore the surrounding countryside.
This book will guide you on 45 different walks that allow you and your dog to enjoy the diversity of the British landscape, and return to the campsite invigorated and exhilarated.

ISBN: 978-1-787110-45-8
Paperback • 22.5x15.2cm • 248 pages • 146 colour pictures

Index

ABC burger 53
Air beam awning 102
Apple crumble (V) 123
Avocado melt (V) 17
Awnings 40
Barefoot Bishop's knob 70
Beaten by the weather 106
Beauclaire 42
Beef Stroganoff (GF) 75
Beef/peppers 119
Beer & chicken 63
Beer can chicken 24
Beetle 74
Best camping pitch 104
Bike rack 92
Biryani (GF) 39
Books vs technology 106
Breakdown 88
Breakfast 15
Breakfast basket 71
Brighton 52
Broken roof 44
Buffalo wings (GF) 37
Camping & Caravan Club 110
Camping rules 14
Campsite etiquette 78
Can openers 87
Carbon monoxide 108
Carburettor 48
Cartwheels 14
Char siu pork (GF) 112
Cheat's tacos 23
Chicken & chorizo (GF) 47
Chicken burritos 41
Chicken fajitas 21
Chicken kiev (GF) 107
Chicken tagine (GF) 33
Children 14, 66
Chips 97
Clock 46
COBB 42
Coffee sachets 72
Colour co-ordination 20

Compression bags 108
Cooking to music 75
Cooking using the van 99
Coronation chicken 64
Crash 44
Derbyshire 110
Disposable BBQ 84
Dogs 112
Double skillet 100
Dressing the part 58
Easy breakfast 71
Easy omelettes 23
Egg fried rice (GF) 112
Fairy lights 16
Festival fiasco 86
Fingy's Outlaws 115
Flags 117
Food thermometer 108
France 68
Fritatta (GF) 95
Fuel gauge 96
Fun weekends 50
Gammon & potatoes (GF) 121
Garages 120
Gazebos 24
Glamping 80
Glasses 46
Glastonbury 113
Goulash (GF*) 67
Gravy in a beer mug 111
Great camp sites 18, 60
Green Hill Farm 60
Happy Hash (GF) 9
Heat diffuser 95
Heaters 98
Houmous & pea fritters (V) 105
Kelly Kettle 36
Lamb kofkas 35
Lamb shawarma (GF) 61
Lamb tzatziki 114
LED lighting 16
Lemon chicken (GF*) 73
Levelling blocks 12

Lightweight camping 26
Looe Bay 18
Lorne sausage 15
Loudest sounds 54
Lowered suspension 10
Magnets 108
Mandy Micra 115
Mechanics 120
Mediterranean chicken casserole (GF*) 83
Mental friends 50
Mexican steak (GF) 81
Missing screw 76
Monte Cristo 27
Moroccan rug 46
Mugs & plates 46
Mull 122
Mushroom burgers (V) 69
Myths & legends 22
Never lose anything again 46
Notebook 76
Number plates 94
Oatcakes 51
Onion rings 97
Onkar's lamb 116
Packing 28 & 108
Packing list 29
Pan haggerty (GF*) 85
Pancakes 11
Pasta 109
Pheasant (GF*) 43
Picnics 62-65
Pizza 103
Plank cookery 91
Pork joint (GF) 101
Porta Potti 30
Portobello mushrooms (V) 79
Pot Noodles 93
Pudding 123
Pulled Pork (GF) 31
Quesadillas 13

Rarebit/Rabbit? (V) 57
Refrigerator 34
Rib of beef 89
Sausage in cider (GF) 49
Saving space 108
Shish kebabs 45
Shooter's picnic 64
Smoked pork (GF) 101
Smoked salmon (GF) 91
Snorting vodka 78
Spam (GF) 87
Spare key 46
Spare wheel cover 94
Squirrel hunting 66
Sun visors 56
Sunday papers 82
Sunny chicken (GF) 25
Sunshades 38, 86
Sweet & sour 59
Takeaway food 82
Tandoori kebabs 55
Tent pegs 32
Tiny stove 7
Toad in the hole 111
Tortilla feast (GF) 77
Tournedos Rossini 99
Trabant 20
Trailer 74
Tupperware 108
Twister! 46
Veg shooter's picnic (V) 65
Venison stew 19
Volkswagen clubs 115
Waldorf salad 64
Weekend meal planner 51
Windbreaks 90
Wooden Skewers 24
Wrapping food 108
Yoghourt eating competition 66